The Hunter in My Heart

A Sportsman's Salmagundi

Robert F. Jones

THE LYONS PRESS
GUILFORD, CONNECTICUT
An imprint of the Globe Pequot Press

For Jeff Piper
and in memory of Roz

Many of these essays, in different form, first appeared in *Shooting Sportsman Magazine, Sports Illustrated, Men's Journal, Sports Afield, Retriever Journal, Stratton Magazine,* and *Game Journal.*

The Lyons Press is an imprint of The Globe Pequot Press.

Printed in the United States of America

10 9 8 7 6 5 4 3 2 1

Design by Compset, Inc.

The Library of Congress Cataloging-in-Publication Data is available on file.

ISBN 1-58574-465-4

CONTENTS

Other Books by Robert F. Jones

Fiction:
Blood Root
Blood Sport
The Diamond Bogo
Slade's Glacier
Blood Tide
Tie My Bones to Her Back
Deadville
The Run to Gitche Gumee

Nonfiction:
The Fishing Doctor
African Twilight
Upland Passage: A Field Dog's Education
Jake: A Labrador Puppy at Work and Play
Dancers in the Sunset Sky
On Killing: Meditations on the Hunt (Editor)

The Market Gunner: A Tale of Loss

A Short Story

FRANK DAVIES RAN away from home when he was fourteen years old. The way it happened, he was minding his own business in the sixth-grade classroom one day when the schoolmaster, a stiff-necked old Dutchman named Mr. Steinbach, accused him of whispering to a classmate. Frank denied the charge. Mr. Steinbach flew into a rage and came at Frank with a hickory stick. Frank bolted. Mr. Steinbach reached out with his free hand and grabbed Frank by the hair. A handful tore out. It was painful. Frank grabbed a slate from Susie Pfefferkorn's desk, whirled around, and smashed it over Mr. Steinbach's head. Frank Davies was big for his age, as tall as Mr. Steinbach. Stunned, the schoolmaster fell to his knees, blood

1

streaming down his face, the wooden frame of the slate itself dangling cockeyed around his neck like the yoke on a draft horse. Chunks of broken slate stuck from his brow, a halo of Indian arrowheads. Frank kept on going. He never went back.

The truancy officer would seek him out at home. Frank headed for the countryside. Life at home, in a tenement near the stockyards on the South Side of Chicago, was no great shakes anyway. The neighborhood stank of blood and cow shit. His mother was a shrew, his father a drunkard. His sisters were snotty little bitches and his older brother, Hendry, the only member of the family he cared for, had long since flown the coop. Hendry was out West somewhere, his latest letter postmarked Sheridan, Wyoming. He was herding sheep, he said, for a greaser in the foothills of the Big Horns. Smelly, stupid animals, he said. Don't get involved with them, Frankie, he said. Frank did not intend to. He hopped a northbound freight in the marshaling yards at Joliet and did not get off until the train had crossed the Wisconsin line. That first night he slept in a hayloft on a dairy farm. In the morning the farmer's wife spotted him when she came out to gather eggs from the henhouse. *Come on down from dere,* she said. She had a German accent. Frank came down. *Do you need a chob?* she said. Frank said he did.

It was coming on harvest time and for the next month Frank worked hard, following the horse-drawn John Deere mowing machine through the fields, shocking corn and later barley, scything and loading hay, pitchforking it up into the loft of the barn, from dark to dark each day save Sundays when he attended church with the Fetzlers. Frau Fetzler was a fat, friendly woman, all smiles and plump red cheeks. She cooked huge meals of pork chops and roast chicken, mashed potatoes or homemade noodles, steaming brown gravy, sliced red cabbage and vinegar, boiled rutabagas and turnips, with desserts of home-baked apple strudel or peach pie, or sweet Italian plums wrapped in boiled dough and served with cinnamon and brown sugar along with a hefty dollop of whipped cream. Herr Fetzler was the strong silent type, a slope-shouldered man with a belly as round and hard as a boulder. He had served as a sergeant in the Second Wisconsin during the war, part of the Iron Brigade, as they called it. He had lost an eye and an ear at Antietam, near the Dunker Church. A son, Willie, had been killed at Cold Harbor. The daughters, four of them, were blond and zaftig. Helga, Annaliese, Hannelore, Alma. They were older than Frank and so paid no heed to him. He slept in the hayloft, dreaming hot dreams of them all through the owlhoot nights.

That winter he milked cows, beheaded chickens, plucked and gutted them. He split small forests of firewood, hauled it in through the blizzards day and night. He hunted deer with Old Fetzler's trapdoor Springfield from the war, or partridges in the mixed hardwoods to the north with the farmer's muzzleloading shotgun. The deer were easy, the grouse almost impossible at first. But Frank soon learned to ignore their explosive rattling flush and take them fast on the wing as they zigzagged out through the timber tops. He learned how to drive the team. He had a way with draft horses. They were big, calm Belgians with soft brown eyes the size of baseballs.

Alma was the youngest of the daughters, maybe a year or two older than Frank. When spring blew in it warmed her blood. One night she climbed the ladder to the hayloft. She pulled her flannel nightgown over her head. It was patterned with faded blue cornflowers. She pulled off Frank's underdrawers. She got down on her elbows and knees, gleaming white in the moonlight. He mounted her like a bull. Well, maybe a baby bull. Two weeks later Old Fetzler caught them at it and pounded Frank bloody. Ordered him off the farm. But he paid Frank every last cent he owed him. Frank headed west with a broken nose, three sprung ribs, and twenty-two dollars in his kick. Plus eighty-five cents extra that Alma gave him on the sly. *Egg money,* she said. She kissed him good-bye.

In Thief River Falls, Minnesota, he got a job in a feed mill lugging hay bales and burlap sacks full of cracked corn or oats ten hours a day and slinging them up onto farm wagons. The pay was fifty cents a day. He was coming up in the world. He lived in a rooming house now, had money to spend on soda pop and Cracker Jacks. He was developing muscles he never knew he had, lugging those hundred-pound sacks around. One evening as he strolled past a saloon, eating Cracker Jacks, he bumped into a drunkard who was leaving the joint. The drunkard staggered, reeled, then exploded into a rage reminiscent of Mr. Steinbach on the day of the slate incident. *You snotnose blankety-blank kid,* he said. *Whyncha watch where you're goin'?* He swung at Frank but Frank leaned back and the punch whistled past six inches from his nose. Frank placed his Cracker Jacks on the board sidewalk, straightened up, and punched the man in the stomach. As the drunk folded Frank hit him on the point of the jaw. The drunk, halfway to slumberland already, collapsed on the boards. Frank picked up his Cracker Jacks and proceeded on his way. A tall, portly stranger in a straw boater and a wasp-waisted linen ice cream suit accosted him. *Son,* he said, *you've got just the punch I've been looking for. How'd you like to get into the fight game? That gentleman you just kayoed is Hunky Horvath. He fought Ad Wolgast.*

Who's Ad Wolgast? Frank said.

Ad Wolgast? the dude said. *Ad Wolgast is the Michigan Wildcat, lightweight champeen of the world, and one of the toughest pugilists ever to don the mitts.*

How did Mr. Horvath fare with him?
Wolgast knocked him out in the third round.
How much did Mr. Horvath get for losing?
The dude told him.

Frank fought sixteen bouts as a lightweight that year, winning ten by knockouts, losing four by decision, with the other two matches adjudged draws. He fought in Sioux Falls, South Dakota; Butte, Montana; St. Paul, Minnesota; Fond du Lac, Wisconsin; Grand Rapids, Michigan; St. Joseph, Missouri. His last fight was out West again, in Danzig, South Dakota.

In the course of training for that contest, Frank ran ten to twenty miles a day along the high-bluffed banks of the Missouri River where it makes a big bend around Danzig. During the course of those runs he noticed that beyond the plowed land seeded with corn and wheat, the tallgrass prairie flanking the road was teeming with wild chickens, big coveys of them, maybe three hundred birds in a bunch. At his approach they rose with a great clatter of wings and a greater speed. They were large plump birds with barred breasts, mottled pale yellow and chestnut brown, short tails, and broad, strong wings, and they flew with alternating wingbeats and glides, covering long distances over the blue-green prairie grass, undulating in the cool dry west wind like the billows on Lake Michigan, settling finally on the far horizon. One day on a run he encountered a wagon laden with these birds. The men driving the wagon were sunburned old-timers, bearded gents who looked tough as harness leather. They had a pair of tall, black-and-tan setting dogs in the wagon with them, and a brace of well-worn shotguns. The sun glinted silver where the bluing had been worn away from the barrels. The reflected light stuck in his eyes like hunks of busted slate. He flagged the men down.

Need a lift, young feller?

Nope, Frank said. *I was wondering what them birds is.*

Why, they're prairie hens, son.

How's come you killed so many of 'em?

We sells 'em to the market in St. Paul and Chicago, one of the men said.

Good eating?

The best, the other man said. He pulled out a fistful of cheroots. *Have a smoke, will ya?*

No thanks, I'm in training.

What for? said the first man.

I'm fighting tomorrow in Danzig. I'm a prizefighter.

What's your moniker?

They call me Farmboy Davies.

We get two bits apiece for these chickens, the other man said to his partner. *Maybe we can afford the price of admission.* He turned back to Frank. *You sure you don't want a lift back to town?*

No. I must keep running until I come to that silo out there on the horizint. My manager says I must. Then I must run back to town. He keeps time on me with his pocket watch.

Well, speakin' of time, we must catch the noon train, the other man said. *Else these birds may spoil on us ere they reach Chicago. Good luck in your battle.*

Thank you, Frank said. *Say, what kind of dogs is those?*

Gordons, the other man said. *Gordon setters. Best durn bird dogs on God's green earth.*

The bout with Sailor Christie went a full forty rounds. It was ruled No Decision. Frank's nose got busted for the third time. His eyes were so swollen that he could barely see, the pain in his ribs allowed him only the shallowest of breaths, and the following morning he found himself pissing blood. He retired from the fight game. He now had six hundred forty-five dollars and fifteen cents in his kick. He was a rich man. He was sixteen years old.

When he had recovered from the pounding and was pissing clear once more, Frank bought a beat-up old buckboard, a team of elderly Belgian draft horses, an ancient 10-gauge W. W. Greener hammergun chased in German silver, five pounds of Du Pont Fg-grade gunpowder and ten of chilled No. 6 birdshot, along with a large round carton containing a thousand copper percussion caps, and set himself up as a chicken hunter. Walking the streets of Danzig, he eyed the stray dogs that roamed the alleyways on the search for garbage. One of them looked like he might be part Gordon setter. He was an old dog, gray around the muzzle, eyes a bit rheumy, but he smiled when Frank stopped nearby to stare at him. He had yellow teeth and what looked like a broken tail. It kinked partway up, about in the middle. The old dog was investigating a garbage can behind Rumpelmayr's Steak House on Main Street, but the lid was weighted down with a paving stone. Frank went into the restaurant and bought a two-pound filet mignon, raw. He went back to the alley. The dog was still there, eyeing the garbage can with sad brown eyes. *Come here, boy*, Frank said. Whether it was love at first sight, or just that the dog had whiffed the filet mignon, Frank never knew, but when he proffered the meat a bond was forged. *From now on your name is Hendry*, he told the dog. Hendry wagged his broken tail. It's all right with him, Frank thought. Just so's I don't call him Late For Dinner.

Daybreak found them ten miles northwest of town, rolling over the prairie. A light dry wind was in their faces. Frank stood on the seat of the buckboard, reins in hand, and scanned the billows of grass for sign of chickens. Hendry seemed to know what they were up to, for he ranged ahead of the team, quartering into the wind with his big square-muzzled head up, nostrils gaped wide, inhaling the breeze. At times, where the ground dipped, he disappeared into the tall bluestem, only his crooked black tail wagging above it. Then he would emerge again to check the position of the wagon.

They hunted in this manner for a mile or more. Then Hendry paused for a moment, looked back at Frank, his eyes bright now and a grin on his grizzled face. He angled off to the north, slowed his pace, crouching forward, tail waving in short arcs at half-mast. He crept forward in a slouch, belly to the grass, then locked up tight. The crooked tail sprang erect like the flag on a rural mailbox. Frank whoa-ed the team and stepped down with the shotgun. It was already charged. He cocked the hammers and applied caps to the teats. *Steady boy,* he said. He walked in ahead of the dog and three chickens got up. Frank swung with them, waiting until their flight paths crossed, then hit the front trigger. All three birds fell. He stepped aside, away from the cloud of smoke from the muzzle. *Steady, steady.* He took two, three more steps, and a dozen birds sprang clucking into the air, shedding shit and feathers. He dropped another pair with the remaining barrel. The dog whined, dancing in place, eager to retrieve. But there were more birds still on the ground, unflown. Frank could hear their puzzled clucking.

Whoa, Hendry, whoa boy. Not yet . . .

Frank pulled the powder flask from his coat pocket, his hands were shaking, recharged the barrels, he was breathing fast and hard, inserted premeasured loads of shot wrapped in waxed paper, rammed them home, recapped the hammers, replaced the ramrod, and walked forward once more. Now a hundred birds got up, thunder on a bluebird day, and he fired into the brown. Five birds fell. A few more flinched to the pattern and staggered on through the air, some of them crashing a hundred yards ahead.

The first covey rise had produced sixteen chickens. These birds were easy, unlike the partridges back in Wisconsin. They rose much slower, flew straight, no dodging or weaving, there were no trees for them to hide behind. Hunting on through the day, Frank improved that total to one hundred and twenty-eight before old Hendry began limping. Frank called him to the wagon and checked his paw pads. Hendry had picked up thorns from the prickly pears that studded the plain. Frank pulled them out, some with his teeth.

As they headed back to Danzig in the red light of the sunset, Frank calculated the day's profits. Two bits a chicken meant thirty-two dollars. If he could maintain this pace, chicken shooting would yield two hundred twenty-four dollars a week. Times fifty-two weeks . . . Why, he might amass more than eleven thousand dollars in a year without holidays. A fortune. And he could do better than that. He considered the possibility of acquiring a faster-loading shotgun. I am penny wise and pound foolish, he thought. For twenty dollars more I might have purchased that hammerless Parker down at the mercantile, a breechloader firing those newfangled waxed-paper shotshells. Sure save time on reloading. With the Parker I'd easily down twice as many chickens each day. He thought of the market hunters he had met on this very road, and the mountain of birds in their buckboard. Two guns working steadily through the day had more than doubled the number of birds he himself had taken. I must find myself a partner, he thought. With two modern guns we would soon be men of substance. But of course they could not hunt all year long. The snows of winter would make the prairie impassable except on snowshoes.

At the hotel in town he looked up Mr. McRae, the agent for the meat markets, hotels, and restaurants back East who purchased game from local market hunters. McRae came out to the wagon, poked the birds, smelled of them, counted them, and paid Frank twenty-eight dollars and eighty cents. *I thought it was two bits apiece*, Frank said. *It is*, McRae said, *but I take a ten percent agent's fee.* He made out a chit and told Frank to take the birds down to the depot, leave them with the baggage master for shipment on the night train.

Frank soon gave up his room in town. The landlady disapproved of dogs in her boardinghouse and Frank did not want Hendry roaming the alleys during the night, hunting for garbage. It might dull his keenness for the hunt come morning, and it was always possible that some angry citizen, fed up with having his garbage cans tipped over, might slip a chunk of meat laced with strychnine into the leftovers. What's more, Frank had grown to love the open prairie. He loved the push of the steady summer wind, the hiss it made through the bluestem, the yip of coyotes at sunup. Buffalo wolves sang the rising of the moon. There were wild turkeys in the timber along the river bottom, while out on the grasslands flocked sicklebills, doughbirds, and upland plover. The buffalo were gone, yes, but he still got a tingle when he found their whitened, black-horned skulls staring up at him blank-eyed from the grass. There were still plenty of mule deer and elk in the brushy draws of the hills, and pronghorn antelope on the flats above the Missouri. In addition to the breechloading Parker he bought a Winchester 45-75 lever-action rifle to vary the constant diet of prairie chicken. Even Hendry was getting sick of it.

The bottomland was thick with ripgut cordgrass and sunflowers, ten feet high, wind-dried now as the summer wore along. Down in the bottoms it was impossible to see more than a few feet ahead. The rattle of the sunflowers in the constant wind and the sudden spatter of their falling seeds unnerved him at first, as did the unexpected flush of migrant songbirds feeding in the brakes—warblers and goldfinches, sparrows and jays, magpies, merles, redwings, and cowbirds. Great golden eagles and chicken hawks circled the plains during the day, and once one of them swooped down from an impossible height to snatch a bird from under Hendry's nose, just as he leaned in to retrieve it. Frank chased the eagle off with a shotgun blast at long range but it did not drop the chicken. Nor did birdshot slow the thief, merely rattling against its feathers.

Every two or three days Frank made the trip into town to sell his birds. The money he kept in a leather satchel bought especially for that purpose, not trusting the banks. At first he and Hendry lived in a tent fashioned from a tarpaulin, but after it blew down a few times in the night wind he excavated a dugout on a south-facing slope well above the Missouri's high-water mark, roofing it over with a weave of hardhack poles, themselves covered with a layer of sod a foot and a half thick. A nearby spring provided cold, sweet water for man, dog, and horses alike. On the dugout's back wall Frank built a hearth and chimney of stones carried up from the river, chinking them with clay from its bank. The clay hardened like cement to the heat of the fire. Beside the fireplace he constructed a bunk of roughly squared timbers. He tacked down boards hauled from town to form a sleeping platform that would keep him clear of the dirt floor. With a moth-eaten buffalo robe for his mattress, a flour sack stuffed with bluestem grass to serve as a pillow, an army blanket or two to cover him, and Hendry curled at his feet, he was cozier than he would have been in Chicago's finest hotel.

Most nights he dreamed of Alma. Perhaps, when his satchel was bulging with dollars, he would send for her . . .

Ranging the prairie, Frank sometimes heard the boom of faraway guns. Other hunters plying their trade. Now and then he saw them in the distance, dark clouds of chickens rising on the hazy horizon, the white puff of distant muzzles, the sky raining birds, then much later the hollow thud of their shots. The market hunters steered clear of one another. There was an ocean of prairie to hunt in, an infinity of birds.

The summer wheeled toward autumn, the grass turned the color of wheat, the cottonwood leaves went yellow as corn. Bur oaks stained the draws like clots of drying blood. Late one cider-sharp afternoon Frank topped a rise and saw another wagon creaking toward him. Two men, no dogs. One of the men had a Sharps rifle across his lap. The bed of the mule-drawn wagon was stacked high with peltry.

Howdy, Frank said when they pulled up abreast.

Chicken hunter, eh? the man with the rifle said, peering into the buckboard.

It's a livin'. Frank smiled.

We're wolfin', the man driving the wagon said. *They're gettin' mighty thin on the ground of late, though.*

A bitter smell of strychnine rose from the pile of wolf pelts. The men were bearded, shaggy, their clothes sun-faded and stained with grease. Hendry trotted up to see what was happening. When he whiffed the wolf scent he wrinkled his flews and growled low in his throat. The rifleman frowned.

Where you headed? Frank asked.

Danzig, the rifleman said. *Sell the hides, then look for some other line of work I reckon.* He spat a stream of tobacco juice. It just missed Hendry, who backed away. *How about you? Done for the day? You got a goodly pile of birds in there.*

No, Frank said, *I only go to town a couple times a week now. The birds'll keep. I got me a soddy out here. Saves time for the huntin'.*

The men stared at him, waiting. In the code of the prairie it was share and share alike.

Why don't you fellers break your trip? Frank said. *Them mules look bone-weary and I've plenty of grub.*

The rifleman's name was Devins, the other one called himself Smith. They were hidemen from the olden days. During the seventies they'd hunted buffalo ("shaggies," they called them) from the Texas panhandle clear up to Milk River, following the herds all through the Great American Desert until they played out in 'eighty-four. Good money, they said. Sometimes as much as five bucks a hide, but even in the worst days, two. Then with the shaggies gone they turned to the buffalo wolves. They laced chunks of spoiled deer meat with poison. Strychnine killed everything. When they checked their baits of a morning they sometimes found, along with a lobo or two, badgers, foxes, skunks, ravens, magpies, even eagles lying nearby, all stiff as boards. Most of the collateral kill was worthless, but you got good money for eagle feathers from the Indian agent at Rosebud. Badgers paid well too. Their stiff bristly fur made excellent shaving brushes.

Hendry sidled up while they ate, cadging scraps. They were dining on fried mule deer liver and beans. When Hendry pushed his snoot toward Devins's plate, Devins shrank away from the dog and swatted at Hendry with his free hand. *Keep that durned mutt away from me,* he said.

Smith chuckled. *Jim don't cotton much to the canine race,* he said. *A half-dead lobo bit him once. Show him the scar, Jim.*

Devins scowled. *Durned if I will,* he said. He clanged his empty tin plate on Hendry's head. The dog slunk away to the shadows under the wagon. Frank got up and poured tin cups of coffee all around.

Jim thought he mighta been pizened by that wolf bite, Smith reminisced. *Oh did he wail. Set a whole durned nation of coyotes to singin', he did.* Smith smiled nostalgically.

Shet yer pie hole, Smith, Devins said.

Smith got up and stretched, then walked over to Frank's dugout and peered inside. *Mighty homey,* he said. *Fireplace, bunkbed, even a durned piller. Jest like downtown. What you got in that there satchel?* He reached in to touch it. From under the wagon came Hendry's warning growl. Smith pulled back his hand.

Oh, just foofaraw, Frank said. *Trifles. Letters from home and the like.*

Home, Smith said. *Don't even remember such a place no more.*

But they remember you, Devins said. He giggled. It was Smith's turn to scowl.

Frank slung the dregs of his coffee into the deepening dark. *Well, boys,* he said, *it's time for me to hit the hay. Gotta be up by first light. Huntin's like farmin'—no rest for the weary.* He snapped his fingers. *Here, Hendry. Bedtime, old feller.*

The dog crept out from under the wagon, gave the strangers a wide berth, and joined Frank in the soddy. Devins and Smith climbed into their wagon, shifted some hide bales, and unrolled their blankets. Soon they were sawing wood. Frank listened to their snores, then pulled Hendry closer to him in the bunkbed. *Bad customers, Hendry,* he whispered. *But they'll be gone by morning.*

They were. And so was Frank's satchel. Frank woke up woozy with a knot on his head the size of a mushmelon. His ears were still ringing. When he sat up, lightning bolts blazed through his brainpan from ear to ear. He swung his legs over the side of the bunkbed and tried to stand. His knees felt soft as soap. The fire glowed under the ashes. To the east the sky was paling toward dawn. Frank chucked kindling on the coals and waited till the twigs flared up. He took deep breaths. His stomach churned. By the light of the newborn fire he saw something lying just outside the soddy door. Red and gleaming. Four legs poked toward the top of the sky. Stiff. The dawn breeze brought the taint of raw flesh and strychnine. Hendry, sure enough. And the bastards had skinned him out.

They'd lured Hendry out of the soddy with poisoned meat, then coldcocked Frank with a rifle butt and made off with the satchel. That must have been how it went.

Frank looked around for his weapons. The Parker and Winchester were gone, and so were his team and buckboard. He looked under the bunkbed and saw that they'd missed the old Greener. That's something, at least, he thought. He dragged Hendry's wind-glazed body to the top of the ridge and scraped out a grave, using a board ripped away from the bunkbed as a shovel. He could not leave Hendry to the attentions of coyotes and vultures. The old dog's yellow teeth were bared in a silent snarl, his eyes stared up at nothing, glazed in death. Frank shoveled dirt over them, looking away toward the sunrise. Then he loaded the Greener from his cache of gunpowder and shot.

Devins and Smith would probably sell what they'd stolen in Danzig, along with their peltry and outfit, then catch a train for parts unknown. But they might have missed the westbound slow freight that pulled out of Danzig at five in the morning. The next train due in was the eastbound express, which arrived in the late afternoon. If he moved fast, Frank had every chance of catching them before they pulled out. He had no appetite but he knew he had a long run ahead of him this morning. He scraped cold beans from last night's pot, washing them down with reheated coffee. Finished, he picked up the Greener and set out for town at a fast jog trot.

He soon fell into a soothing rhythm that helped ease the pain in his head and his heart. It was like training for a prizefight, this run, like in the days before Sailor Christie. Like the run when he met those first market gunners and decided to change the direction of his life. Goddammit, he missed Hendry. It wasn't the money so much, it was the dog. Frank felt the fire rekindle in his heart. He'd gun them down on sight, Devins and Smith, splatter their guts all up and down Main Street. Then skin them out like they'd done to Hendry . . .

No, maybe not. Townsfolk would be watching. The law would hang him. No jury would understand what he felt right now. Though Hendry was better than any man he had ever known—braver by far, uncomplaining, more trustworthy, loving, honorable, and always reliable—dog murder was still not justifiable cause for manslaughter. The wiser course would be to report Devins and Smith to the sheriff. They were thieves, plain and simple, and horse thieves to boot. The owner of the mercantile would remember the guns he'd sold to Frank, and the knot on Frank's head would be evidence of their theft. So too would be the corpse of Hendry, though Frank shuddered at the thought of exhuming it.

But then he considered all the time it would take if he behaved like a good citizen and followed the slow but exceedingly fine-ground course of justice. By the time Devins and Smith were convicted, if ever they were, Frank's rage would have cooled to a mildly nagging memory. Hendry would have subsided into the mists of yesterday. And what sort of sentence would Devins and Smith get from the court, even if they were convicted? Horse theft was no longer a hanging offense as it was in days gone by. In the modern West, they might end up in the state pen for a year or two, if that. Do-gooders from the East had changed things. Vengeance is mine, saith the Lord? What mealymouthed Christer wrote that? What a theft of satisfaction from the human soul in its moment of loss, crying out—blood for blood.

When he got to town, Devins and Smith were long gone. Frank sold the Greener at the mercantile, realizing just enough money for a train ticket back East. It would take him as far as Des Moines. Harvest time in corn country. He could pick up work on a farm easy enough, if not he'd go back to the fight game.

The sun was setting, weak, piss yellow over the rolling plains, as the cars rolled into the oncoming night. Snow would be coming soon, and the bitter winds of winter. At least he'd miss that. Off on the far horizon Frank saw a faint, shifting haze, pale gray then thickening to black then fading again, rising and falling as it moved out toward the tallgrass prairie. Chickens in flight, a vast, wild flock of them. Frank blinked his eyes and shrugged his shoulders. Market gunning had been a bad idea. He turned up his collar and scrunched himself down in the hard wooden seat of the Pullman car. It would be a long, cold ride back to nowhere.

THE LONG AND THE SHORT OF IT

For more than half a century I've been hunting upland gamebirds, ruffed grouse and woodcock primarily, from the Rockies to the Canadian Maritimes, from Wisconsin, Minnesota, and Michigan clear down to Virginia and Georgia. I've hunted them behind pointing dogs and flushing dogs— from Irish, English, and Gordon setters, through English and German shorthair pointers, to springer and cocker spaniels, Brittanies, golden retrievers, and Labradors of all three colors. Eventually I settled on Labs as my favorites. Three great representatives of the breed convinced me, two yellow and one black.

Simba, the first of the yellows, was a huge dog—105 pounds without any body fat to speak of. He was better suited to the water—big water, rough water—but he worked beautifully in the uplands, in tandem with a German shorthair I had then by name of Max. They cruised the overgrown stone walls and popple brakes of southern New York and Pennsylvania like some Eastern version of the California Highway Patrol, hard-eyed and deadly. When Max would lock up, Simba would check back on me, give me the eye, wait until I was in position, and pounce in for the flush. He never lost a bird, and his only fault was an unbreakable insistence on devouring the first bird of every season. He'd only eat that first one, though, and he wasted not a feather, bless his heart. (Occasionally he relented, as if knowing I used the feathers to tie trout flies, and puked up a pile of them for me in the truck on the way back home.)

The most dedicated of the three Labs was the black one. His name was Luke, and he had the uncanny ability not only to alert me when he had a ruff pinned, but—with two of every three grouse he put up—to flush the bird back toward me, allowing an easy straightaway shot as the bird blew past. Simba had taught him the basics, but Luke developed this flush-back trick on his own. I certainly had nothing to do with it. When I began to puzzle over the phenomenon, I checked my game logs. I keep fairly thorough details on each flush and shot, and over the dozen seasons he hunted with me Luke flushed 3,423 birds (1,749 grouse, 1,674 woodcock); slightly better than sixty-three percent of the birds he put up came back toward or over my gun.

When Luke was eleven and nearing the end of the line, I had a chance to get a yellow Lab pup from a kennel in Zeeland, Michigan. My good friend Dan Gerber had just lost an old yellow Lab named Lily and had tracked down her antecedents. A litter was due shortly, and Dan asked me if I'd like to have one of the pups, a littermate to his dog. He named his female Willa, after Willa Cather. I named mine Jake. Over the next two seasons, Luke taught the pup all he knew, then died. I still can't think of that splendid black dog without tears coming to my eyes. But Jake is the next best thing, a wonderdog in his own right. He flushes just under half the birds he puts up back to me, and that's no bad thing. He's bigger than Luke was (eighty-five pounds to the black dog's sixty), and better on waterfowl. I've seen him work dozens of blind retrieves in whitecapped water or flooded timber, where the wind was away from the downed birds and Jake had no clue to where they'd fallen but the knowledge of where my muzzles were pointed when I fired.

But mainly I hunt the uplands here in southern Vermont, and Jake does just fine. When he was three years old I had an opportunity to pick up a pup from a litter of Jack Russell terriers. Friends of mine on Maryland's Eastern Shore had a fiery little bitch named Mrs. B, and like all Russells, Mrs. B was a piece of work. I'd never owned a terrier, but these murderous minidogs won my heart, so I brought home an eight-week-old female whom my wife and I named Rosalind Russell, after one of our favorite old-time movie stars. Roz may not have the legs of her namesake but she does have her feistiness, along with a great gift for comic timing.

Terriers are "earth dogs," deriving their generic name from the Latin root terra, and Jacks were bred to run with English foxhounds, then when and if Reynard went to ground, to dig it out of its den. They did the same with European badgers, which are even tougher than foxes. The titanic battles that raged beneath the ground were something else again. Many a Jack never reemerged from those dark, dank chambers, or if they did, often returned to the sunlight with an ear or an eye missing.

Though I never had any notion of making a birddog out of Roz, I proved too softhearted to leave her home alone when the season rolled around. She was only three months old, her head didn't even clear the tops of the grass, but I brought her along with me and Jake anyway, figuring at least

to give her a feel for the woods, and increase the bond between us. During one of those first hunts she inadvertently
blundered on a close-lying woodcock not three feet from
where I stood. It sprang skyward like a windup toy—I'm always reminded, when a woodcock flushes, of Paul Klee's
weird painting *The Twittering Machine*—and Roz watched it
fall to my shot with wonder in her eyes, then hied off after it.
Jake, of course, does the retrieving honors in our family and
quickly disabused her of the contemplated usurpation. But
when Roz came back in to me, her joyful eyes seemed to say:
"Do it again, Dad!"

So, God forgive me, I did. The result is that I now have
the strangest looking brace of upland bird dogs in New England. An Odd Couple, indeed. Or as I often describe them,
The Long and the Short of It.

And they make a fine team.

In my experience, the grouse of interior New England—
far more than those of the Rockies, the Midwest, or even
nearby New York state—are extremely loath to hold for a
point. I've had many more open shots at them when working
behind flushing dogs than with pointers or setters. My theory is that over the past 250 years the grouse have been
hunted so hard by the perennially poverty-stricken, meat-
hungry countrymen of interior New England that all the
dumb genes were killed off long since. The only birds that
survived to breed were the ones who instinctively walked
off, or more often ran, at the first hint of man or dog in the
vicinity. Grouse are said to "freeze" when they sense a threat
out of an instictive fear of raptors: If they run or fly, they
might be hooked from above by a stooping hawk or owl. But
early New Englanders shot off all the hawks and owls they
came upon, along with the "pa'triges." So the wise birds of
today simply leg it away from any large animal's approach,
and then flush wild when they're well out of range.

I've taught all my Labs to work close, checking back with me every minute or two to see where I'm headed and what piece of cover I'm thinking of hitting next. By overlapping a trained Lab with a pup, the younger dogs have learned these tactics more quickly than if I were training them solo. Just as Simba taught Luke to work close and check back, so too did Luke teach Jake. And—wonder of wonders—Jake taught Roz.

Because of his size and despite his bull-like strength, Jake simply can't get into some of the tighter pieces of cover—interlaced multiflora rose thickets, for instance, or the impenetrable fox-grape hells that festoon our sunny-slope hillsides. Roz, though, stands only ten inches tall at the shoulder and can—with her stubby legs—snake her way into these spots like a weasel. I've even known her to tunnel her way into those hells, throwing a great, tan, rock-filled roostertail behind her. Often a grouse or woodcock will be forced to fly at her churning, clattering approach. I've learned to wait on the shot until they're clear of the thorns or vines so that Jake can fetch it back to me. For Roz doesn't retrieve—having learned her lesson only too well from her big brother, who truly lives for the work and chastizes her quite gruffly when she tries to fetch back a fallen bird. (Though I'm certain that she would like to, and just as sure that she'd do it well.)

It's different, sure enough, hunting with this strange pair of dogs, and I'm certain that the ghosts of Burton Spiller, Dr. Charles Norris, and William Harnden Foster must be spinning in their graves every time my Odd Couple flushes a gamebird.

QUEST FOR QUIET

Silence is a rare stimulus in most sports. The high points of organized competition are generally punctuated with whistles, thuds, cheers, jeers, groans, whacks, screeches, and boos. Now and then, during the lung-tied instant before a crucial field goal, free throw, or three-and-two pitch, silence heightens the tension, but those situations are remarkable largely because of their rarity—and for what usually follows. Yet there once was an area of sport where silence was the key, the prime turn-on to an excitement that required reflexes as quick as a linebacker's or as subtle as an NBA guard's. That silence began with the first frost of autumn. It heightened as the leaves began to brighten and fall. It was bracketed by the steady tolling of a gundog's bell and

25

the sharp bark of gunfire. The most precious moment for most of us began with the sudden stillness of the bell. I first became aware of the magic in that moment some thirty-five years ago near Calais, Maine. We were hunting woodcock, of course, and the bell ceased its toll many times. Each silence seemed immortal.

"Well, we'll just get out and take a stroll up along that rim of alders and we ought to find a few birds in there. Why, goodness gracious, I recollect when we first started working dogs on woodcock back about thirty-eight years ago, maybe thirty-five, we might point a dozen birds in as many minutes up here, you'd just kill one and go to pick it up and with your next step why you'd put up another and kill it too, and then another until if you didn't have that old dog with you, oh dear, oh dear, well you'd never pick all of 'em up—get on around heah, you Duke, around *here!* Yes, good boy, in there is where they ought to be, *jeezum!*—but as I was saying, that was long ago and whilst most guides today'll tell you that you should ought to of been here last week, well, I'll tell you you should ought to of been here twenty years ago, my goodness, and it's waxing worse, yes it is, it's waxing worse," said Asa Sprague.

Then suddenly there was quiet.

"Duke's on point," Asa said. "Get on in there!"

Hunting woodcock with Asa Sprague and his ancient pointer Duke was a study in silence. Contrary to the stereotype of the taciturn New Englander, Acey talked incessantly, while the cowbell on Duke's collar clanked an erratic accompaniment to his master's voice. Lulled by words and bells and the scent of rotting apples, caught up in the rhythm of a daylong march through the bright autumn woods, I pounded many miles of rolling country as if in a dream. Then, instantly, silence fell. The dog's bell had stopped; Acey had stopped; time too had ceased for the moment.

Walking in ahead of the point, I could feel the tension build. The woodcock was in there, I knew, mottled body pressed flat to mottled leaves, only its big, black eyes, each of which could cover 180 degrees, shining wet in the under-brush as a modest giveaway. I realized that when he erupted with that heart-stopping whistle of wing feathers and zigzagged through the upper reaches of the alders, there'd be only about three seconds in which to swing and hit the trigger. I walked in ahead of old Duke, his eyes wide, nostrils flared, belly almost to the ground, every muscle tense and al-most quivering. The woodcock jumped, I shot. The bird fell . . . The flat bang of the gun had broken the silver silence and Acey's monologue resumed as quickly as it had ceased.

Like most woodcock addicts then as now, Asa Sprague sought more than meat for the pot. The birds themselves, like many of us who hunt them, are recluses, preferring the tangled depths of an alder brake or aspen thicket to the easy, open fields where the more gregarious of our breed hunt quail or pheasants. Back in the early nineteenth century, breeding populations of woodcock existed throughout the eastern United States. Year-round shooting and intense hunt-ing pressure, particularly from market hunters, wiped out most of the locally breeding birds before the Civil War. Frank Forester, an early American outdoor writer, reported killing upward of 150 birds in a day's shooting on the Jersey Mead-ows back in the 1830s and argued (in vain) for closed seasons on the timberdoodle long before governments recognized the need for them. Finally, with local birds shot off, large populations of breeding woodcock could only be found in northern New England, New York, the upper Midwest, and the Canadian Maritime Provinces. But the woodcock is a mi-gratory bird, moving south just ahead of the frost line to spend the winter in Georgia, Alabama, northern Florida, or Louisiana. They're hammered at every stop along the way.

En route the birds fly anywhere from ten to a hundred miles a night, refueling during their rest stops on earthworms. Their long bills, jointed near the tip, are especially adapted for grabbing worms. I'd like to see one tackle a bowl of spaghetti.

As a target for the wingshooter, the woodcock demands a sharp eye, a sharper ear, and quick reflexes. "You'll usually hear him before you see him," Sprague said, "and you'd better be up on him before he clears the alders. He'll pause at the top of his ride and then cut out through the upper branches like a singed ferret." A close-working dog is a must. Older or slower dogs—Brittanies, Labs, cockers, springers, and elderly pointers or setters—are preferable to young, rangy ones. Acey's pointer Duke filled the bill.

Duke was eleven human years old at the time, which would have made him about seventy-seven in dog years. Acey himself admitted to being "in the sixty-ninth year of my age," but local townsmen allowed he was probably more like seventy-two. The combined bird-hunting wisdom of that grand old hunting team totaled nearly a century and a half of woods lore. For all their gray hairs, though, neither man nor dog flagged perceptibly during three days of hot, heavy hunting. Duke's chest and belly were ripped raw by the briers, and unseasonably warm temperatures (eighty degrees was the high one afternoon) sent him searching for water, what Sprague called "Adam's ale," in every rill or mud hole. Then, recharged and dripping, he dashed off into the thickets, bell clanking and tail wagging.

Because of the heat and a month without rain, the highlands were too hard for good worm digging, so the birds we found were widely scattered through the moist, lowland coverts. These were local birds, Sprague said, the migration not yet having begun, and there were still too many leaves on the alders for clear shooting. Still, Asa remained as spry as his dog. On three separate occasions, when a bird flushed wild between us, the old man flung himself to the ground and bellowed, "Shoot!" His rolling, bowlegged gait, almost identical with that of his dog, carried him through the thickest tangles at a pace that left me breathing hard. And I was a quarter century younger than he was. "Well, feller," he'd bellow in his Titus Moody accent, "you can't hit 'em if you can't raise 'em, and you can't raise 'em by standing still."

But it was, as always for me, the country and not the killing of birds that dominated the hunt, both physically and psychologically. I suspect that it's not for lack of erudition that the folks around Asa's hometown pronounce it *Callus*. After three days of pounding the worn-down granite mountains that flank the Bay of Fundy my feet were as hard and horny as Huck Finn's. Throughout the region, the failure of the nineteenth-century American homestead was writ large upon the land. Weathered barns leaned away from the northeast wind. Iron stoves, red with rust, flaked away their half-lives in the stone cellars of collapsed farmhouses. Studded like sudden oases through the tilted hills, abandoned orchards brought forth their plenteous fruit for nature's consumption. Twice we jumped deer and grouse feeding on the bright windfallen apples. Resting on a hillside as the day got hotter, I munched on a crisp, white-fleshed, pear-shaped apple as Acey pointed to the gray ruin of a farmhouse down below and recalled its past.

"This was Nell Berry's place," he said. "She was an old widder woman who used to raise state charges here—orphans. A fine and gentle woman, old Nell, full of love. Those apples back there on the hill were the finest in this corner of the country. I used to come up here and talk to her, with one eye on the apples so's to nail me a pa'tridge when they flew up to feed. Over there is Breakneck Mountain, oh I pounded over it many a night after jacking deer, and down there"—he pointed to a blue flash of water through the golden blur of poplars—"is Meddybemps Lake, where two of my best buddies drownded. They was running deer with dogs, killing up to a hundred a year for the market. In those days, you couldn't earn a living wage around here—hell, you still can't—so you had to hunt for it. Well, it was a day just like this one. No wind, bright, hot, dusty. The dogs ran the buck into the lake, and they went out in their canoe to shoot it. Clayton, he had a withered arm, and I reckon that when he rose up to shoot, the canoe rolled over. Neither of those boys could swim so good. They come up through the ice the following spring. You could spot them from the black bulges in the ice. Well, they was *deteriorated* some."

From the cover down below we could hear the tinkle of another gundog's bell. Duke stopped panting and stared downhill. "More bird hunters," Acey said. "Well, that's okay. Plenty of birds in these hills." We heard the bell clank closer, closer. Then . . .

Silence. Down the slope about two hundred yards the other dog was on point. Even at that range, I could sense the tension building until the climactic wing whistle and shot reopened the conversation. The downhill hunters turned out to be a pair of older, white-haired woodcock enthusiasts from Ohio whom I'd met the previous evening in Calais. I still like to think of them as typical of the breed. John J. Adams was a labor lawyer from Cleveland who'd learned the book on upland gamebirds by walking them up dogless as a kid. He'd bought his first gun with the money he earned on a paper route—a 16-gauge Model 12. His partner, Jack Klages, was president of an auto parts company in Columbus, Ohio. As they hiked up the hill to join us, birdless so far, neither seemed dismayed. "Some tasty apples down there," said Jack, munching one.

As the morning wore on, Duke and the Ohioans' dog pointed plenty more woodcock and we three managed to miss nearly as many. From time to time Jack and John launched into historical monologues, as spiky with learning as the wild rose thickets were with thorns. They commented on the "blueberry hay" the farmers had laid down on their fields, hay that will lie rotting and composting for a year before it is ignited to return its nutrients to the earth. "We burn off our fallow material too fast in the rest of America," John said. "Early retirement and all that. We should let talent age before sending it up in smoke. This blueberry hay could stand as a kind of metaphor." He was a man of careful words, judicious insights. By contrast, Jack was an enthusiast, an avowed "covered-bridge freak," and he filled a ten-minute uphill hike with a detailed account of a visit he'd made with his wife to "the world's longest covered bridge" (1,282 feet) in nearby Hartland, New Brunswick. True sportsmen, neither John nor Jack was in a slathering rush to kill birds, and the low-key nature of their hunting proved as refreshing as the windfall apples picked up along the way.

By day's end, though the dogs had pointed more than thirty woodcock, only one of us had killed a five-bird limit. But as Acey emphasized, that's not what it's all about anyway. "Well, boys, it doesn't bother me much that we haven't wiped them all out," he said, his wild, white roostertail of hair defying the north wind. "I've killed my share of meat in these woods, oh yes. I've lugged big hunks of moose and bear over these ridges, and if I had a song for every bird I've rubbed out, why, I guess you'd be callin' me Elvis. Jeezum shucks, if I never kill another bird, I won't cry about it. Glory, but it's a nice way to spend a day."

No one contradicted him. Silence prevailed . . .

And nowadays, whenever I hear a pointing dog's beeper blatting away in the distance, or a four-wheel ATV blaring through the woods, I cherish that old-time silence all the more.

MUDBATS FOREVER!

On what should have been a quiet evening last spring I went out behind the house at dusk, into our fifteen-acre meadow, to catch the Woodcock Sonata. The time was 8:35 P.M., the evening windless and mild; the last light of day was fading to blue velvet.

Down the road about a quarter of a mile, a pack of half-wild dogs, the pride and joy of a sentimental neighbor lady, was barking with its customary frenzy.

At the same time, another neighbor came roaring up the road in his truck at forty miles an hour—an event that can occur as many as twenty times a day. When this neighbor, a volunteer fireman, arrived in his driveway, he sounded a brief burst on his siren (paid for in part with my tax money)—*whoop, whoop, whoop!*—and got on the loudspeaker (ditto) to coo a few words of baby talk to his coon hounds, which responded in kind with excited yips and whoops of their own. It's a little game they play.

Meanwhile, a third neighbor was shooting a last-light round of hoops with his ten-year-old son. Added to the whoop of dogs and sirens and loudspeakers came the tympanic thump of a basketball against the newly installed backboard.

And on top of all this, what should I hear but the angry burbling hiss of my blood, coming rapidly to a boil . . .

But then, just in the nick of time, came the sound I'd been praying for: the faint, nasal, rasping peent of a woodcock announcing the sky dance that constitutes his courtship. The buzzing call was infrequent, about once every ten or twenty seconds, and lasted for three or four minutes overall. Overture complete, the bird launched itself on twittering wings straight upward into the empyrean. Up, up he spiraled, twittering all the way—one hundred feet, two hundred, three . . . Then he dive-bombed the earth in a long zigzag glide, burbling his flight song, a series of wild, liquid chirps . . .

The woodcock landed just about where he'd launched from, and soon the peenting began again. By now the neighbors and their dogs and sons and sirens and basketballs were all indoors, where they belonged. For the next half hour the avian Romeo and I had the evening to ourselves.

Eventually, I knew, these aerial serenades would attract a female of the species to the edge of the meadow. After mating, while Romeo flew off in search of another conquest, his erstwhile Juliet would scratch a crude nest in the field, sometimes close to a scraggly shrub or two but more often right out in the open. A woodcock nest is nothing fancy, a mere scrape edged with a low berm of twigs and grasses. In it she'll lay four buff-colored eggs, mottled a rusty brown, that look too large for such a small bird. She incubates the eggs for about three weeks. The hatchlings can follow the hen on foot and actually feed themselves only a day or two after hatching, probing the mucky ground for worms just like Mommy. In four weeks they are full grown and flying, and by eight weeks they are entirely on their own.

Yet during the brief time the young spend with their mother, she attends them much more carefully than many other female birds, covering the chicks from rain and snow, protecting them with her subtle camouflage from wandering predators. Indeed, the nineteenth- and early-twentieth-century literature on the woodcock, admittedly anecdotal, reports many cases of Mother Woodcock actually *carrying* their young away from danger, and on the wing at that.

Edwyn Sandys, an expatriate English hunter-naturalist whose book *Upland Game Birds* (Macmillan, 1902) is one of my most prized possessions, writes:

> ... I have good reason to believe that I have seen one carried off. The nest in question was on a bit of level ground amid tall trees. The sole suggestion of cover was a lot of flattened leaves which lay as the snow had left them. Perhaps ten yards away was an old rail fence about waist-high, and on the farther side of it was a clump of tall saplings. A man coming out of the wood told me he had just flushed a woodcock and had seen her brood, recently hatched, and pointed out where they were. I went in to investigate, and located one young bird crouched on the leaves. It ran a few steps and again crouched, evidently not yet strong enough for any sustained effort. I went off, and hid behind a stump, to await developments. From this shelter the young bird was visible and it made no attempt to move. Presently the old one came fluttering back, alighted near the youngster, and walked to it. In a few moments she rose and flew low and heavily, merely clearing the fence, and dropping perhaps ten yards

within the thicket. Her legs appeared to be half-bent, and so far as I could determine the youngster was held between them. Something about her appearance reminded me of a thing often seen—a shrike carrying off a small bird. I carefully marked her down, then glanced toward where the youngster had been. It was no longer there; and a few moments later it, or its mate, was found exactly where the mother had gone down. . . . These details are dwelt on because many writers have disputed the carrying of the young. My impression is that the bird had removed the other children before I got to the place. They certainly were not beside the one, but the search for them was brief, owing to the fact that there was a nasty possibility of stepping on them.

An odd bird indeed is my friend *Philohela minor*. Oh yes, I know the taxonomists recently changed his name to the uneuphonious *Scolopax minor*, but I'm an old curmudgeon now and I'm damned if I'll obey orders. Known colloquially as timberdoodle, bogsucker, even mudbat, the woodcock is the strangest, dearest bird I know, and I won't change his name on a whim of mere science.

Consider this oddball object of my affections:

A woodcock's brain, for some reason, is mounted upside down.

Its ears are located forward of its nostrils.

Its huge, dark, bulging eyes, which sit high on the rear of a tiny, pinched-in head, can see a full 360 degrees, the better to elude its enemies—which are legion. Were our eyes as large in proportion, they'd each be the size of a grapefruit.

Add to this a disproportionately long bill—two and a half inches in the male, three in the female—a bill that is flexible at the tip and as sensitive as a pair of human fingers, allowing the woodcock to grasp its favorite food source, earthworms, as deftly as you might an errant strand of pasta on a slippery plate; a virtually nonexistent tail; a pair of dainty, coral-pink feet; wings that look too broad and long for a bird that weighs only a little more than six ounces—wings more suitable to a barn owl or a small hawk—and a wondrous, dodgy, batlike agility in flight, and you have an unlikely object for human affection.

The woodcock and his larger mate (females of the species weigh eight ounces or more) can cover two or three hundred miles a night during their migrations, but usually they fly alone, or with a few close friends—leisurely spring or fall flights of no more than twenty to fifty miles each, depending on the weather.

A woodcock can eat twice its weight in worms each day in preparation for these seasonal flights.

The animals that like to eat *him*, not to mention his wife and his progeny (either eggs or chicks), include owls, hawks, crows, ravens, shrikes, bobcats, coyotes, foxes, dogs, house cats, snakes, raccoons, skunks, weasels, and the odd human hunter. Yet his worst enemies are the land developer and those misguided flatlanders who oppose clear-cutting.

Though the woodcock is not yet in danger of extinction—nearly two million birds a year are bagged legally by hunters over the woodcock's migratory range, east of the Mississippi from southern Canada to the Louisiana bamboo thickets hard by the Gulf of Mexico—they've been declining over the past dozen years or more at an annual rate of 3 percent. The main reason for this is loss of habitat. To thrive, woodcock need young successional forests dotted with brushy, overgrowing meadows, but we are allowing our woodlands to get too damned old—not just in my home state of Vermont, but throughout the Northeast.

The boom time for woodcock in this country occurred from the turn of the twentieth century through the Great Depression of the 1930s. During those years family farms were abandoned at an ever-increasing rate as the nation turned

more and more to city life. As a result, in the emptying countryside, vast patches of cleared pasture slowly returned to
woodland: thick stands of sprouting aspen clouded the once-
bald New England hills, and mucky, worm-rich alder brakes
clotted the brooks and burns and bottomland that drained
them: Timberdoodle Heaven.

By the 1960s this process was already reversing itself.
Aspen had matured to pole timber and was being edged
out by invading hardwoods like ash, oak, swamp maple,
and beech. Alders had aged past the stage where woodcock could profit from them. The malling of America also
contributed its bit to the decline of grouse and woodcock
habitat: The cheapest land was boggy or swampy, and devel-
opers had only to drain it to throw up a new shopping center.
And it was on the edges of those very bogs and swamps that
woodcock had found their happiest worm-hunting ground.
Too, people fed up with life in the tumultuous cities of the
Northeast and their stultifying suburbs were moving into the
countryside of rural, interior New England, where land was
still cheap and building costs not yet excessive. Inevitably
the sites these people chose for their new homes were the
very places where ruffed grouse and woodcock had found
their best living: wooded hilltops with brooks running
nearby. The former cityfolk brought with them fallacious at-
titudes regarding woodland and wildlife. Clear-cutting,
which could have brought back the successional stages of
woodland recovery so necessary to continued woodcock
populations, was and remains anathema to most flatlanders.
Even selective logging, which does nothing to improve game
habitat, is frowned upon, though it's often grudgingly accepted by city types to improve the "landscaping" of their
acreage.

The only new growth that's benefited from this urbanite
invasion in my neck of the woods is the new Vermont state
flower, with its colorful orange-and-black blossoms gracing

every quiet backwoods road and brook and hillside clear up to the Canadian border: *Postatus signatorus* (the POSTED sign).

Soon, though, if habitat continues to decline the way it's going, such warnings will no longer be necessary. There'll be nothing left to protect but squirrels and owls. And then they too will be gone.

A SNIPE HUNT

When I was a kid just starting to hunt, the dogs and I used to jump snipe quite regularly. They frequented the same marsh meadows, pond edges, and low-lying riverside fields where we came to sneak-shoot ducks. It was always a bit of a jolt to be pussyfooting quietly through the tussocks and reed beds, ears all atip for the telltale babbling of ducks on the feed, when all of a sudden a snipe or two, or ten, sprang up from underfoot—skeap, skeap, skeap—to go dodging out low over the marsh grass. They were tempting targets, fast and elusive, just the type of gamebirds that cry out to be shot at, but of course—with ducks on my mind—I didn't dare swing on them and pull the trigger. That would have alerted all the waterfowl in the county, and besides I was usually loaded with No. 4s, a full charge of which would shred a snipe like so much coleslaw if I managed to connect.

But woodcock, grouse, and pheasants could sometimes also be found on these cooler, wetter grounds, especially in the hot weather of early season, so when I could afford it I carried a pocketful of lighter loads and, once the ducks had stopped flying, hunted the upland birds on my way back from pond or river. And of course, soon I was wasting my precious rounds on snipe. I say wasting because I hit only about one of every ten I shot at—and that on a good day.

With its long bill and outsized wings, *Capella gallinago*, the common snipe (in those days it was designated Wilson's snipe), looks like a slimmer, white-breasted version of the woodcock. Both birds hold close to a pointing or flushing dog, or even a man approaching clumsily on foot, and both are quick off the ground. But where the woodcock, usually found in dense, tall cover, leaps straight up for about fifteen or twenty feet before beginning the dodgy portion of its escape routine, the snipe lines out low and fast, dodging from the get-go. I once hunted woodcock in northern Georgia, along the banks of slow brown rivers lined with tall trees and very little undergrowth: The woodcock we jumped there also flew low, zigzagging right from the flush. All my life I've had trouble with low-flushing birds—that is, birds that fly out and away from me below the plane of my eyeballs. I tend to shoot over them, or sometimes not at all. Perhaps I'm unconsciously afraid of hitting a dog or even another hunter who might be out there, unseen by me in the tight-focused concentration of the shot. The ruffed grouse of my New England home coverts seem to know this, and when they flush low I usually end up apologizing to the dog.

Whatever the reason, my score on snipe remained abominable. The few I did manage to bring to bag, though, were delicious eating—a bit smaller and less meaty than woodcock, but not quite as strongly flavored, even though the snipe too is primarily a worm-eater. It was not until twenty years after I first started wasting shot on the species that I had a really bang-up day on snipe. Early one autumn during the 1970s, I'd flown into Yakutat in the southeast Alaskan panhandle to fish the coho salmon run on the Situk River. It was a dark, splendidly wild country of black spruce and naked rock, quaking bogs and glacial muck and rushing blue-white water, all overseen by the glowering face of the Malaspina Glacier. In addition to huge salmon runs, this area was also famous for its "blue bears," a color variation of the black bear also known as the glacier bear, and the lodge we stayed in had a full body mount of a rearing bruin, its great paws outstretched, jaws agape, just inside the entryway. It was as blue as if it had been daubed with woad—rather like Mel Gibson's face in the battle scenes of *Braveheart*.

Unfortunately for our angling plans, an ugly storm system had blown in from the Gulf of Alaska along with us, and the Situk was out of its banks, discolored and likely to remain that way for the next few days. The fishing was abominable, especially for the bright, fresh-run salmon that we'd come for. We managed to fish the headwaters of the river system, where the water was still reasonably clear, and caught more than we cared to of the earlier arrivals, big fish that had already gone dark and offered little in the way of fight. It rained and rained, then rained some more.

"Fine weather for ducks," I gloomed to my guide, a tough little guy named Bobby Fraker.

"Ducks, you say?" He lit up like a Christmas tree. "Why didn't you say so earlier? Hell, we could run up to Dry Bay in my big boat this afternoon, the tide will be just right, kill us a couple of limits—not just ducks, but geese too. There's a bunch of 'em just blew in, Canadas lest I miss my guess."

And thus it was arranged. After lunch we fared forth in Bobby's "big boat"—which proved to be an open, sixteen-foot outboard. But the seas in the gulf were calm, and we couldn't get any wetter than we'd been so far. Or so I imagined. It was a long, loud, bumpy ride along a shoreline piled high with driftwood and flotsam. Bald eagles circled and swooped over the inshore waters, snagging dead salmon or stealing live ones from the ospreys that went through the dirty work of catching them. At one point we saw a bear shuffling along the beach above the sea wrack, but it was just a plain old garden-variety brown bear, slightly larger than a Volkswagen, where I'd been hoping to see a bright blue bruin like the one that guarded the lodge.

As we entered Dry Bay, Bobby began nosing slow and easy into the shallow inlets, the motor idling quietly, while I stood in the bow with his backup gun, a battered old Winchester Model 12. Ducks jumped skyward—mallards, spoonbills, widgeons, pintails. More rain fell than ducks that afternoon, but it was fast, exciting shooting and soon I had my limit. Wherewith we traded places and Bobby filled his in half my time. Now for the geese.

We ran deeper into the bay, the ice-cold water turned milky blue with glacial till, pulling up finally to tie off under a pile of driftwood on the shore of a long rock-studded spit, half sand, half quaking bog meadow. "The geese should be feeding on the lee shore," Bobby whispered. "We'll lay the sneak on 'em."

The weather had cleared suddenly, the cold rain ceased and a weak, wan sun tried to peek through the thinning cloud cover. Alaskan coastal weather, winter and summer all jumbled together. In wool socks, long johns, hip boots, and T-shirts, we crouched our way across the bog meadow. It was uneven going. One step you'd be on solid bottom, the next knee-deep in foul-smelling tidal muck. But the tension was keen nonetheless. Suddenly a snipe went up from the marsh grass under my muddy boot, then another, then six, seven, eight of them—*skeap, skeap, skeap!* Dodging, twisting, begging me to shoot. Old habits die hard. It was all I could do to keep from swinging on them.

Whether the snipe alerted the geese or not, they were gone by the time we reached the lee shore. We could see them circling out over the deeper recesses of the bay, then cupping in a mile away.

"Dammit, I want me a couple a them Canucks," Bobby said. His face was grim, his eyes wild. Marsh mud streaked his face, in this watery light like so much Celtic woad. "Let's go back in the woods some, circle around, see if we can't jump 'em from that side."

I thought of bears. I thought of wolves. I thought, suddenly, of the tide.

"Do we have time?" I asked. "When does the tide turn?"

"Aw hell, we got plenty of time."

"Why don't you go ahead," I said. "I can kill geese anywhere but I haven't shot snipe in many a year. While you're gone I'll renew my acquaintance with the species." I'd noticed some 7½s in the ammo box of the boat—rounds Bobby used on teal and spruce grouse, he'd told me.

"Okay," he said, "but give me about twenty minutes before you start shooting, and try to hunt the far side of the spit. That way maybe you won't spook the geese on me."

I waded back through the shallows around the point to the boat, had a cup of coffee from the thermos, emptied the No. 2s from my gun and loaded with the lighter rounds, stuffing my pockets with the rest of the box. I looked at my watch, then started hunting.

The snipe got up by squadrons. To my amazement and delight, I dropped the first three I shot at—clean kills at thirty to forty yards. It took a while to find them in the tall marsh grass without a dog. Having no shooting vest, I stuck their heads through my belt loops, just the way I had as a kid with woodcock and grouse, and walked on, waiting my shots, trying not to shoot too fast with the tight-choked autoloader. My score mounted, no misses so far. What accounted for my unaccustomed accuracy on these birds? It could have been the gun—the Winchester was heavy, long-barreled, slower to mount, and steadier of swing than the light upland guns I'd shot on snipe in my early days. It could have been the naïveté of these young, far northern birds, which didn't seem to dodge as much as the birds I remembered. No doubt they would wise up the farther south they proceeded on their annual migration, so that by the time they reached the latitudes where I had earlier gunned them, they'd know all the tricks of surviving a hastily thrown shot pattern. But I think the reason for my newfound success on snipe was Alaska, plain and simple. Subconsciously I knew there could be no dog, no other hunter, in the path of my low-flung shot patterns. That day at least, I simply couldn't miss . . .

By the time Bobby returned, lugging two big Canadas over his back, the sun was sloping down fast toward Japan, far to the southwest. We got out of there in a hurry. The tide was turning, in fact had already turned. At one point on the run out we ran aground on the mud bar that guarded the mouth of the bay. We both had to get over the side and push the boat through the glaucous glacial muck for what felt like half a mile. A new rainstorm had moved in from the gulf, adding to our woes. Dry Bay? You could have fooled me. Then it was a high-speed ride for home, bucking the wind, the chop, and the icy rain, cold and shivering and soaked through, both of us, despite our rain gear. But it had been worth it. Even more so that night, when—showered and shaved and dressed in warm wool and flannels—Bobby and I tucked into a skilletful of braised snipe, piping hot and swimming in a rich, sherry-laced cream sauce. You get what you pay for.

THE SLIDE TOWARD
SENESCENCE

Just as we bird hunters, like it or not, eventually grow decrepit, so too do our favorite coverts. I've been feeling the effects in both regards lately. When I moved to Vermont in the spring of 1979, I was a mere stripling in the forty-fifth year of my age. During that first summer I scouted the turf around my new home, pounding the hills and slogging the swamps nonstop in search of prospective bird coverts. It all looked ideal.

At the top of a twelve-acre meadow directly behind the house was a vigorous stand of young aspen from which my dog, a black Lab named Luke who was then not quite two years old, routinely flushed three or four ruffed grouse in short order whenever we entered it.

Along Oven Brook, which bisects my thirty-five acres, alders grew thick and tangled. Resident woodcock fed there every morning and evening, while during the day they used the brushy edges of the field, hanging tight in the doghair popple until Luke nosed them into the sky.

On the steep slope across the road, flanking a stand of spruce and white pine, was an old apple orchard that was slowly being smothered out of existence by thorn hells of blackberry and multiflora rose. Grouse budded in the apple trees; woodcock could always be found in the wetter ground along the rills and brooklets that laced Shatterack Mountain.

Indeed the entire eastern face of Shatterack was prime bird cover. So too was the western slope of Bear Mountain, which rose some three thousand feet behind my property. Not half a mile from my back door stood a knob called the Haystack, with a similar mix of decaying apple orchards, fresh aspen stands, alder and hardhack and thorn apple and wild grapes: Burnt Ridge, the Bear's Den, upper White Creek, the Owl's Head, Canary Brook, the Hay Flat—the coverts were strung up and down the winding road I lived on like jewels on a necklace.

Ten minutes up the road toward Sandgate I spotted a big meadow studded with clumps of young popple. Come fall, I knew, those "Woodcock Islets" would be thick with migrant mudbats. And so it proved when the bird season opened.

I don't like to hunt the same covert two days in a row, preferring to allow at least a week between visits, but here I had at least eight or ten nearby coverts at my disposal. Eventually my list of reliable spots grew to fourteen. Some of them Luke and I could "frisk" in half an hour of careful hunting; others we'd hunt all day if we chose, and often we did.

All of these coverts peaked in the late 1980s. Then they began a slow slide toward senescence. The alder brakes topped out and thinned, rather like the hair on my own balding pate. The aspen thickets as well. Where once I could count on sixteen grouse and/or woodcock flushes in an hour of hunting, the numbers began to decline—ten, eight, four, three, sometimes none at all. My gunning log tells the sad tale. Meanwhile POSTED signs blossomed along the roads as more and more wealthy suburbanites from New York and Boston bought property in the Green Mountain State, almost all of them anti-hunters. They were also anti-loggers. The idea of clear-cutting for habitat improvement was as odious to them as, say, a rusty pickup or a junker parked in the barnyard. Their idea of good habitat was tall, stately, parklike woods with no nasty understory of brush and brambles to impede them in their Reeboked romps thro' the sylvan glades.

One wealthy woman who bought four hundred acres just down the road from me, but comes up to her Vermont pied-à-terre only three or four times a year, razed a perfectly wonderful woodcock cover to plant it in Christmas trees. Her POSTED signs meant business, too. She proved to be a strident, nay, a hysterical anti-hunter.

One of my most productive coverts, just off the Ebenville Road near a place I call the Pine Plantation, also changed ownership. The guy who sold the property had been a deer hunter, but welcomed bird hunters so long as they filled him in on what they'd seen by way of buck rubs and scrapes as the deer season approached. His successor, a lawyer from New Jersey, dabbled in grouse hunting but was loath to post his land. Since he only came up to Vermont on the odd weekend or during long holidays, I continued to hunt that covert, until one day he called me at home, long distance from Jersey City, to say he now had a paid "spy" in the neighborhood who'd reported to him the presence of myself, my dog, and my pickup truck in the vicinity of his domain. "Now I don't want to get 'legal' on you," he said, "but I'd appreciate it if henceforth you stayed off my property. I'd like to have at least *some* of my grouse left. I bring clients up here from time to time and it would be nice to have something left to shoot at."

His grouse? And he was afraid that I would *shoot them all out?*

Some bird hunter.

I knew who his spy was—a local who lives half a mile down the road from me and whose apt nickname is Weasel. He'd fink me out for sure, so I decided to avoid the Ebenville covert from then on. What the hell, I had plenty of others to hunt.

Or did I?

The Woodcock Islets were no longer producing—the last bird I shot there fell in 1991.

The Shatterack coverts had gone by.

Even my favorite upland patch, a two-mile-long stretch of endlessly varied cover dominated by a knob called the Pinnacle, was no longer holding as many birds as it once had. Again the same old story: overly mature aspens and alders. Pole timber: good deer and bear and turkey woods, but no understory left.

No edge without a new house and a satellite dish looming nearby.

I kept my own property in good shape through all this by clear-cutting small patches, an acre or two at a time, but thirty-five acres isn't much covert, not for an entire season. So I began again to scout new ground. There wasn't much left, and those few spots I located were posted to the nines.

Then I met salvation in the form of a guy called Ed Carmel. Ed, who is nearly sixty now and a bachelor, moved to our town from Massachusetts more than twenty-five years ago. A Vietnam vet and an ardent deer and turkey hunter, he told me time and again, when we happened to meet at the general store, of the abundance of gamebirds on his sixty-five acres. He also leases the hunting rights on an adjacent two hundred acres. "I don't hunt birds myself," he said, "but I'd love to walk the property with you and your dogs sometime, just watch and see how you go about it."

I generally prefer to hunt alone, me and the dogs poking along and following our noses, sometimes shooting at what gets up, sometimes not, as the mood strikes me. I long ago gave up hunting for high body counts. During the bird season I'm usually starting a new novel and half the time I spend afield my head is in the clouds, living in the world of my fiction. But what the hell, I really needed some new coverts. I finally agreed to Ed's proposition.

It proved to be Upland Heaven. The lower half of the acreage was an ancient apple orchard—old-timey varieties like Sheepsnose, Yellow Transparent, Pearmain, and Northern Spies—interspersed with young popple, yellow birch, and stands of alder in the seeps and swales. A lot of the thickets were wreathed in healthy, productive grapevines. Every year or two, for the past quarter century, Ed had brush-hogged winding lanes through the brambles and sumac that threatened to strangle the covert.

He'd brought along an old Stevens 16-gauge side-by-side, a turkey gun, choked full and modified. I offered him the use of a more open gun, an old 20-bore Winchester Model 23 of mine choked improved and modified, but he just laughed. "I don't want to kill anything," he said. "Just watch. Hell, I only carry the gun for balance anyways!"

What more generous a hunting companion could you ask for?

Ed's reluctance to kill, I knew, derived from the fact that a few years earlier he'd been diagnosed with prostate cancer. Prompt surgery and follow-up radiation therapy had given him a respite, but he told me he knew he would die— "sooner rather than later."

He said this without a trace of self-pity.

We've hunted together on his property this season at least once a week, usually for two or three hours at a stretch.

In that time it's not unusual to move twenty or thirty birds of both varieties. I've killed a few, to be sure, but mainly I enjoy Ed's eager company. For all his physical problems he's tireless in the woods, preferring to beat the toughest covers by himself, through vines and briers and thorn apple jungles, allowing me to work the more open areas where I can get a decent shot.

He exults each time I drop a bird, studies it in hand with the rapt awe of a youngster, and when I miss he laughs out loud—"Ya gotta love it!" he says. (No you don't.) He shoots at a few himself but hasn't connected yet. "They don't give you much time to aim," he grins. Though he'd never eaten grouse or woodcock before in a long hunting life, Ed discovered a real gusto for them one night when my wife and I had him over for dinner.

He is one of the kindest, most decent men I've ever known, and certainly one of the bravest. Now if I can only get him a more suitable upland gun and teach him how to wingshoot, I'll have found not only a great new covert when I need it most, but a hunting partner as well.

THE ROYAL MACBOB

Tired of the same old same-old? Here's a thought from our British cousins: Jaded outdoorsmen might consider spicing up their sporting lives by attempting to score a "Great Macnab," i.e., catching a salmon, shooting a stag, and bagging a brace of grouse, all in the same day. The truly bored could add a fourth element to the challenge—bedding the cook at the shooting lodge to cap the day's performance. This feat, according to Britain's foremost outdoor magazine *The Field,* elevates the accomplishment to the status of a "Royal Macnab."

Ungodly sexism aside, I found the notion interesting on two counts. First off, the source of the Great Macnab challenge stems from one of the most delightful sporting yarns I've ever read: John Buchan's 1925 novel *John Macnab*. The Scots-born Buchan (1875–1940), best known today for his thriller *The Thirty-Nine Steps,* which was made into a popular 1935 film by Alfred Hitchcock, was a sportsman, soldier, barrister, member of Parliament, prizewinning author, and, later in his eventful life, governor-general of Canada.

The novel is purportedly based on a real-life feat performed in 1897 by a Scottish sport named Captain James Brander Dunbar. Buchan's version, embroidering on the actual event, deals with the merry misadventures of three eminent—and eminently bored—British sporting gentlemen who, in an attempt to shake their ennui, journey to the wilds of Scotland, where they issue written challenges to the lairds of three game-rich but closely patrolled estates. "Sir," reads one such missive, "I have the honour to inform you that I propose to kill a stag"—or a salmon as the case may be—"on your ground [on a specified date]. The animal, of course, remains your property and will be duly delivered to you. . . . In the event of the undersigned failing to achieve his purpose he will pay as a forfeit one hundred pounds, and if successful fifty pounds to any charity you may appoint. I have the honour to be, your humble servant." All three letters are signed with the nom de chasse "John Macnab."

In other words, "Catch me if you can!"

The ensuing pages are filled with stalking lore and poachers' tricks, hair's-breadth escapes and wonderful descriptions of the bleak, beautiful, heather-clad Scots Highlands in all kinds of weather. In the course of the narrative, one of the adventurers falls in love with the lissome daughter of a victimized laird, which must be what gave the editors of the *The Field* the idea for the final fillip of the Royal Macnab.

Though Buchan didn't include grouse in the prey his poacher-heroes sought, *The Field* wisely did. Most Scottish grouse, of course, are shot from butts after having been "driven" by beaters until they take flight well in advance of the line of guns. They come through high and fast, very challenging targets. What the Brits call a "rough shoot"—where the individual gunner and his dog walk up the birds, American-style—is considered déclassé, so perhaps that's why Buchan, who was an avid and accomplished wingshot but a bit of a snob (he later became Baron Tweedsmuir of Elsfield), did not include a grouse challenge. A single furtive gunner couldn't very well hire beaters to drive the birds to him without giving himself away. But *The Field,* by adding a brace of grouse to the challenge, made its version of the Macnab far more difficult an accomplishment, especially in the course of a single day.

I know because I tried it.

Some years ago, shortly after I'd first read Buchan's novel, I found myself in a position to go for what was later to be termed a Macnab. I was still bowhunting at that time—in those years before the woods began to fill up during the early arrows-only deer season with neophytes carrying compound bows and shooting at everything that moved—and early one crisp, bright October morning in Vermont I managed to drop a buck within the first hour of hunting. My "stag" was nothing spectacular—a fork-horn that dressed out at 115 pounds—but through arduous preseason scouting I'd anticipated its habitual feeding patterns, got in the right position on opening day, and killed it with a close, clean neck shot. But by the time I'd "gralloched" it, shifted the carcass out of the woods, hung it from the meat pole in the cool, shady barn, skinned it, and covered it with cheesecloth to discourage blowflies, I still had the whole day ahead of me. And energy to burn.

On my way out of the woods with the deer, I'd crossed Oven Brook, a quick little mountain stream—what the Scots would call a burn—and noticed a decent-sized brook trout holding in a clear, cold, spring-fed pool not far from my back door. The "native" was in full spawning colors, red, black, green, and ivory, and looked to go about fourteen inches, which was big for this little rivulet. Okay, so it wasn't a salmon fresh in from the salt, with the sea lice still on it—I'd have to travel to Maine or the Maritimes for one of those—but it was America's best-tasting and most beautiful salmonid, our classic cold-water fish, revered in song and story since colonial times. I decided to emulate John Macnab and have a go for it. And with an ultralight fly rod at that. Orvis had recently developed a short 1-weight rod, which the company was touting for small-stream fishing. I strung mine up and, disdaining waders, proceeded to stalk my prey à la mode de Macnab.

Creeping through the ferns on hands and knees, I approached the shadow-dappled pool. Was the trout still there? The floor of the pool was paved in broken chunks of marble, flaked off the bedrock of Bear Mountain over the twelve thousand years since the retreat of the last glacier, and—coupled with the lacy amoeba-shaped whorls of foam that danced on the surface—that made the viewing difficult. A fortuitous caddis hatch was occurring, and when one of them fell on the water, struggling, my trout appeared as if by levitation from the depths to inhale it. Heart pounding like a schoolboy's, I tied on a Henryville Special and had at him. To stand up would give the game away, so I was forced to cast from a squatting position, and with a very short line at that. But on the third drift of the fly down the pool, the brookie rose and took it.

I'd like to describe for you a monumental battle, line screaming off the reel, the trout taking me deep into the backing, wading upstream after him over spillway after spillway, finally gaining on him, socking the gaff home just as the hook was about to tear free. But the whole fight lasted thirty seconds at best and I certainly didn't need a gaff. Still, it had been a delicate stalk and a difficult presentation, and the fish, once I had him on the bank, was drop-dead gorgeous. He'd taste even better than he looked, poached in white wine and bay leaf, chilled, then served cold over a bed of watercress with a little of my wife's homemade mayonnaise on the side.

I looked at my watch. Not quite 10 A.M. The way to crown these successes, of course, would be with a brace of plump, sidehill ruffed grouse, the royalty of North American upland gamebirds. My black Labrador Luke was an eager accomplice. One of our most productive beats at that time of year lay across the gravel road from my home. There, on the overgrown lower slopes of Shatterack Mountain, an old, abandoned apple orchard trailed steeply uphill through young aspens and collapsing stone walls for half a mile. Grouse congregated there in the fall to feed on windfallen apples, most of them varieties no longer grown commercially. This was a good apple year, tree limbs heavy with red and yellow fruit, and the spring had been kind to grouse broods as well. If we were unlucky with the birds, I could always fill my game pockets with apples, which my wife would convert into the best applesauce I'd ever tasted.

We crossed the road, hiked through the meadow, crossed Oven Brook and a rusty barbed-wire fence that divided my land from that of a friendly neighbor, and suddenly Luke got birdy. His black coat gleamed as the guard hairs came erect. His tail came up. His nostrils opened wide to the scent of game. "Hunt 'em up, boy," I whispered. He broke toward the first big apple tree. Three grouse roared out from under it, using the tree for cover. What with the leaves still clinging green to the branches, I had no shot. Thus it often is in early season. But I got a good line on the birds, and we pounded uphill, hoping for a reflush.

A hundred yards farther on we came into a cluster of aspen whips interspersed with old apples. Again Luke got birdy. This time one of the grouse flew straight through a break in the trees. Big mistake. I dropped the partridge in a halo of feathers—a bird of the year, young and naive. He'd be tender and juicy. This is too easy, I thought. It's not even noon. I'll be home in time for lunch . . .

Like hell I would. The sidehill ruffs of interior New England are a cagey lot. All the dumb birds were killed out of the gene pool years ago by hungry hardscrabble farmers and market hunters, who thought nothing of shooting them from bare tree limbs, where the birds came to eat apple buds and popple catkins of an evening or early morning. The daily bag limit on Vermont grouse is four, and I'm not at all embarrassed to admit that in twenty years of hard pounding I've never filled it. I certainly didn't that day.

Luke and I worked Shatterack from bottom to top and then back down again, getting flush after flush with no shot possible. The grouse had an uncanny knack of flying low, to keep a stone wall between them and the muzzle, or exploding behind me, going the other way, or waiting until I was bent over, ducking a tree limb, before launching themselves into blurred invisibility. My game journal shows twenty-two grouse flushes in the course of that hard, hot, leg-deadening six-hour day. I missed four shots along the way. We got up a number of woodcock as well, and I killed a limit of three, but I wanted—needed—that final grouse to complete my "brace."

As so often happens, we got the bird only after I'd pretty much given up and shaped our course homeward. We were pushing through heavy cover to the edge of a field when Luke—who was nearly as weary as I was—perked his ears, lifted his tail, and lunged into a tussock of grass concealing a fallen barbed-wire fence. A ruff rattled out into the open field, a clear straightaway shot. I missed with the right barrel, cursed myself and the whole race of *Bonasa umbellus*, hit the back trigger, then exulted as the left barrel knocked the bird tail over tip, to fall with a gratifying thump some forty paces out from the wire.

That final bird revitalized us. When we got back to the house my wife was home from work and already preparing dinner. "I saw the buck in the barn," she said, smiling as she put a casserole in the oven. "Nice work."

"Did you see the trout in the refrigerator?" I showed it to her, then emptied my game pockets. She was duly impressed.

"Looks like you had a great day," she said.

"I know how to make it even better," I said. "Come on up to the bedroom. There's something I want to show you."

She grinned. "I guess I have a few minutes to spare," she said. "Catch me if you can."

It was one of the best days of my sporting life—the day I scored the Royal Macbob.

CLOSE ENCOUNTERS OF THE WORST KIND

Chances are you know the feeling. You're pushing through the woods, or up the mountain, or across the prairie, and suddenly the hair on the back of your neck rises. Something is watching you. A poacher? A pot farmer? A bloodthirsty maniac? Or is it just paranoia? You turn and scan the immediate surroundings. Very carefully. Nothing's there, but as you continue on your way the feeling persists, intensifies, turns the whole day into something about as delightful as a dental appointment with novocaine in short supply . . .

My pal John Holt had that experience not long ago on Hay Creek, a tributary of the North Fork of the Flathead River in north-western Montana. He was up there in the conifers one fall day hunting spruce grouse and ruffs. No dog, just his 20-gauge Beretta for companionship. The sudden feeling that somebody was in the woods with him wasn't pleasant—images of Freemen sprang to mind—and though John had already flushed a few birds with the morning still young, he found himself heading back toward the dubious safety of his beat-up old Toyota pickup. "Then, in one of those low wet grassy swales, I saw a footprint. Unshod. Big. *Waay* big. The toe pads in a line straight across. Claw tips well forward of the toes. A griz for sure. And the track was still filling with water."

All the way back to the truck he found more grizzly tracks, and then a "steamer"—a fresh, pungent pile of dung. "Could be he was just letting me know he was there," John says. "They'll do that, you know. But then again maybe he was one of those 'dinner bell grizzlies' you read about, the ones that hear a shot, figure there's meat on the ground, and come at a gallop—maybe hoping for an elk, or at least a gut pile. There are plenty of elk hunters up there that time of year. Maybe he'd bullied his way into a good meal before. I got out of there, fast."

It's not the sort of close encounter we normally associate with the gentle art of bird hunting, yet it does happen. We should be aware.

I had an experience similar to Holt's a few years back, but with a black bear, thank God, not a griz. My dog and I had been frisking the popple thickets for grouse near a rounded mountain spur called the Owl's Head, just south of my house in Vermont, and we'd managed to scratch down a couple of birds. The early October day was stoking up, too hot for good dog work, and we were heading for home past an alder brake alongside Oven Brook. Figuring maybe there'd be a woodcock or two in there, laying up in the cool, damp shade, I sent my black Lab, Luke, into the cover while I skirted the edge of the thick stuff hoping for a shot. I could hear Luke crashing around in there, when suddenly there came a deep, loud woof. Much deeper and throatier than I'd ever heard from the young dog. Luke came shooting out of the alders like a cork from a champagne bottle. Tail between his legs, ears down, eyes rolling as he tried to look back behind him. Deep in the shadowed maze of the alders I saw a darker shadow, slowly rising as the bear stood up to get a better look at us. Like Holt, I cleared out as quick as I could. There were no objections from Luke.

I was put in mind of both these episodes the other day while reading Scott McMillion's scary book *Mark of the Grizzly*. It relates the gruesome details of eighteen separate grizzly attacks—some of them fatal—over a recent twenty-year period. They range in locale from Alaska through British Columbia and Alberta to Montana and Wyoming, and all of them—if you can stomach the horror—hold valuable lessons for anyone venturing into bear country. Only one of the incidents involved a bird hunter, but it's a doozy.

On October 20, 1996, a Sunday, Kyle Schoepf—an active young Montana horse trainer and outdoorsman, bored at the prospect of a day watching NFL football—decided to chase pheasants near the Ninepipe Reservoir on the Flathead Indian Reservation south of Kalispell. The Ninepipe country, which lies in the flats below the spectacular Mission Range, prime grizzly habitat, is probably the only place west of the Continental Divide where the big bears and the gaudy roosters feed side by side. The bears are drawn by the fruit orchards of Mission Valley—apples, plums, and pears galore, along with plenty of buffaloberries, hawthorn, barley, wheat, and sunflowers for the gamebirds. It was a slushy, windy day with intermittent showers of heavy, wet snow, the beginnings of a murderous winter throughout the northern Rockies. Schoepf and his young German shorthair, Charley, flushed only hen pheasants in the first covert they checked, so they headed for another down the road, hoping for roosters. Instead they found sheer hell.

In the second covert, Charley started acting "goofy," ranging out too far, running at frantic random without his customary quartering pattern, sometimes backtracking and hunting behind Schoepf—something he'd never done before. They were pushing through high, thick grass, flanked by dense brush and trees. No birds got up. Then, about twenty-five minutes into the hunt, Schoepf heard a strange noise behind him. He looked over his shoulder and saw a huge bear coming at him in full charge, head low, huffing and chuffing, not twenty feet away. He spun and fired his 12-gauge Winchester Model 12 the only way he could at that distance—from the hip.

As McMillion writes:

> The gun went off, blood blew back on his face, and then the bear was on him, her head at his feet but her body somersaulting, slamming into his, crushing him into the soft ground as she contorted. . . . The bear was yelling and bleeding and waving all four legs, all twenty claws, reminding Kyle of a blender. She was incredibly heavy, and she covered him with mud and gore and hair. . . .
> She sounded, sadly, like a pig in torture.

Schoepf's lucky load of steel No. 6s had taken the 370-pound sow square in the throat, tearing out a two-inch chunk of her jugular. The muzzle blast probably also blinded and deafened her. It was the only fatal shot from a smoothbore that could possibly have saved him from a mauling, and probable death.

When Schoepf managed to squeeze out from under the grizzly, he and Charley ran off 150 yards at record speed and looked back at the dying bear. She rolled, stood, screamed, flopped down again on her back, swatting at her head to drive off the horror that had turned her life to black agony and looming death. To no avail.

Schoepf, covered with bear blood, dung, and hair, raced back to his truck, Charley at his heels, and drove to a nearby farmhouse to report the incident. The grizzly is a threatened species in the lower forty-eight, and killing one unnecessarily is an actionable offense. Investigators arrived quickly and found the bear dead where Schoepf said it was. They also dug Schoepf's Model 12 out of the mud, its barrel bent about fifteen degrees to the left from the bear's impact. That and the light plastic shotshell wad, embedded nearly two inches deep beneath the bear's hide, convinced the authorities that it had been a close encounter indeed. The sow also had two nearly grown cubs with her, providing a clear-cut reason for her charge. The cubs drifted off into the Mission Mountains before they could be captured, and one hopes they made it safely to their denning grounds without being killed and eaten by a male grizzly, a common fate for orphaned bears. Grizzlies, and black bears too, become "hyperphagic" in the fall, driven by instinct to fatten up for the long winter's sleep, sometimes eating up to twenty thousand calories a day. In the world of the great bear, cannibalism is not an actionable offense.

What could Schoepf, or any bird hunter for that matter, have done to prevent the attack? Conventional wisdom in avoiding such confrontations says that no one in bear country should wander through tall grass or thick brush if they can possibly avoid it. But if you must, be sure to make plenty of noise to alert a prospective attacker. Most bears, unless guarding a carcass or suddenly surprised within their flight-or-fight range (conservatively estimated at about one hundred yards for grizzlies), will clear out if they know a human being is approaching. But bird hunters always seek out tall grass or thick brush, because that's where the birds are.

McMillion doesn't say whether Schoepf's shorthair Charley was wearing a bell, but even if he was, it might not have provided sufficient warning in the loud wind blowing that day.

Experts say that the mere presence of a dog in its vicinity, belled or unbelled, can provoke a bear to attack. But what bird hunter worthy of the name would be afield anywhere without his gundog? And a scared dog usually returns at speed to its master. A chilling thought: If I'd been living in Montana instead of Vermont when I sent Luke into that alder thicket, there could have been a grizzly in there instead of a black bear. And when my noble Lab came clanging back to Daddy for protection I might well have been confronted with a situation similar to Schoepf's—but armed with only a puny 20-gauge double charged with low-base 8s, and nowhere near Schoepf's reflexes.

Should Schoepf have been carrying a can of pepper spray? The oleoresin capsaicin spritzed from such cans—and there are plenty of brands on the market—has proved more effective than gunfire in halting grizzly attacks before they carry through into the dangerous (i.e., mauled or dead) phase. But Schoepf certainly didn't have the time to use the stuff, with the bear almost on top of him before he saw it. Still, if you're hunting sharptails or Huns or chukars in open country that could harbor grizzlies, say near Yellowstone or Glacier National Parks, carrying a jumbo-sized can of pepper spray in a quick-draw neoprene holster could prove quite helpful, provided you saw the bear far enough away to draw it before he or she was on you. But unless you're hunting pheasants in the Mission Valley, you're more likely to run on a griz in blue grouse, spruce grouse, or ruffed grouse country, the high country, tangled and thick, where you'd get little warning before an attack. Even Clint Eastwood would be hard-pressed to outdraw a charging grizzly in cover like that. It's reassuring to know that my friend Tim Linehan of Libby, Montana, in years of guiding bird and big-game hunters in the Yaak Valley, one of the wildest portions left of lower forty-eight America, has not yet run afoul of a grizzly, though there are twenty or thirty occupying that terrain.

Incidentally, pepper spray doesn't seem to have much effect on black bears—indeed, one authority says they grin their way right through it like mist from a lawn sprinkler.

The best anti-bear weapon that a bird hunter can carry is alertness. If you see or hear a congress of crows, ravens, or coyotes in an area you're hunting, it could mean a bear is guarding a carcass in the vicinity. The bear will guard it with his life, even if it means taking yours. Clear out. Of course, if you find fresh bear tracks or scat, ditto. God forbid you should see a bear cub. That always means Mama's nearby. And if your dog starts acting goofy in bear country, call him in and head for the truck. It's better to heed that uneasy feeling that something's out there, maybe watching you, something bigger and tougher than you are, than to press your luck and regret it later in the hospital with a chewed head and a packing of gauze where your butt used to be. Or worse still, not to regret—from six feet under.

There are plenty of good books available that can tell you what to do if you're confronted by an angry bear, fascinating data and supposition about false charges and true ones, about the efficacy of playing dead or climbing trees to escape injury (grizzlies *can* climb, though not with the agility or to the height of black bears, so you'd better remember your ape heritage in a hurry if you take to the upper branches), and about your chances of scaring off a nasty bear with shouts, gestures, shots in the air, and other such tactics, including pepper spray.

The best overall account I've read is Dr. Stephen Herrero's *Bear Attacks: Their Causes and Avoidance*. Unlike McMillion's book, which deals only with grizzlies, Herrero's discusses black bear attacks as well, including an ominous chapter on "The Predaceous Black Bear." According to Herrero, who has researched close to a thousand separate bear attacks, more than 90 percent of black bear–inflicted injuries have come about when the bear was actually stalking its human prey with dinner in mind. (Grizzly predation is much, much rarer.) Most of those hunted were on the small side—children or women—and the attacks came with little or no warning.

His most chilling account is of an attack on a woman geologist, Cynthia Dusel-Bacon, in the summer of 1977 near the top of a brush-grown ridge some sixty miles southeast of Fairbanks, Alaska. The woman had been dropped on the ridge by helicopter for a routine day of geological field mapping in the Yukon-Tenana Upland. No sooner had the chopper whupped away than Dusel-Bacon saw a black bear pop up from the brush not ten feet beyond her. As she'd done in the past, she tried to scare off the bear—a small one—by yelling and clapping her hands. No go. Banging on boulders with her rock hammer, she retreated slowly uphill, but the bear slipped around her, above and out of sight. "My next sensation was that of being struck a staggering blow from behind," she later recalled. The bear was on her in an instant, tearing great chunks of muscle from her outstretched arms. She reached for her walkie-talkie and managed to get off a quick cry for help to the helicopter pilot—"Ed, this is Cynthia. Come quick, I'm being eaten by a bear"—before it chewed her biceps off. When the chopper pilot got her to the hospital, she had no flesh remaining on her left arm for five inches between her shoulder and her elbow, and her right forearm was chewed to pieces. Today she wears two artificial arms.

Running away wouldn't have helped much, even if Dusel-Bacon had had time and terrain in her favor. Running only triggers a bear's pursuit response, and a healthy bear is faster than any Olympic sprinter, capable of covering forty-four feet per second in full charge, which would clock out to about seven seconds over a hundred yards. Yet any bear, black or brown or blue or cinnamon, can be as stealthy as a panther in its stalk. Fighting back once you're in a bear's clutches might be your last resort, but bear muscles are twice as dense, hence twice as strong, as those of even an NFL tackle, so hand-to-jaw combat would offer only a faint hope at best.

Yet Old Ephraim doesn't win 'em all. Take the case of angler Knn Bates, a burly wood sculptor from Dubois, Wyoming, and the grizzly bear he bumped into on the Snake River one recent Easter Sunday. Bates, whose oddly spelled first name reflects his Sioux ancestry, was having a fine day's fishing—four trout on his first four casts—when he heard something behind him.

"I turned around and there was the bear," Bates says, "about thirty feet away—staring at me, popping his jaws and whining." A male griz, maybe four hundred pounds, with blood in his eye. Bates, who himself weighs 260 pounds and carves bears with a chain saw for a living, has great respect for the species. He's hunted them all his life and knows their behavior. This, he sensed at once, was a clear case of predation. The bears of nearby Yellowstone Park had emerged early from hibernation and there wasn't much to eat. Bates knew he was on this bear's menu.

He dropped his rod and creel, picked up a few rocks, and retreated slowly toward a nearby bridge. The bear batted the creel a few times and then came after him.

Bates backed out on the bridge, figuring to vault into the river if need be. When he turned to climb the rail, the griz sprang forward and snagged his arm. Fortunately he was wearing a fluffy, down-filled jacket, and the bear's teeth just grazed his flesh. Bates now knew that the only way to save himself was to fight. "I spun around and slugged him in the mouth with everything I had," he recalls. Much to his surprise, he decked his adversary. "The griz let go and kind of set back on his rump. It shocked me. I didn't think I could knock a bear down."

For good measure, he bounced a rock off the grizzly's head and kept bombarding it as the griz retreated.

But at that critical moment a car appeared and started pushing the bear right back across the bridge—toward Bates. The tourists drove up and asked what was happening. All they got from Knn was cuss words.

At last the driver beeped his horn and herded the griz off the bridge, then kept on driving—though Bates was bleeding from a fang wound in his arm and his knuckles were dripping blood. His right arm, he discovered later, had suffered a linear fracture from the force of his knockdown punch, and he had to undergo an agonizing series of seventeen rabies shots.

"People say I'm lucky it was a small bear," Bates says in wry retrospect. "Like hell. The difference between a four-hundred- and a six-hundred-pound griz is like the difference between a slug to the chest with a 20-gauge versus a 12-gauge shotgun."

From now on when he goes into bear country, Bates will carry two cans of alcohol-based pepper spray and a flare. "If the spray doesn't work," he says, "I'll torch him."

It all sounds pretty grim, yet there are few outdoorsmen—whether hunters or anglers, mountaineers or cross-country skiers, hikers or bikers or weekend wildflower collectors—who would opt for a world without bears. Maulings and fatalities are in fact quite rare. More humans are killed each year by bee stings than in a century of bear attacks.

And after all, the knowledge that a bear might be lurking just around the next bend in the trail, or snoozing in the next patch of bird cover, adds a spice to the outing that I'd sorely miss. Long live *Ursus arctos*—but please don't chew on me.

THE VERMONT EVERGLADES

If your life has become too fast or distracted, get thee to a bog or marsh.
—John Eastman, *The Book of Swamp and Bog* (1995)

It's good advice. No better natural habitat exists for the study of minutiae. Swamps are slow, secret places, quiet and maybe a bit ominous. They catch and hone your attention. They demand concentration. No babbling brooks or splendid vistas, no roaring, high-peaks winds to distract you. You have to watch your step in a swamp—the bottom can fall out from under you at any moment, sucking you down into the primordial ooze. There might be a snake sunbathing in disguise on that snag your hand is reaching for. That knobby log just ahead might prove to be the nostrils of an alligator. The mossy rock dead ahead that looks like a good, firm place for your next footfall could be a snapping turtle—a big one . . .

71

Thoreau once wrote: "I enter a swamp as a sacred place." But until recently few Americans would agree. Over the past two or three centuries more than half of our bogs, fens, marshes, quagmires, and swamps have disappeared under the bulldozer blade of progress—drained, filled, and paved over to become housing tracts or shopping malls or industrial areas. Through the ages the very word *swamp* and its various synonyms have become code words for horror. Think about it. The Swamp Thing. The Blob. The Creature from the Black Lagoon. The Mystery of the Fens. The Making of a Quagmire. Nowadays, in an effort to reverse this negative imagery, green-thinkers refer to such places as "wetlands." It sounds a lot cleaner, healthier, nicer. But they didn't have to convince me. Since childhood I've been an inveterate swamp rat, a born bog-trotter, warts and all.

One of my favorite hangouts when I was growing up was a small, fetid bog near the Milwaukee Road railroad tracks not a mile from my home in Wauwatosa, Wisconsin. In its bug-infested environs my friends and I played Tarzan and Bomba and Jungle Jim, swung from grapevines, sloshed through the stinky black mud, caught polliwogs, wrestled make-believe crocodiles, and gigged actual bullfrogs whose succulent legs we skinned out and deep-fried in a nearby hobo jungle, using an old frying pan rescued from the town dump and some lard swiped from our mothers' kitchens. The deep black water in the swamp's center was home to some very large, very dark largemouth bass, but we never landed one. On hook-up the bass merely had to dive, wrap the line around a drowned tree limb, and *pop!*—instant freedom. In the fall we jump-shot plump mallards in the same flooded timber and flushed snipe or woodcock from the speckled alder brakes that surrounded the swamp. It was a growing boy's mucky, smelly version of paradise.

All of this is by way of introducing the Vermont Everglades—a sprawl of dark water, cattails, and wood-duck nesting boxes on either side of Vermont Route 7 just south of the town of Manchester Village. It's the closest thing we have to the Glades in tiny, chilly Vermont. Granted, ours are a bit smaller than their Florida namesake—80 acres as against 2,560,000. But then again, Small Is Beautiful as the ecoactivists tell us. The actual name of this marsh is the Kesick Swamp Wildlife Management Area. It was acquired by the state in 1994 and falls under the aegis of the Vermont Natural Resources Agency.

"It's still pretty much pristine, a virgin swamp," says biologist Scott Darling of the Fish and Wildlife Department. "Not many alien invaders. No phragmites or Eurasian water milfoil yet, though there's some purple loosestrife probably brought in on tire treads when the highway went through." Purple loosestrife, a tall, rather pretty weed that grows densely in low, wet areas along highways, is a European "exotic" that arrived on our shores before 1850, probably in ship ballast. It reproduces prolifically, forming dense colonies that crowd out such native flora as blue-joint, cordgrass, cattails, and water parsnip. Most birds and insects won't eat the seeds and muskrats disdain using the stalks, even to build their lodges. Bees suck its nectar but the honey produced is dark green, though it's said to be quite sweet.

The best way to explore a swamp is by canoe, so one spring day not long ago my friend Hubert Schriebl and I lugged one down to the quaking banks of Kesick Swamp for a look-see. It was a cool, sunny morning in late May. The hardest part of the journey was finding a way into the place. You can't simply park on the shoulder of Route 7 and drag a canoe down to the nearby water—to state troopers that's a no-no. After circling the swamp and finding nothing but private driveways leading in to homes perched on the edge of the boggy ground, with the water still hundreds of yards away, we finally found a gravel side road just north of the Chiselville covered bridge in East Arlington. The gravel led us in to a house, just short of which a rutted two-track peeled off to our left toward a power line. From there the trail coursed downhill to a locked gate. Another hundred yards or so farther we could see the glint of water, and the roof of an empty cabin. This hunting camp the state had purchased when it bought the swamp. We lifted the canoe, a red Mad River whitewater model, over the gate and carried it down to the cabin.

A couple of muddy, brush-choked trails led to the water's edge. As I bushwhacked in to scout the situation, a beaver slapped its tail on the water ahead of me and and I saw it dive. A flock of killdeer buzzed me, then zipped off in tight formation to circle the marsh before pitching in on the far shore. "This is it," I called back to Hubert. "You're going to love it."

We embarked in the wobbly canoe—Hubert, a world-class skier and photographer, is ill at ease in watercraft, especially when he's lugging along his heavy camera bags. But we managed not to capsize. The swamp spread before us—a sprawling glint of shallow, tea-brown water scrimmed with a yellow ruff of ragged cattails. Red-winged blackbirds and grackles bounced on the slender reeds and serenaded us in metallic disharmony. Flimsy mats of aquatic vegetation dotted the surface: Large islets of swamp smartweed (*Polygonum coccineum*) poked their conical pink flower clusters skyward, fringed with narrow lanceolate floating leaves; round-leafed water lilies with bulbous yellow flowers floated nearby.

Swamp smartweed, a member of the buckwheat family, is a preferred food source for deer, muskrats, migratory seed-eating songbirds, and, of course, waterfowl. Every web-footed wanderer of the skies from tundra swans and Canada geese to black ducks, mallards, teal (both blue- and green-winged), and wood ducks will chow down in a marsh full of smartweeds. "Only the bulrushes rival them as a seed source for wildlife," says John Eastman in his valuable guidebook to wetlands lore, *The Book of Swamp and Bog*.

The yellow-flowered water lily, I later discovered by consulting my field guides, was the bullhead lily *(Nuphar variegatum)*. Schools of fathead minnows shaded themselves under the lily pads. Muskrats and beavers eat the underground, rootlike stems (rhizomes) of various water lilies, the beavers stashing them in their lodges for winter consumption. Deer and porcupines will grub out the roots and eat them. Moose also love them, and the Kesick Swamp is a preferred sloshing—I mean stopping—place for Bullwinkles on the prowl in the intervale between the Green Mountains and the Taconics. Motorists frequently stop along Route 7 to watch tall, black, bulb-nosed moose foraging belly-deep in the marsh, water lily roots dangling from their mouths like gobs of spaghetti.

The skeletal trunks of drowned trees rose throughout the swamp, and as we paddled around on the fringes of the cattail stands, trying to grab snaps of a pair of Canada geese that kept just out of camera range, I noticed a big, messy nest of sticks wedged high above the water in a tree fork. I kept my eye on it, glancing over from time to time, and soon my patience was rewarded: a gawky, long-billed, feathered head rose from the nest rim and peered around at the world outside. Soon another head joined, then a third one. They swiveled around and gawped at us. "We're being watched," I told Hubert. He looked over at the nest, grabbed up a different camera lens from his bag, and with eager eyes said, "Let's ease on over there."

They were young herons—great blue herons—and eventually we counted four of them. At first they were quite shy, but soon got used to our presence. I'd spotted a dead trout lying on the bottom, its body torn by the bill of some wading bird, so while Hubert snapped the herons' portraits I rigged up a fly rod I'd brought along and cast a small Adams dry fly, hoping the swamp might hold some brookies. But the water was already too warm, which I discovered when I stuck my hand in. Scott Darling later told me that brookies used the shallows of the swamp in cooler weather—in April and the fall months—but the lack of rain in recent weeks had sent them back up into the chillier, better-aerated waters of the swamp's Green Mountain feeder streams.

It had gotten quite hot by now out on the water, and with the sun clocking toward the zenith we decided to call it a day.

We returned to the Vermont Everglades several times during the ensuing months, both singly and together, and on each visit found something new to watch or photograph or just chuckle at. A full-grown American egret fished the swamp for a while—testament to the species' recovery from the depredations of plume hunters at the twentieth century's beginnings, who almost reduced the bird to extinction so that women could adorn their hats with the long breast feathers. On a visit in late June, getting on the water at 6 A.M., we found the swamp shrouded in low ground fog. Mount Equinox was hidden in the haze. As we launched our craft—a wide-beamed, flat-bottomed aluminum johnboat this time, a better platform for stability and thus for picture taking—a ruby-throated hummingbird buzzed out of the fog, hovered inches from my face, then decided I wasn't quite the flower he'd hoped for and disappeared as quickly as he'd come.

Rowing out toward the heron nest we flushed a noisy raft of mallards and wood ducks off the water. There were only three herons in the nest this time, but they'd grown to double their size. We never did see the parents. They must have been fishing more productive waters. Later, when the fog burned off, we spotted the fourth heron nestling, already a teenager in bird years, stalking the muddy shallows where the cattails grew, obviously hunting up a nice juicy breakfast of minnows. We rowed over to the wood-duck nesting boxes closer to the highway and found them occupied not by woodies but by aggressive squadrons of tree swallows. The swift little birds strafed us continually, then soared off into the sky to dogfight with one another like so many miniature MIGs.

On the way back in we surprised a female teal—a green-wing, I think—that was towing a string of downy ducklings. She immediately went into the broken-wing routine, paddling frantically away from us, hoping to lure these awesome predators after her while her young paddled with amazing speed to hide themselves in the bankside foliage. On a hummock of decomposing cattail stalks about twenty yards from the shore we found a goose nest holding one large, off-white, unhatched egg. Next to it lay the gutted corpse of a black-spotted leopard frog—done in, no doubt, by one of the many minks that make a living here. Nature at work . . .

In the fall, Hubert visited one last time and found the vegetative prize of the year—a gorgeous fringed gentian *(Gentiana crinita),* just bursting into bloom. The wild gentian is increasingly rare in this world so hostile to swamps. A small-scale delight, of course, and though we hadn't had any great adventures in the Vermont Everglades—no roaring bull alligators, not a single run-in with a snake, poisonous or otherwise, no piranhas or bog-trotters or hulking moss-backed monsters—we emerged from its primordial ooze with heartiest best wishes for the swamp's continued good health and survival.

Since that first visit I've made it a point to revisit Kesick Swamp each fall during waterfowl season. Crouched behind the reed walls of a crudely built blind in the predawn chill, with my yellow Lab Jake at my side, we await first light and the arrival of the ducks. The dog suppresses a shudder of excitement as the whistle of wings tears the stillness. The happy babble of incoming mallards soon follows as the ducks circle our set of decoys—once, twice . . . a third time for good measure. Then they cup their wings and pitch in, feet extended, wobbling slightly to scrub off speed. *Drakes only* is my self-imposed rule. I stand and fire. Two shots, two mallards. The rest of the flock is gone in the wink of an eye.

"Fetch 'em, boy."

This is the moment Jake lives for. He's out of the blind in a flash, having marked the fall of the birds by their heavy splashes. When he's brought them duly to hand and shaken himself dry (thus drenching me sodden), I smooth the glossy feathers, admiring the gleam of early sunlight on their dark green heads, the midnight blue of their specula. I wipe down the gun and zip it back into its sheepskin case, then pour a cup of hot coffee from the thermos. A pair of ducks is enough for us these days.

For the next hour or two we sit quietly in the blind, watching the swamp come awake and ply its mucky trade. Muskrats putter to and fro like furry motorboats. A heron stands tall and still as a snag, then strikes like a rattlesnake to swallow a small brook trout. In the distance we hear the rasp of beaver teeth at work on a popple sapling, followed by the slow crash of its fall. Migrating fall warblers pour through the thickets along the shore, brighter than the autumn leaves. Across the swamp a cow moose stands knee-deep in the muck, munching waterweeds, black and angular against the far foliage. High overhead a long string of Canada geese etches a wavering V across the pale blue sky, yapping like the hounds of heaven. More ducks pour in to our decoys but we do not disturb them.

Yes, Thoreau considered a swamp to be a "sacred place." At moments like these, Jake and I agree.

GOOD-BYE, OLD PAINT?

There's a marvelous Bill Mauldin cartoon from World War II that says it all: A cavalry sergeant is standing next to a disabled jeep, mired deep and decrepit in the mud. His back is to the vehicle, his left hand covers his eyes, and in his right he holds a cocked .45-caliber Colt automatic aimed at the jeep's hood, square between the headlights. Yes, it's end-of-the-road time, and he's about to deliver the coup de grâce to his faithful steed . . .

I know the feeling. My own "shooting brake," a brown-and-tan 1981 GMC half-ton, is heading for the last roundup. I call her Old Paint. Time, hard use, and—mostly—the rust bugs that infest the backcountry where I live and hunt have taken their toll. The sills on both doors are rotted out; great blotches of rust are metastasizing their way across the doors and the flanks of the bed panels. The seats are shredded thanks to a decade and a half of attention by dog claws. The tailgate rattled so fiercely last fall that I removed it.

Oh sure, I know I should have gotten rid of the old gal long ago, traded her in on something younger, trimmer, and comelier, a Tahoe or a Suburban, say, or at least a Subaru Forester, but I'm a sentimentalist (and, if truth be told, something of a tightwad). After all, I keep telling myself, her motor still fires up hale and hearty whenever I flick the ignition, even in the coldest weather. And in terms of travel Old Paint is still a youngster, with only 118,860 miles on her odometer. I know guys who routinely drive their trucks to the two-hundred-thousand-mile mark. So I hang on to her. But here in Vermont every vehicle has to pass a stringent state inspection, and I've known for years now that it was only a matter to time before my faithful steed would fail.

Such was my state of mind last month as the dread date neared: Soon I'd have to drive the machine down to Tim's Garage in town for what I was certain would be the fatal look-see. The night before the inspection I lay abed, sad and sleepless, recalling some of the many adventures I'd shared with Old Paint over the years.

Otter Creek in Spate . . . Soon after I'd gotten the truck, I decided to check out a good-looking bottomland covert I'd spied from Route 7 near Danby, Vermont, about three-quarters of an hour northeast of my home. The flats along the creek were mixed hardwoods and popple, studded with old apple trees in fruit. The sky was overcast as I drove through a shallow ford across Otter Creek, which drains north nearly the length of the state to empty into Lake Champlain. A good, firm gravel bed at the ford. Across the creek I parked, belled the dog, grabbed my gun, and started exploring. An hour later, it started to rain. Soft at first, then harder, finally a downpour. But we were into birds—two woodcock and a nice, fat, apple-fed grouse in my game pocket already. We hunted on in a wide circle through the wet second-growth woods. Three flushes and one bagged woodcock later, we swung back to the truck. Both Luke the Lab and I were sopping and muddy. The truck windows fogged over quickly as we drove back to the ford. Through the mist I could see that Otter Creek had swollen some, but not until we were halfway across did I realize that the river had risen at least a foot since our arrival. I could feel the gravel shifting and grumbling under the truck tires. Water lapped at the door sills. Deeper water lay ahead. Then upstream about fifty yards I saw a whole uprooted tree wallowing toward us. I looked at Luke; he looked at me. Should I back up or fare forward? To go back would mean a cold, damp night in the truck. But forward, we might have to swim for it. "God hates a coward!" I said aloud, and floored it. Luke grinned his approval. Old Paint surged ahead like an amphibious tank, a bone in her teeth and a roiling, muddy roostertail surging behind her. We just made it before the tree rumbled past . . .

And who could forget the Incident in Yellow Branch Bog? About ten years ago I decided to check out Vermont's Northeast Kingdom for both birds and fall trout. Luke accompanied me in the truck. One day up there we followed a logging track up the Yellow Branch of the Nulhegan River into some of the finest, vastest stands of young popple I've seen this side of Minnesota. Woodcock galore. The flight birds were down, and we had an afternoon of great shooting. In fact, I limited out fairly early, then pushed on solely for grouse. They were fewer, tending to flush a bit wild, so we hunted on until the sun was just kissing the tops of the aspens to the west. In the dusk, heading back to the highway, I took a wrong turn, and soon the tires were slurping mud.

Then deeper mud. Yellow, glutenous, with a grip like a giant squid. Stumps impeded our progress, but Old Paint stepped over them with a laudable hauteur, as if they weren't even there. Soon the mud was hubcap-deep, though, and I put the truck in low range. We crawled forward. Occasionally, through the leafless thickets ahead, I could see distant head-lights zipping along what had to be the paved highway, Route 105 between Island Pond and Bloomfield. We forged ahead toward it. Then, just after I saw the first bats of the evening flickering through the gloom, a huge, dark shape loomed ahead, about a stone's throw to the right of the two-track. I flicked up the high beams. A moose. Neck swollen with the rut. What looked like a chandelier of a rack on his big mulelike head. Luke growled, his ruff up. "No way," I told him as I hit the gas. A rutting bull moose, mistaking the truck for a rival, would have made short work of us all. I could swear I glimpsed, through the rearview mirror, the bull trotting after us as we split for the highway. Fortunately, the track firmed up over the last quarter mile to the pave-ment, and Old Paint fairly flew us to safety. We lost the tailpipe to a stump during that last mad dash, so maybe it was the roar of O.P.'s unmuffled engine that gave the moose pause. But I doubt it.

Then, only two winters ago, there was the Night of the Awful Ice. My dogs and I were coming back to Vermont from a week of late-season geese and ducks at my friend Joe Judge's place on the Eastern Shore of Maryland. About halfway up the Jersey Turnpike it started to rain. By the time we hit the Palisades Parkway flanking the Hudson, with Manhattan glittering eerily through the mist to the east, the rain turned to sleet. When we reached the New York Thruway, I put Old Paint in four-wheel drive and turned the defrost to high. The cars coming toward us in the dark gleamed like diamonds, sheathed as they were in ice. At every bump I could hear whole panes of the stuff flaking from the sides and hood of the truck to go tinkling merrily beside us in our progress. Dicey, yes, but Old Paint was sure-footed. I kept a steady foot on the throttle, made no sudden moves with the steering wheel. In the course of that night-mare ride we danced lightly past eighteen-wheelers jack-knifed along the shoulders, blew off sedans, sports cars, and even once, I'm nearly certain, a flame-red Maserati cutting doughnuts on the ice down the center of the northbound lane.

Not until we reached the dirt road that leads from my home village up the mountain to my house did we meet our comeuppance. The worst feature of that road, in any season, is a steep incline called Sap House Hill. In mud season it's a rutted, bottomless quagmire; in winter a luge run. Halfway up, at about thirty miles an hour, the right front tire hit a rut that slewed the truck sideways toward the drop-off to White Creek, looming twenty feet below and fanged in anchor ice. I downshifted and tapped the brake. Old Paint whoa-ed obedi-ently, just at the edge of the drop-off. The glare ice was too slick for O.P.'s engine and clutch to pull her out of there, even in four-wheel drive. The night was gelid. Though my yellow Lab Jake was unmoved by the chill, Roz Russell, my feisty lit-tle Jack Russell bitch, was already shivering. Only a mile to home. The dogs could walk the road on paws like studded snow tires, but with that ice I'd spend half the distance falling on my butt. Then I thought of the unplucked ducks and geese in the cooler that lay in the truck bed. I quickly ripped wads of plumage from the birds, wedged them under the wheels that weren't getting traction, laid broken brush atop the feath-ers, and fired up the engine. Toeing the clutch and the gas pedal with balletic delicacy, I spurred Old Paint forward. Yes! A piece of cake! Five minutes later we were home after the most harrowing ride of my life. All thanks to Old Paint.

Well, to my vast relief after all that nostalgia, Old Paint got a reprieve this year: She passed her inspection. She's good for another year of hauling firewood, dump runs, fishing excursions, and daring probes into the grouse coverts of the East, both birdy and not so birdy. Maybe with a fiberglass fix-up, a couple of new doors, and a new bed liner, she'll be good for another couple or three years. If not, I think I'll put her out to pasture—literally, Vermont fashion. Drive her up into the meadow behind the house, mount her on blocks in a place of honor, pull the tires and battery, drain the oil and gasoline, and just let her sit there until she melts into the countryside . . . and my fond, sweet memories fade.

RAMBLINGS OF A DOGMAN

Outside of a dog, a book is man's best friend.
Inside of a dog, it's too dark to read.
—Groucho Marx

Here's a dog story for openers. This guy comes home from work hungry and his wife's still out. But he knows that when she's going to be late she usually leaves something in the icebox for him. He peeks inside and sees a plate covered with waxed paper. It looks like a nice slab of meat loaf, so he spreads it on some saltines and eats it. His wife comes home, all embarrassed at having forgotten to leave him at least a snack.

"It's okay, honey," he says. "I had that meat loaf you left in the refrigerator."

"That wasn't meat loaf," she says. "That was leftover dog food from Fido's supper!"

"Well, I don't care," he says, "I like it. Get me some more."

Next time she goes to the grocer's she orders six cans.

"What's this, Missus?" that worthy asks. "You got a new dog?"

"No, but my husband ate some of this stuff the other night and says he likes it."

"I don't know, Missus," the grocer says. "You better be careful. Dog food's not for people—God only knows what's in it."

"Well, my husband is very stubborn. He says he wants more, and that's that."

The grocer shakes his head and fills her order.

This continues for about six months. Then one day the woman comes in and orders just one can of dog food.

"So your hubby finally wised up, did he?" the grocer says.

"Oh no," she says, "it's not that. The other night poor George was up on the couch licking his balls. He fell off and broke his neck."

Well, I don't care. I'm a dogman and proud of it. For more than half a century now I've lived with dogs, walked behind them over hill and dale, through alder hells and brier patches, swamps and prickly pear deserts. I've taken them with me whenever and wherever I can. I've laughed at them and with them, and squirmed while they laughed at me. I've exulted in their doggy triumphs, been embarrassed by their gaffes. I've slept with them in cold, wet, miserable wilderness camps, and been warmed by them at home in the depths of a New England winter. I've mourned their inevitable deaths more keenly even than those of my own blood kin, and been comforted by them in turn in times of distress.

I've even been known to eat dog food, though only on a dare, and it wasn't too bad apart from the aftertaste. And I haven't yet broken my neck, though I damned near did not long ago. In 1993, on Vermont Route 315 between Dorset and

Rupert, while manuevering at speed to avoid killing a partridge, I hit a patch of gravel and skidded head-on into a utility pole at thirty-five miles an hour. The chest strap on my seat belt gave way and I was thrown against the steering column. When I came to, the windshield was starred and my Jack Russell, Roz, was sitting in my lap licking blood from my face. My fogged brain was pleased with this: A dog's saliva is said to contain a mild antibacterial component, hence the old comparative "Cleaner than a hound's tooth." I looked around to check on my big yellow Lab, Jake, fearing he might have been injured in the crash. But no: He sat quietly in the backseat, concern writ large on his noble phiz. Dogs are fatalists. Yet when I turned to look at him he grinned with relief and wagged his tail as if to say, "Whew, I was worried there for a minute."

It's said that with time we grow to resemble our pets. Like my dogs, I love to wallow—though in facts and theories rather than mud, horse manure, or deer droppings.

DOG NUTS

In *The Devil's Dictionary*, Ambrose Bierce defined the canine race thusly: "Dog. A kind of additional or subsidiary deity designed to catch the overflow and surplus of the world's worship."

Over sixty-seven years I've owned twelve dogs, ranging from tiny terriers and a bugle-throated beagle to rangy pointers and big, burly retrievers. That's really not many by the standards of the true dog nut, some of whom—people who ride to hounds, compete in dogsled races like the Iditarod, hunt raccoons or coyotes or mountain lions or bears— will own dozens at a time.

A woman who lives down the road from me—and it's a remote dirt road, five miles from the nearest hamlet—takes in any stray that wanders by. She does not hunt or herd with them, she just loves them. The word must have spread on the doggy internet because at any given moment she has any- where from eight to twelve dogs living in clean, comfortable wire kennels around her doublewide trailer. They range from nondescript but healthy, well-fed mutts to a pair of beautiful Brittanies, with stops at such breeds as a spitz, a golden retriever, two basset hounds, and a sprawl of Labradors. Their chorused voices ring out eerily on a moon- lit night when coyotes are singing in the surrounding hills.

In a wealthier town just over the mountain, it is fashion- able among the doggy set to throw birthday parties for one's purebred pooch, replete with festive, conical paper hats, party favors, and a huge birthday cake fashioned from Alpo, with beef jerky "candles" for the birthday "boy" or "girl." Little Tiffany, a charming bichon frise, had just turned two. She had fourteen sticks of jerky on her cake—one for each of her canine pals.

Even in death, some of us treat dogs as we would people. Pet cemeteries abound throughout the Western world. The Cemetery of Dogs, located on the forested islet of Asnières in the Seine River near Paris, was founded in 1899 by the French feminist Marguerite Durand to relieve that dulcet stream of its burden of dead, rotting dogs, thrown into it every day from the banks of the City of Light. Some forty thousand canines lie there today in eternal rot—I mean rest—some of those from the turn of the century in moss- grown marble mausoleums styled on the classical doghouse, while the graves of today's new residents are marked by ma- chine-tooled headstones with laminated photos of the loved ones. The biggest and oldest dog cemetery in the United States can be found in Hartsdale, New York, a suburb of Manhattan. The dog graves cover nine acres of meadow and willow trees, and on Memorial Day, according to Mary Eliza- beth Thurston in her fine book *The Lost History of the Canine Race*, hundreds of people dressed in their mourning finery parade through the grounds carrying bouquets of flowers to place on the graves of their late pals. One woman, in keeping with her Jewish faith, waited a full year before placing a headstone on the grave of her Doberman pinscher, Apollo.

In their wills, many disillusioned humans leave their entire estates to the dogs.

That's a lot of dog biscuits.

ON GRIEF

Dogs die and break our hearts.

We die and they mourn us.

In his book *Dogs Never Lie About Love,* Jeffrey Masson, the former director of the Freud Archives and an unabashed animal lover, suggests that some dogs actually "commit suicide out of despair" over their master's death. He cites the case of a six-year-old boy whose cowboy suit ignited near a bonfire. While the boy lingered near death in the hospital, receiving eleven blood transfusions, his dog, whose name was Woodsie, refused to eat. The boy finally died, and the dog followed him two hours later.

Greyfriars Bobby was a Skye terrier sheepdog in Scotland. When his master, Old Jock, died in 1858, Bobby was still young. He followed the funeral procession to the Greyfriars cemetery in Edinburgh and after Old Jock had been planted, Bobby lay down on the grave. He stayed in that graveyard year after year, kept alive by the food people brought him once his story was known—little snacks at first, then leftovers from their own suppers, sometimes even whole roasts. Bobby lived there for fourteen years. He died in 1872. A statue on Candlemaker's Row in Edinburgh commemorates Bobby's vigil. It was donated by the Baroness Burdett-Coutts and stands above a drinking fountain built for wandering dogs.

A friend of mine, the best upland bird hunter I've ever known, gave up the pursuit of ruffed grouse and woodcock after his great dog Ruff died. Landy couldn't bear to go into the coverts again; the memories were too painful. For a few years he didn't hunt at all. Then he bought a beagle and began chasing cottontails and snowshoe hares. Now he's the best rabbit hunter I've ever known.

ON THE SENSES OF A DOG

"If you eliminate smoking and gambling," wrote George Bernard Shaw, "you will be amazed to find that almost all an Englishman's pleasures can be, and mostly are, shared by his dog." Dogs, though, are far more unbuttoned than most Englishmen. They're true voluptuaries, orgiasts when the opportunity arises, and like all consummate sensualists they have the senses to bring it off. Though dogs can indeed see color, if only in muted shades, because of the predominance of rods over cones in their eyes, they are far better at spotting movement in dim light than we are, and they can hear sounds far beyond our range (thirty-five thousand cycles per second to our twenty thousand). My dogs can distinguish the sound of our car when my wife is still half a mile from home, wherewith they begin their Happy Dance, singing at the top of their voices.

But the organ from which a dog derives its greatest pleasure is of course its nose. Any dog's idea of a great day is to walk its nose through the world, the wider the range the better. They're admirably suited for this work. Where we have only 5 million olfactory cells per human nose, the average basset hound has 125 million, a fox terrier 150 million, and a German shepherd some 220 million. Back in the early 1950s, a meticulous German scientist named Walter Neuhaus designed an "olfactometer" and after extensive tests of both dogs and men, concluded that canine noses are one million to one hundred million times more sensitive than human beezers.

What's more, the dog has a secret weapon: the tiny (two and a half centimeters) Jacobson's organ, located between the roof of its mouth and its nostrils near the front of its face, which allows it to simultaneously sniff and taste everything it encounters. If what it encounters smells/tastes good enough, your dog will eat it, and is equipped to chase it for a good long way to do so. If the object encountered smells to a male dog like a bitch in heat, then chances are your male will want to hump it. If it smells like another male, he'll probably fight to establish dominance. If it smells like excrement, more often than not he'll roll in it—nobody knows for sure why.

ON THEIR INSOUCIANCE

"The great pleasure of a dog," says Samuel Butler, "is that you may make a fool of yourself with him and not only will he not scold you, but he will make a fool of himself too."

Dogs have a great sense of humor. As Turgenev says in *A Sportsman's Sketches:* "It is well known that dogs are capable of smiling, and even of smiling very charmingly." They love to have fun—especially at our expense.

We were hunting our way through a late-season blizzard, a mixture of sleet and big, fat flakes that cut visibility to about ten yards. My yellow Lab, Jake, of course had four-paw drive and studded snow pads, so the slippery going didn't bother him a bit, but with each step I was skidding on the brink of disaster. Every now and then I'd catch Jake looking back at me with what seemed a wicked, anticipatory grin, hindquarters wriggling and tail out of control. He knew where we were going, I thought . . .

We'd just topped a rise and were heading downhill toward a stand of dense young aspen whips—a patch of cover that had been good to us, grousewise, in seasons past—when my booted heel hit a buried slab of raw Vermont marble covered with wet, ice-crusted leaves. Sure enough, my feet went out from under me and I fell splat on my butt.

Jake's grin widened and he seemed to chortle at my embarrassment. He clearly said: *"Haw, haw, haw!"*

What I said was unprintable.

The dog was laughing at me, I was sure of it.

I'd always suspected it, and now it seems that it's true: Dogs *do* have a sense of humor. A recent study by Professor Patricia Simonet, a psychologist at Sierra State College in California, detected not only canine laughter, but also subtle sounds that could be the doggy equivalent of human giggles, chuckles, cackles, and titters. "To the untrained human ear," she says, "it sounds like a pant, a 'huh, huh.' "

Professor Simonet conducted her study by hanging around parks with a powerful microphone, taping the sounds made by dogs at play. It wasn't an easy task, she says. The dogs were willing to cooperate but the people often interrupted her recording sessions by asking what she was up to. Nonetheless, Simonet found that dogs use at least four sound patterns: barks, growls, whines, and laughs. Only the laugh is reserved for playtime. When Professor Simonet studied her recordings, she found "a wide range of nuance and tone"—subtleties lost to humans, she says, since the frequency is beyond our ears. The key to her experiment was testing how dogs respond simply to the noise of other dogs laughing. Professor Simonet played the *huh huh* sound to a group of puppies, one by one. On hearing the broadcast they picked up their toys and jumped for joy.

Subtleties, hey? After reading of Professor Simonet's landmark work, I took my dogs aside and tested them with the subtlest dog story I'd ever heard.

"This fellow's bird dog has died," I told them, "and he's in the market for a new one. He sees an ad in the paper for 'good gun dogs' and goes out to a nearby farm. The farmer shows him a kennel full of pointers, setters, and Brittanies.

" 'How's about that big Gordon, over there?'

" 'Oh, he's not for sale,' the farmer says. 'He's my own personal bird dog—too valuable for me to sell.'

" 'Listen, let me at least see him work. I'd be willing to pay plenty for a good dog.'

"The farmer takes the Gordon out into a patch of likely-looking cover on the back forty and tells him: 'Okay, Mac-Gregor, find the bird!'

"The Gordon takes off into the brush, locks up on point, then barks once.

" 'That means he's pointing a single,' the farmer says.

" 'Oh, come on,' says the would-be buyer. 'Dogs can't count.'

" 'We'll see,' says the farmer. He goes over to the dog and kicks the brush. A single cock pheasant blasts out of the cover.

" 'That was just a fluke,' the buyer says. 'Let's see him do it again.'

"The farmer hies the dog on. A few steps later, MacGregor locks up and barks—four times.

"Same deal as before, but this time when the farmer kicks the cover four pheasants flush.

"The buyer is sold. He forks over fifteen hundred dollars for the dog.

"A few weeks later the farmer has to go to town and decides to stop off at the guy's house to see how his dog is doing. Pulls into the driveway, no sign of the dog. The guy comes out of the house, looking kind of miffed.

" 'How's MacGregor coming along?' the farmer asks him.

" 'It didn't work out,' the guy says. 'You sold me a bill of goods. On opening day I took him to my best covert. He got about two steps into it and started barking like crazy. Then he ran back and began humping my leg. Next he picked up a stick and started shaking it at me.' The guy shakes his head sadly. 'He'd obviously gone nuts, so I shot him.'

" 'You durn fool!' the farmer says. 'He was telling you there's more effing birds in here than you can shake a stick at!' "

I waited for the telltale *huh, huh.* No soap. Jake yawned. Roz, my Jack Russell, decided to chase the cat. Clearly this dog humor was more subtle than I'd figured. You can't expect to elicit a heartfelt whoop with a feeble joke. Man's best friend finds different things funny in different ways. Perhaps earthy humor was more to their liking, so I gave them my best shot—a bit of English doggerel:

THE DOGGIES' MEETING

The doggies called a meeting;
They came from near and far.
Some came by motorcycle
And some by touring car.

Each doggie crossed the portal,
Each doggie signed the book,
Then each unshipped his asshole
And hung it on a hook.

One dog was not invited,
Which sorely raised his ire.
He dashed into the meeting hall
And loudly shouted, "Fire!"

This threw them in confusion
And, without a second look,
Each grabbed another's asshole
From off another's hook.

And that's the reason why, Sir,
While walking down the street,
And that's the reason why, Sir,
When doggies chance to meet,

And that's the reason why, Sir,
Wherever they may roam,
Each sniffs the other's asshole:
To see if it's his own.

I waited for at least the equivalent of a doggy titter. Even a groan would have been welcome. Alas, no sale—though kindhearted Jake did indeed smile at me with what looked suspiciously like canine pity.

Next day we were hunting one of our favorite coverts, a hillside that usually teemed with woodcock and grouse. With my ear now trained, thanks to Professor Simonet, I listened for every subtle nuance of doggy humor. As we entered the top of it, I thought I could detect the two of them chuckling gleefully. Wickedly, it seemed. Or was I getting paranoid?

They led me down the slope through a stand of ancient apple trees where often, at that hour, we found a partridge or two feeding on the ground amid the windfallen fruit. It had been a good apple year, and the pomes lay on the ground like a carpet of outsized ball bearings. You had to duck to get under the lowest of the apple boughs, and of course keep your gun in one hand, ready to mount at the first flap of a grouse wing. I was just bending down to pass under one of these low sweepers, feet already skidding on the apples underfoot, when it happened. I heard the chain-saw rip of grouse feathers, stepped forward and raised the gun, and my feet went out from under me once again.

Thump!

I must have created a quart of applesauce when my tailbone hit the ground.

When I looked up, buttsore and humiliated by this pratfall, I saw both dogs not ten yards away, looking at me—eyes filled with glee, ears cocked, grins on their faces. Both of them were going *"Huh, huh, huh!"*

Then, as if to explain the joke, Jake shook his head, his flapping ears sounding just like a grouse flush. They'd set me up, the rascals. Led me into a spot where they knew my footing was unsteady, then faked the whole situation.

Yes, where humor is concerned, dogs prefer slapstick.

Fair warning: Be prepared.

They're totally lacking in inhibitions and unless taught otherwise (a rolled newspaper, a stern command, the repeated words "No! Bad dog!" are good educational tools) will do whatever strikes their fancy, whenever the mood is upon them. They'll gladly copulate in the middle of Main Street at high noon, or in the nave of a cathedral during the sermon at Christmas services. Dogs will defecate in the park or in your living room if left to their own devices. Given the proper amount of rotten roadkill in his belly, a dog will redecorate the backseat of your car, or the front if you allow him up there, in the pattern our British cousins call "dog's dinner mauve." Only rarely, though, will a mature male dog urinate in either your house or your car. He's saving that valuable commodity for better things: to mark every tree, post, bush, weed, or grass stem with his calling card. He especially loves to mark car or truck tires, seemingly aware that they will carry his byline out into the wider world—possibly fulfilling some deep doggy dream of immortality.

ON THEIR UNCANNY SENSE OF DIRECTION

Phrenologically and figuratively speaking, the Bump of Locality stands tall on a dog's otherwise flat-topped skull. Canine lore is full of stories about dogs slogging hundreds of miles to rejoin families that had moved far away, leaving poor Rover behind. My dogs have led me back to truck or camp through stygian gloom after many an evening's hunt. They have no problem finding their unerring way home on the rare occasions when we get separated in the woods.

But the best story I've read about this still-unexplained directional sense appears in a book titled *War Dogs: Canines in Combat* by Michael G. Lemish (Brassey's, 1996). During the Vietnam War, a U.S. Army scout dog named Troubles and his handler, PFC William Richardson, were airlifted out of An Khe into a landing zone some distance back in Indian Country. Richardson was severely wounded in a firefight soon after they landed and dusted off in a medevac chopper. The patrol they'd been working with left Troubles behind when they too were evacuated. As Lemish tells it:

> Three weeks later Troubles was found back at the First Air Cavalry Division Headquarters in An Khe. The dog, tired and emaciated, would not let anyone get near him. Troubles then slowly went to the tents comprising the scout dog platoon and searched until he found Richardson's equipment and cot. The dog then simply curled up alongside his master's belongings and fell asleep. If the pair had walked into the jungle, Troubles's return would be easy to explain: the dog followed his master's scent home. . . . But the pair had been airlifted in, and Richardson left by helicopter, so no scent trail could possibly have been left behind.

Just how Troubles found his way home, and where he had been for three weeks, remains a mystery.

I've seen my own dogs do some amazing things. Last November, along the Blackwater River on Maryland's Eastern Shore, I was hunting ducks in flooded timber. Just before dawn Jake and I were huddled in a skimpy blind in the middle of a swamp. There was skim ice on the water, and we could hear the chortle of puddle ducks everywhere. My friend Stony Stonebreaker set out the decoys while I and Duke Cunningham, a Republican congressman from La Jolla, California, perched on a brace of upright two-by-fours driven into the mud with six-inch-wide blocks of wood nailed across the top. It might have been comfy to Stony, who's part Indian, and for Duke, a former navy fighter pilot who was America's first ace in Vietnam, but for this overweight, sixty-something white man it felt more like a torture stake. Jake sat in hip-deep swamp water, his back to the decoys, watching my every wince. Just at legal shooting time, Stony said: "Here they come!" We heard the whistle of teal, the heavier rip of widgeon wings through the graying darkness, ducks circling the dekes. They cupped in, swift, dim shadows against the fading night. "Take 'em," Stony said.

As I stood to shoot, I saw Jake's eyes locked on mine. I fired twice, Duke twice, Stony three times with the pump gun—long, ragged lances of flame igniting the darkness. We could hear ducks fall, the crackle and splash of their bodies on the iced-over water.

Jake's eyes were still on me.

Stony gestured me to release him for the retrieve.

"Fetch, boy," I said. Jake rose, spun on his heels, and hit the water with a great cold splash. He hadn't seen a single duck fall. Not a one was visible from the blind—they'd all dropped behind hummocks of marsh grass and drowned trees—and the wind was at our backs, so he couldn't have smelled them. Yet Jake swam strong, unerring, without hesitation to each of the five birds on the water. He'd no sooner bring one back in than he'd turn and hit the water for another. We gave him no direction. After the fifth bird, he sat down in his icy hip bath again and began to groom himself.

How had he known where to go? I believe he could tell where they fell from the angle of my gun when I shot, and from the expression in my eyes if I'd hit or missed. He may have also seen from the corners of his eyes the shots of my companions. Moreover, all dogs have an inner ear that can shut down to filter out extraneous background noises, so Jake may well have concentrated only on the splashes of ducks hitting the water, and from those sounds gotten a rough idea of their range and direction. But did he actually count seven shots and know we'd killed five birds?

I have to believe he did.

ON TRAINING

The books available on dog training, in English alone, would fill a small library. The theories are even more abundant. But when it comes to hunting, I'm convinced that a dog's best coach is an older, woods-wise dog. For years I've always kept an older Lab and a young one for just that purpose. My yellow Lab Simba taught Luke all he knew about birds and cover; Luke taught Jake, and now Jake has converted my Jack Russell, Roz Russell, into, of all things, a bird dog. She can flush woodcock with the best of them. Sure, I can teach a pup—any pup—simple obedience: sit, stay, come, down, heel, fetch, or kennel up. And most dogs, even nonhunting breeds, will quarter instinctively while running ahead of their master in field or woods. But an older dog that's learned the haunts and tricks of gamebirds, and that's amply rewarded with praise and head rubs when he finds game, will soon earn the envy and emulation of the younger one, thus shortening the hit-or-miss stage in a single pup working alone. Even a finely bred pointing dog, when he locks up on a pheasant or a covey of quail, will often compel a younger, untrained dog to honor that point by the sheer force of his personality—coupled with fear of the disapproval the older dog will show if the pup dashes in and bumps the bird.

The use of shock collars in modern field dog training more often amounts to abuse. I've seen frustrated amateur trainers get so angry at themselves when their dogs don't do what they hope the pups will that they zap them again and again. By not trusting the dog's nose they inadvertently teach the pup to avoid pointing a bird, and for a very good reason: It doesn't want to get zapped again. Not long ago a neighbor of mine who once played in the NFL strapped a shock collar around his neck and zapped himself to see what it felt like. Paul's a big guy—six foot five by 250 pounds. The blast, he says, dropped him to his knees.

ON MORALS

Dogs are nonjudgmental. You can be doing anything—driving a car, cooking, going to the toilet, hammering nails, typing, even making passionate love—and your dog will sit there watching with a mild, slightly quizzical look in his eyes. He's waiting to see what's going to happen next, and wondering—hoping perhaps—that it will involve him and the out-of-doors.

A dog doesn't even care if you're robbing a bank or stealing from the poor box, even committing murder, so long as you take him with you. He'll be by your side through thick or thin, willing to help if called upon, mourn if you fail. Bill Sikes in *Oliver Twist* is a cruel, warped man, a lowlife and criminal. He beats his dog without mercy, never even gives it a name. Yet the dog follows him everywhere, and when Sikes inadvertently hangs himself at the novel's climax, the dog— some kind of pit bull, judging by Cruickshanks's drawings— who's been crouching on the roof slates, watching events unfold, howls pitifully and leaps for his master's shoulders— only to miss and fall to his own death on the cobbles below.

Mad Dog Roy Earle's dog, Pard, in the movie *High Sierra* insists on joining his master during Earle's last stand in the mountains. Roy puts down his Lewis gun and is reaching out to help the dog up the last pitch of rocks when a waiting police sharpshooter kills the man with one shot from a scoped rifle. Poor Pard whines in sorrow.

I'm sure even Hitler's beloved German shepherd Blondi, who died with him and Eva Braun on April 30, 1945, in the Berlin bunker, thought the world of the *Führer* even as the poison went to work.

DOGS AND FAMILY VALUES

Woodrow Wilson once said: "If a dog will not come to you after he has looked you in the face, you ought to go home and examine your conscience." Dog's are nature's true conservatives. They prefer the status quo and would like it to prevail. They want the men, women, and children in their lives to remain together, never changing, never leaving, never growing older, always ready to feed them when suppertime rolls around, always loving each other. When my wife and I are working toward an argument, our dogs excuse themselves from the room. Our tones of voice must tell them what's coming: subtle changes of tone that begin before we're even aware that contention is brewing. Dogs, like us, would probably like to live forever. They want things to continue as they are—food, love, sex, sleep, warmth, other dogs, and adventure. Can we fault them for such a dream?

If all mankind disappeared tomorrow, whisked from the earth without a trace, what would become of our dogs? Many would die, of course, having grown too reliant on us to feed them, too soft to deal with the hard truths of survival. It would, for a while at least, be truly a dog-eat-dog world.

But dogs breed twice a year. In six years, a single litter could produce sixty-seven thousand offspring. In perhaps a hundred or maybe a thousand canine generations the distinctions we know as breeds would slowly meld back toward the dog's prototype. The animal that would emerge would be clever, yellowish tan, weigh about thirty-five pounds, with ears erect or perhaps tippy at the top: a marvelous sniffing machine ready at a moment's notice to mate, to eat, to fight, or just to take a snooze. Maybe a grin now and then. Soon the nights would be filled again with howlsong.

I'd like to think that somewhere in that chorus a note would ring out in mourning for the bipedal fools whom once they loved and served so well.

The nineteenth-century French poet Alphonse Marie Louis de Prat de Lamartine once wrote: "When man is lonely, God sends him a dog."

But what if a dog is lonely?

If you don't have a dog . . . well, think about it.

FIRST AID FOR FIDO

Nothing can wreck a bird hunt quicker than an injury to your gundog.

A few years ago, the writer Steve Bodio was hunting pheasants on the plains east of Lewistown, Montana. It was a cold November day—below zero at dawn—with a breeze sharp as a skinning knife working across the grasslands, and Steve's strong, hard-charging springer spaniel, Bart, had hunted full-speed-ahead, as usual. He'd been in and out of ice-cold water during the morning, and all afternoon he'd coursed the bald, brown hills at an eager run. But Bart was eleven years old. Late in the day he suddenly collapsed. By the time Steve got up to him the spaniel's eyes were glazed and rolling. Mucus oozed from his mouth. Steve and his soon-to-be-wife Libby Frischman raced Bart back to town, and the nearest veterinarian.

"It was a close call," Steve says, "but the vet pulled him through. What had happened was that Bart had suffered a sudden onslaught of hypoglycemia—an exhaustion of the blood sugar in his system. It'd never happened before, but there's a first time for everything. Hypoglycemia isn't all that rare in older dogs." From then on, at the vet's suggestion, Steve and Libby always carried a squeeze bottle full of Karo syrup in one or another's game vest whenever they had Bart out working. "You have to dilute it in the colder weather," Libby says, "or else it gets so thick that you can't squeeze it into the dog's throat quickly enough." Another remedy, she adds, is to bring along a small supply of Gainesburgers and feed one to your older dog every now and then. "Gaines-burgers have a lot of sugar in them."

Over the years, most of the injuries to my own dogs, young or old, have involved barbed wire—an invention I've come to think of as the Devil's Dental Floss. It's everywhere in the country I hunt, usually old barbed wire, rusty to the point of decrepitude and cleverly disguised in those ancient New England pastures by thick growths of vine, brush, brambles, and weeds. My dogs go charging ahead at full speed, as is their wont, only to be stopped cold by a twanging strand of rust-brown webbing on which the half-inch prongs are still wickedly sharp. The twang and the yelp are nearly simultaneous. The wounds these barbs inflict are impressive: sometimes half a foot long, on chest or shoulders or throat, and deep enough so that you can see the raw flesh gaping within. Sometimes you don't even notice the wounds—and the dogs certainly don't seem to worry about them—until blood starts streaking their fur. But I've learned now to carry in my game pocket a bottle of Quick Stop, a powder that works on the principle of the styptic pencil men use to stanch razor cuts inflicted while shaving. Pour a few shakes of the powder on the ugliest gash and you'll see the blood stop flowing almost instantly. For $10.95, the Dunn's catalog offers a sixteen-ounce bottle of a liquid called Cut-Heal Medication, which serves the same purpose.

It's a good idea to wash the wound with hydrogen peroxide and apply a coat of over-the-counter antibiotic ointment—something like Bacitracin, Neomycin, or Polymyxin—*before* applying the styptic medication.

For really severe cuts there's a device available through veterinary suppliers called a surgical stapler, which you can use to pin the edges of a gash together and thus prevent excessive blood loss before you can get your dog to a vet for proper stitching. Best check with your vet for lessons in how to use the stapler. It's good to realize that an average-sized gundog can lose up to a pint of blood before serious trouble sets in.

Another problem I run into at least once each season is thorn punctures. Inevitably when we're pushing a thicket of thorn apples for grouse or woodcock, especially in the early season before their pads have toughened up, one or another of my dogs will come out of the covert on three legs—the fourth held high off the ground and a heartfelt plea for succor in his eyes. Sure enough, there's usually the butt end of a two-and-a-half-inch sticker protruding from the hurt foot. I once tried to remove a thorn with my fingers but couldn't get a good enough grip on it, and ended up using my teeth! Now I carry either a heavy-duty tweezers or a small needle-nose pliers in my game pocket for such emergencies.

A partial preventive measure is to precondition your dog's pads before the bird season opens. Plenty of mutual exercise is the best approach, but if you lack the time you can get by applying a pad conditioner like Tuf-Foot ($8.99 for an eight-ounce bottle from Dunn's). Still, no matter how horny the pads on your dog's feet, thorns and cactus spines can always find their way in through the thin, sensitive skin between the pads. In truly wicked country where everything bites—South Texas, for instance, or the prickly pear wastelands of the West and Southwest—you might want to consider dog boots, taped around the top to prevent their slipping off. I prefer the ventilated rubber boots: a full set of four from Dunn's for $29.99. They seem to turn back the spikes more effectively than either Cordura leather or suede, and in my opinion give better traction on wet rock as well.

Now and then, through his nonstop exertions, one of my dogs will pull up lame during a hunt. What I fear most is a fractured long bone or sprained "wrist" in one of his legs. Usually the dog won't start limping right away, but when you notice even the slightest hint of a limp call the dog in, make it sit until it's calmed down some, then go over the leg carefully.

Begin with the toes and see if a nail is split (if so, a canine nail clipper, some disinfectant, and an application of antibiotic ointment is in order, followed by a wrap or three of adhesive tape over the trimmed-back toenail stub).

Next check the dog's pads and between his toes for cuts, abrasions caused by rough rocks, thorns, or iron nails. An application of Quick Stop and/or a wraparound bandage can help temporarily.

Finally, feel the leg carefully for a possible sprain or fracture.

Sometimes, especially with an older dog early in the season, it's just stiff muscles that's causing the problem. We all know the feeling. But if your dog winces or yelps when you probe or manipulate a particular spot, it's time to call it a day and get to the vet. I always carry an Ace bandage in my game pocket, along with a roll of adhesive tape and a bottle of Bufferin. Wrap the injured joint firmly but not so tight as to restrict circulation, feed the dog a single Bufferin or enteric-coated aspirin (stick it in a Gainesburger to make it go down easier!), and head for the truck. Working a dog on a fractured or even on a sprained leg will only compound the problem. He could end up out of action for the season.

Always remember that dogs are a lot tougher than we are. When their blood is up, in the heat of the hunt, they don't feel pain, or at least their eagerness—their heart—causes them to shrug it off. It's up to us, their masters and disciples, to keep a close eye out for danger and injury.

The most frightening accident that ever occurred to me in the field happened one beautiful October day a few years back when I was hunting a favorite Vermont covert with Charles Gaines and Chris Child, who were visiting from New Hampshire. Charles had his great Brittany Tucker along, so I left my black Lab Luke in the front seat of the truck while we hunted the Brit on our first swing. Sure enough, Tucker pointed a grouse not twenty-five yards from the truck. Charles walked in and killed the bird within sight and sound of the truck. It fell in some heavy brush along a stone wall.

Next thing we knew—Luke was nosing his way into the thick stuff for the retrieve! I looked back at my truck, aghast. At the shot, he'd busted out of "jail" by smashing clean through the driver-side window, leaving a hole like a six-teen-inch naval rifle shell in the thick safety glass. When he'd fetched back the bird I checked him over for cuts but could only find a few drops of blood on his lower lip. Nonetheless I raced him down to the vet in town for a thorough check. Amazingly, the examination revealed no wounds. The blood on his lip had been that of the grouse. We were back in the woods within an hour, and filled out a bang-up day with no harm done.

ROUGHING IT

Bird hunting is usually a day-trip experience, but from time to time over the years I've found it both expedient and productive to trek into remote country and camp out for a few days in pursuit of our feathered friends. My first outings of this sort, when I was a teenager, occurred in northern Wisconsin, where my quarry was mainly ruffed grouse and woodcock, with a few puddle-jumped ducks thrown in for variety. Necessarily I traveled light: a bedroll, a tarp, a knapsack containing a frying pan, a can of lard, a box of wooden matches, an ax, and a few staples—Heinz pork and beans or chili con carne, bread, coffee, fruit preserves, and salt.

The camps were rough. The Nicolet and Chequamegon country had been cut over only forty years earlier and was coming back in dense thickets of popple and jack pine, alder and sumac and blackberry bramble. Ideal bird habitat, but scruffy to look at, painful to walk through, hardly the setting for an idyllic *National Geographic*–style campsite. The lakes that studded the region were cold and brown, tasting of iron. The few mature trees still standing lacked the interlocked root support of their long-since-fallen neighbors and had a tendency to topple at the blast of November storms. A kid I knew had camped under one of these surviving hundred-foot-tall white pines on a stormy night, wrapped himself in his blankets, gone to sleep, and never woke up. The tree fell on him sometime before dawn.

There were other hazards to solitary camping in those crude, preplastic days. If your ax slipped and you split your foot while chopping firewood, you might well bleed out before you could get to the nearest road. A sudden blizzard could freeze you to Popsicle status despite your tarp and army surplus blankets. You might bog down in a muskeg and never get out. And of course a shotgun chambering low-base 7½s was hardly the weapon of choice when confronted by an angry black bear (though I saw only three of them in all those years, each at a great distance and already heading away from me in supercharged overdrive).

Still, it was the faint, sulfurous hint of danger implicit in these outings that made them memorable. Camped out on a chilly night in the Chequamegon, stars winking like ice chips overhead, the campfire burned down to dull red coals that snapped now and then like pistol shots, I would lie under my blankets against the stump of a great, long-since-felled pine, my belly full of pan-fried grouse and beans, and drift off to sleep dreaming of windigos and hodags. Owlhoot made it all the better. In my sleep the hodag would creep close, all fangs and horns and scales, his serpentine tail scuffling through the pine duff. I'd start awake, reach for the shotgun . . . but it was only the night wind.

Oddly enough, though, the closest I ever came to death in a hunting camp was a quarter century later, on a luxury safari in East Africa. We were camped along the Tana River not far from Mount Kenya, bird hunting. I was over that way for *Sports Illustrated,* covering the East Africa Safari Rally, a three-thousand-mile road race that in those days traversed most of Kenya, northern Tanzania, and southern Uganda. After the rally I took an extra couple of days for a taste of the fabled safari life. My professional hunter, Bill Winter, ran a first-rate operation, replete with mess tent, shower stall, a Bedford lorry to haul the camp gear, a cordon *bleu* chef, individual green canvas tents for the clients, and a staff of polite, well-trained, crisply uniformed African "safari boys."

That morning we'd hunted sand grouse. Not far from the river was a hot spring, a *maji moto* in Swahili, and we walked in quietly through a low ground fog, armed only with 20-gauge shotguns. Soon the sand grouse would be flying. Lambat, the head tracker, led the way, peering intently into the mist. He raised a hand: halt. We heard a chuffing sound in the fog, then dimly made out two dark bulky shapes. *"Kifaro,"* hissed Lambat. *"Mama na mtoto."*

Either the fog thinned or adrenaline sharpened my vision, for suddenly they came into focus: a big female rhino and her calf. The mother whuffed again, aware that something was wrong but unable with her weak eyes and the absence of wind to zero in on the threat. She shook a head horned like a Mexican saddle and shuffled off into the haze, followed by her hornless offspring, which looked at this distance like an outsized hog. I'd often jumped deer while bird hunting in Wisconsin, and once a moose got up and moved out of an alder swale I was pushing for woodcock near Greenville, Maine, but rhinos are somehow different. If only for the heightened pucker factor.

The sun bulged over the horizon, a giant blood orange, and instantly the fog was gone, sucked up by the dry heat of day. But then it seemed to return, in the whistling, whizzing form of a million sand grouse, chunky birds as quick and elusive as their distant relatives, the white-winged doves and mourning doves I'd shot back home.

These were chestnut-bellied sand grouse, *Pterocles exustus,* the most common of the six species that inhabit the dry thorn scrublands of Africa. They fly to water each morning, hitting the available water holes for about an hour soon after dawn, fluttering over the surface to land, drink, and soak up water in their throat feathers for their nestlings to drink during the dry season.

I promptly began to miss them, overwhelmed and wild-eyed at their sky-blackening abundance. Then I settled down as the awe receded and began knocking down singles and doubles at a smart clip. It was fast, neck-wrenching shooting with the birds angling in from every direction. I stood under the cover of an umbrella acacia, surrounded by shell husks, the barrel soon hot enough to raise blisters, shooting until my shoulder grew numb. Bill stood nearby, calling the shots and laughing at my misses.

"Quick, behind you, Bwana!"

I spun around to see a pair of sand grouse slashing in overhead, mounted the gun with my feet still crossed, folded the lead bird, and then leaned farther back to take the trailer directly above me—*pow!* The recoil, in my unbalanced, leg-crossed stance, dropped me on my tailbone. But the bird fell too.

"Splendid," Bill said with a wide, white grin. "Just the way they teach it at the Holland & Holland shooting school. The Classic Twisting, Turning, High-Overhead, Passing, Fall-on-Your-Arse Double. Never seen it done better, I do declare!"

But that wasn't the scary part. The scary part came that night, after a gourmet dinner of grilled sand grouse breasts, rice pilaf, plenty of white wine, Devonshire clotted cream for dessert, and a few postprandial brandies accompanied by Bill Winter's forte: an hour or two of nonstop X-rated puns and limericks. My partner on this safari was a photographer named Tony Triolo, a stout, balding, witty Sicilian American and a world-class snorer. I too, I've been told, have been known to gurgle a bit after a hard day's hunting, a full meal, and a sip or two of the grape. Tony and I were sharing a tent and I knew that if I didn't beat him to bed and get to sleep before he arrived, I'd be in for a sleepless night. But Big Tony stole a march on me. By the time I zipped the mosquito net and crept into my comfy cot, he was sawing logs. No, he was sawing the whole damned Chequamegon forest.

After lying sleepless for an hour under Tony's thunderous barrage, I despaired of the effort, grabbed my pillow, mattress, and blankets, and repaired to the only unoccupied abode in the camp, the mess tent. There I dossed down and sank into the arms of Lethe. At last the night was quiet, and from this distance Tony's snores were no louder than the murmuring mud-brown Tana River.

Toward dawn, though, the camp's assistant chef, a Kikuyu named Wamatitu, was awakened by a series of loud, ferocious, ravening growls emanating from the mess tent. He got up, went over to the tent, peered through the screened door, and saw to his horror not a northern Wisconsin hodag, but what was obviously an East African hyena thrashing around in the gloom. Gobbling the food supplies? Must be. Could a creature that produced such noises be anything else? Wamatitu, an otherwise gentle and kindly soul, repaired to the arms safe, withdrew a Remington Model 700 rifle chambered for 7 mm magnum, loaded it with solids, and went back to the mess tent to dispatch the gluttonous despoiler of all that was tasty.

By the time he returned, thank God, dawn was breaking. In the strengthening gray light of a new day, Wamatitu discerned the writhing, supine shape not of Bwana Fisi, the Ravenous Hyena, but that of Bwana Bob, the Tana River Snoring Champion.

He stayed his fatal round.

Let this story be a lesson to you: It's safer to rough it alone.

HELL WITH THE FIRES OUT

From George Washington, who loved nothing better than chasing the red fox hell-for-leather over hill and dale on horseback, through Dwight Eisenhower, a dedicated quail hunter, to Bill Clinton (of all people), who not long ago actually shot a duck in rural Maryland, not to mention the bird-hunting Bushes, père et fils, many of America's presidents have been hunters. But none was keener for field sports than Theodore Roosevelt, and probably no president of the future ever will be. Not only did Teddy of the Big Teeth hunt at every opportunity, he also wrote some fascinating books about his days afield. African Game Trails (1910), which recounted the bloody details of his six-month shooting safari in British East Africa the previous year, is still a good read, as well as testament to the fact that TR, thanks to congenital myopia and total blindness in his left eye due to a boxing injury incurred in the White House in 1904, was a lifelong lousy shot.

But the best of his outdoor writing can be found in an early trilogy about his experiences in the Wild West: *Hunting Trips of a Ranchman* (1885), *Ranch Life and the Hunting Trail* (1888), and *The Wilderness Hunter* (1893). In 1884, following the death of his wife Alice in childbirth, the desolate twenty-five-year-old TR took leave from the New York state assembly, where he'd already made a name for himself as a fiery reformer, and lit out for the Badlands of Dakota Territory. A year earlier he'd bought a 30,000-acre ranch called Chimney Butte on the Little Missouri River, hard by the Montana line, intending to invest in the cattle boom brought about through the opening of the country by the Northern Pacific Railroad, and now he established another, the Elkhorn.

The Badlands was grim country—"hell with the fires out," as one early visitor called it—and not for nothing had the river that formed it been dubbed the Little Misery. Corpse-blue clay alternated with red scoria; the sandstone bluffs and chimneys were veined with strata of black lignite that burned deep beneath the warped surface, ancient, sulfurous fires set by lightning; steam seeped from fissures in the buttes and crags, while backward-flowing creeks, footed in quicksand, cut the country into a mind-boggling maze. The creeks came and went with the seasons and what water there was usually puckered the mouth with its bitter alkaline taste.

Yet the place was a paradise for wildlife, great and small. In Roosevelt's day a few remnant buffalo still wandered the draws and the flat shortgrass prairies atop the buttes. Grizzlies and black bears abounded. Elk, black-tailed deer, and pronghorn antelope were everywhere. But best of all, to my mind, the country was home to a superabundance of game-birds: plover and curlew, ducks and geese in season, sharptails and sage grouse in particular.

In chapter 3 of *Hunting Trips,* titled "The Grouse of the Northern Cattle Plains," TR takes a clear-eyed look at prairie gunning more than a century ago, and in the process gives a clue to the westerner's historical lack of enthusiasm for wingshooting. "I would no more compare the feat of one who bags his score of ducks or quail with that of him who fairly hunts down and slays a buck or bear," he writes, "than I would compare the skill necessary to drive a buggy with that required to ride a horse across country; or the dexterity acquired in handling a billiard cue with that shown by a skilful boxer or oarsman."

Though he hastens to say he's not decrying the shotgun, TR explains that in the West of those days, full of outlaws and warlike Indians, the weapon of choice was the rifle or the revolver, even for hunting. "Large game is still that which is sought after, and most of the birds killed are either simply slaughtered for the pot, or else shot for the sake of variety, while really after deer or antelope." A page later he elaborates:

> As already said, the ranchmen do not often make a regular hunt after these grouse. This is partly because most of them look with something akin to contempt upon any fire-arm but the rifle or revolver, and partly because it is next to impossible to keep hunting-dogs very long on the plains. The only way to check in any degree the ravages of the wolves is by the most liberal use of strychnine, and the offal of any game killed by a cattle-man is pretty sure to be poisoned before being left, while the "wolfer," or professional wolf-killer strews his bait everywhere. It thus comes about that any dog who is in the habit of going any distance from the house is almost sure to come across and eat some of the poisoned meat, the effect of which is certain death.

A wealthy man by nineteenth-century standards, Roosevelt always carried the best of weapons. His standard armory during his Wild West days consisted of a 40–90 Sharps "for very long range work;" a six-shot, lever-action 50–115 Bullard Express "which has the velocity, shock, and low trajectory of an English rifle," and ("better than either") a 45–75 Winchester Model 1886 with a half magazine—"by all odds the best weapon I ever had . . . having killed every kind of game with it, from a grizzly bear to a big-horn." He also owned and used, though infrequently, a 10-gauge hammergun by Thomas of Chicago, a hammerless 16-gauge by Kennedy of St. Paul "for grouse and plover," and his "little ranch gun," good medicine for either fur or feather: a 16-gauge drilling with twin 16-bore tubes mounted atop a 40–70 rifle barrel. With one or another of these weapons, plus his long-barreled .45-caliber Colt revolver and a sharp, sturdy-bladed hunting knife on his belt, "Old Four Eyes" as the cowboys called him was loaded for anything.

Most of the sharptails or sage grouse he killed by snapping their heads off with a rifle or pistol bullet "at the expense of considerable ammunition, I might add."

One morning, though, after "a succession of ludicrously bad misses at deer," he went out on horseback with his shotgun—probably the 10-bore:

> While riding through a barren-looking bottom, I happened to spot some prairie fowl squatting close to the ground beneath a sage-brush. It was some minutes before I could make out what they were, they kept so low and so quiet, and their color harmonized so well with their surroundings. Finally I was convinced that they were grouse, and rode my horse slowly by them. When opposite, I reined him in and fired, killing the whole bunch of five birds. Another time at the ranch our supply of fresh meat gave out entirely, and I sallied forth with the ranch gun, intent, not on sport, but

on slaughter. It was late fall, and as I rode along in the dawn . . . a small pack of prairie fowl passed over my head and lit on a dead tree that stood out some little distance from a grove of cotton-woods. They paid little attention to me, but they are so shy at that season that I did not dare to try to approach them on foot, but let the horse jog on at the regular-cow-pony gait—a kind of single-foot pace, between a walk and a trot,— and as I passed by fired into the tree and killed four birds. Now, of course I would not have dreamed of taking either of these shots had I been out purely for sport, and neither needed any more skill than would be shown in killing hens in a barn-yard; but, after all, when one is hunting for one's dinner he takes an interest in his success which he would otherise lack, and on both occasions I felt a most unsportsman-like glee when I found how many I had potted.

During casual walk-up hunts with the 16-gauge of no more than a hour or two, it was common for TR to return to the ranch house with bags of twelve to fifteen birds.

"But the best day's work I ever did after sharp-tails was in the course of a wagon trip which my brother [Elliot] and I made through the fertile farming country to the eastward." They had spent the night at the cabin of a hospitable Norwegian wheat farmer and fared forth at dawn the next morning in their light covered wagon with two dogs: an elderly, arthritic pointer whom Teddy calls Old Stub Tail and "a wild young setter pup, tireless and ranging very free." The entire countryside was fenceless in those days, and the tall bluestem spread before them like a slow-heaving sea, studded with yellowing islets of wheat in which the sharptails fed morning and evening.

With Old Stub Tail nailing point after staunch point, and the setter pup in his enthusiasm inadvertently bouncing whole coveys before Teddy and Elliot could get within range, they still had a bang-up day. "The actual killing the birds was a good deal like quail shooting in the East," Roosevelt wrote, "except that it was easier, the marks being so much larger."

The day's only mishap occurred during a two-hour lunch break, "for shortly after noon the stub-tail pointer, for his sins, encountered a skunk, with which he waged prompt and valiant battle—thereby rendering himself, for the balance of the time, wholly useless as a servant and highly offensive as a companion." The wild setter pup filled in ably, though, and by the time they put up their guns an hour before last light, the wagon was fairly groaning with the fruits of the day's harvest: "When we came in at night, we had a hundred and five grouse, of which sixty-two had fallen to my brother's gun, and forty-three to mine. We would have done much better with more serviceable dogs; besides, I was suffering all day long from a most acute colic, which was anything but a help to good shooting."

Such abundance of course will never come again. Reading Roosevelt, or any other decent writer on nineteenth-century bird hunting for that matter, makes me yearn for a time machine, but one that would excise my contemporary qualms about game hoggery even as it whisked me back to those the bloodthirsty days of yesteryear.

THE FLYING BUFFALO

I am quite willing to admit that the flesh of an aged
sage-hen doth possess that sageness one might expect
with advancing years—nay! I will even go farther and
acknowledge the flavor of it to suggest a rare blend of
ancient duck dressing, old moccasins, and pulverized
brick. . . .
—Edwyn Sandys (1902)

Two mind-boggling problems confront
the would-be sage grouse hunter: (1) How
do you find them in the vast sea of
sagebrush that constitutes their age-old
habitat; and (2) What do you do with
something that rank, tough, and smelly once
it's on the ground?

The Great Plains has always been a sagebrush hell—an MMBA as my friend John
Barsness calls it, for Miles and Miles of
Blooming *Artemisia*—and since sage grouse
are less dependent on water sources than
any other species of tetraonid, the birds
could be just about anywhere in those flat-
lands that stretch from horizon to horizon. A
strong pointing dog that works big can be of
some help in locating a covey, but he'd better be long-winded and hard-footed. If you
use a dog, bring along plenty of water as

well as tweezers and a snakebite kit, because sage hens live in the heart of prickly pear and rattler country. My former brother-in-law and still sometime hunting buddy, Roger Marlow of Casper, Wyoming, learned the snake lesson the hard way. His beloved gundog Ollie ran fatally afoul of a rattler a few years back. Roger hadn't the heart to get another pooch, so now he hunts alone and afoot, walking ten or fifteen miles a day over sunbaked, windswept, waterless, foot-tangling sage flats in hopes of flushing a covey of the big birds.

I'd shot representatives of all the other North American grouse species—ruffed, sharptail, prairie chicken, spruce and blue grouse, and ptarmigan—but never a sage hen. Looking to achieve a Grouse Grand Slam before I shuffle off this mortal coil, I accompanied Roger on several of his marathon jaunts one recent fall. In the process, the prairies damned near slammed me, and grandly.

The sage grouse, *Centrocercus urophasianus*, sometimes called the spiny-tailed pheasant, is the largest grouse in North America. A big "boomer"—the male of species—will weigh from five to eight pounds, twice the size of an average hen, bringing it nearly on a par with the European capercaillie or *Auerhahn*. "Buffalo with wings," Barsness calls them, and he has a point: Like bison, sage grouse are superbly adapted to the prairie life. Though they'll eat such Great Plains goodies as wild legumes, weeds, grasses, clover, alfalfa, dandelions, ants, beetles, weevils, and grasshoppers, the bulk of their sustenance comes from the small, gray-green, ultrapungent leaves of the *Artemisia* plant—sagebrush. It makes up nearly 100 percent of their winter diet. Sage also provides the birds with ideal cover. Their mottled light tan and black feathers blend perfectly with the yellowing sage of autumn, and with the grasses that intersperse it. You'd think a bird that large would stand out like the proverbial sore thumb, and when they're walking undisturbed through their realm, they do. But at the first sign of danger—coyotes on the prowl, hawks in the air, hunters tottering toward them with guns in hand—they'll usually freeze and flatten themselves like so many nubbly doormats. Getting airborne is a last, desperate resort. Like turkeys, sage grouse are notoriously slow and wobbly on the takeoff, cackling hysterically, shedding loose feathers as they rise, emptying their cloacas in long, liquid squirts that stink to high heaven. A strange and somewhat comical bird, indeed.

So's my ex-brother-in-law. We both grew up in rural Wisconsin, hunting and fishing right from the get-go. When Roger married my sister, I was delighted. She wasn't, and about twenty years later they split, at her insistence. Since then (apart from a brief but disastrous second marriage) Roger has lived the life of a confirmed bachelor. He crams as much hunting, fishing, and camping into a prairie year as any man alive. Now and then, though, you'll catch him at home, where he repairs occasionally to watch his TV favorites: *Monday Night Football, Beavis & Butthead,* and *ER.* His son, Eric, who got him hooked on that video fare, is now an M.D. in Indiana, and has prescribed a game-meat and vegetarian diet for his aging pa (Roger is seventy and retired from a career as an awning salesman). A veggie dinner *chez* Marlow often consists of a heaping plate of mashed potato buds topped with a can of creamed corn. Thank God, though, there's plenty of antelope, deer, and elk meat in his freezer, along with an abundance of gamebirds and trout, so we ate well enough while I was with him.

"Sage grouse, is it?" he says when I arrive at his doorstep one late September day. "Good. They open on Saturday. I've been scouting all spring and summer and I think I've got some located." On that blustery, rainswept opening day, we hie ourselves off in Roger's dark green camper-topped Toyota to the sage flats west of the dying town of Bairoil (population about thirty-five, down from its boomtown numbers of four hundred). You pass a big industrial plant just as you approach the town. "Now and then they have a leak," Roger says as I eye the ominous warning signs posted along the road. "If those red lights are flashing, you better not drive through. The poison will kill you with a single whiff." Most of the houses in Bairoil are boarded up and empty. A part-time saloon equipped with nonfunctioning gasoline pumps sits at the edge of town. "I think they open it sometimes on Saturday nights," Rog says.

Beyond Bairoil we bump our way down a two-track to a dinky, weed-streaked, half-acre impoundment. "Lost Soldier Reservoir," Rog says. We look out on the bleak, wind-bent sage flats of the Buffalo Buttes escarpment surrounding the lake. "Easy to get lost out there, soldier or civilian, particularly on a day like this with no sun to guide you."

We grab the guns and start hiking. Three hours later the only thing we've flushed is a white-tailed jackrabbit. My feet are raw and chafed—new boots—and twice I've been tripped up by the tanglefoot sage, so my butt is sore as well. We arrive full circle back at the reservoir. "Guy took a twelve-pound trout here earlier this year," Rog says. We string up the rods and start battling the twenty-mile-per-hour west wind. I take a couple of ten-inch rainbows and a slightly bigger brookie on a grasshopper pattern. Roger, fishing a spinning rod rigged with a plastic bubble and a silver spoon, takes a fourteen-inch 'bow. We drive an hour into Rawlins, to the south of us, and have a restaurant fry them up. It's better than potatoes and creamed corn à la Marlow, but not by much.

Roger and I had a great antelope hunt south of here twelve years ago, a whole week of it, living in a big canvas wall tent and going out each morning on our separate ways, picking and choosing among vast numbers of prongbucks and rattlesnakes, even flushing a few sage grouse from time to time, and rendezvousing again at sunset in camp. Eventually, we each killed an antelope with better than fifteen-inch horns. Now I'm wondering if I shouldn't have brought a rifle instead of the smoothbore . . .

Next day the weather clears but the wind is really howling. All week long we hunt in promising sage country well west of Casper, flanking the old Oregon Trail (you can still see the wagon ruts on Overlook Hill)—up coulees and dry washes, seared by the wind, circled by vultures and hawks, dancing with dust devils, pounding ten or more waterless miles each day. Without a single flush. We're jumping pronghorns and mule deer over every rise, but no sage grouse.

We head east to spend the day and a night at the Thunder Basin, a two-hundred-thousand-acre national grassland administered by the forest service, between Wright and Douglas. Roger has drawn an antelope tag, and while he scours the prairie for a suitable pronghorn I walk the sage for birds. Nothing. One night in camp a small herd of elk trots past us, not fifty yards away—four cows, a three-quarter-grown calf, and a nice six-point bull. On one of my walks up a box canyon, I nearly come nose to nose with six mule deer does and a fork-horn buck. We stand not twenty feet apart, watching each other. Then I stamp my foot and blow. The deer turn, flag, and trot uneasily up the canyon wall. I decide to sit down and plot my next move and plunk myself squarely atop a cluster of unseen prickly pears. Next morning Roger nails a nice prongbuck after a quarter-mile stalk through an arroyo beyond which a Sinclair pump jack is clanking and hissing like some mad, mechanized praying mantis. The 125-yard shot takes the buck square through the base of the throat. He has odd-shaped horns, the tips bending straight back like fishhooks. We butcher him, pack the meat in a cooler, and move on.

Still no sage grouse.

My time is running out. In two days I'll have to head north again to Montana for my flight back East.

"We'll give it one more shot," Rog says. "There's some public land we can hunt over in the Hat Six country, near Muddy Mountain. Should be grouse in there."

I'd heard that before.

At dawn the next day we're parked at the end of a two-track that peters out under a pale ridge of rimrock flanked by deep, truck-swallowing arroyos. Black Angus cattle are trailing and feeding along a muddy rivulet called Clear Creek. A cowboy on a handsome chestnut gelding trots over to us, and as he dips a lipful of snoose from a tin of Copenhagen, we tell him we're looking for sage grouse—has he seen any?

"I don't pay much attention to hunting," he says. "Cattle's my life. But if I see anything, I'll flag you."

And an hour later, good as his word, he does. The wind is howling, as usual, but looking up I see a lone rider waving to us from the top of the rimrock. I wave back. He points down at his pony's feet and raises a bunch of fingers.

We head up the rimrock. Rog has legs of iron and soon outdistances me. I plug my way up the broken rocks, huffing and puffing as my ankles buckle like overcooked pasta. Then I hear the hollow sound of a 12-gauge shotgun, muffled by the wind, and look up in time to see a gigantic bird topple from the sky. Then another. I break into a lung-searing trot. As we hunt out side by side to the end of the rimrock, finally I see them ahead of me: They look like nothing so much as two emus and an ostrich.

They're waddling as fast as they can, peering back at me as I gain on them—reluctant to fly, just as the experts say. But when I'm up within twenty yards of them, they have no other choice.

The ostrich flushes first—squawking maniacally, shedding feathers and shit right and left, wobbling like a flak-hit B-17 as he rises. I swing and shoot. I'd swear the ground shivered under my feet when he hit—a grand slam indeed.

Picking him up, I get a whiff of his sagey reek that nearly sets my head reeling. And heavy? Later we weigh him in at just under eight pounds.

"A big old boomer," Rog says, grinning. "The biggest I've ever seen. He'll be a bit tough, but tasty enough after a couple of hours in a good marinade. They don't have crops like other gamebirds; they digest the sage leaves entirely in their stomachs, so you've got to remove it within half an hour, otherwise they taste too strong."

Lugging him back to the truck is the boomer's revenge, but just as Roger said, he's tasty enough that night when we eat him replete with a side dish of mashed potatoes and creamed corn. But I wouldn't want to rely on sage grouse for a steady diet.

A HIPPIE-DIPPIE BIRD HUNT

Over the years, for better or worse, I've taught many people the art of shooting-flying: friends, family, neighbors, young and old. Or perhaps *attempted to teach* would be a more accurate description. With some I had success. Others couldn't hit the proverbial broad side of a barn. But the drop-dead ditsiest experience I ever underwent as a shotgun pedagogue came in the fall of 1970 when I found myself in the unlikely role of shooting instructor to a hippie commune in the wilds of central New Mexico.

I'd recently moved from *Time*, where I'd been the magazine's de facto "counterculture editor," to *Sports Illustrated*, a far different publication then than it is today. *SI* in those years was a "writer's magazine," and few of us contributing to it back then—including such fine, far-out craftsmen as Thomas McGuane, Jim Harrison, William Hjortsberg, Dan Gerber, and Russell Chatham—considered ourselves "sportswriters." Rather we wrote offbeat features about what really interested us, provided the subject had at least some remote or tangential relationship to the broad portmanteau word *sport*.

So it was no problem to get the editors' okay on a trip I proposed to the counterculture's rural enclaves, the "communes" that were springing up all over the country back then, particularly in the Mountain West. "Let's see what these longhairs do for fun other than sex, drugs, and rock-'n'-roll," I suggested. The editors sent me on my way with a casual wave of the hand and a full expense account.

I traveled west with a gentle Manhattan longhair named Roger Ricco, one of the founders of an urban "tribe" called The Group Image, whom I'd met and befriended during my research for the 1968 *Time* cover story that introduced the word *hippie* to the public at large. Roger had friends in three or four newly founded communes in New Mexico, so we concentrated our initial forays into the country north of Albuquerque. We brought along a minimum of gear: sleeping bags, cookware, a tarp in lieu of a tent, and I packed along my fly rod and a sweet-pointing little C. J. Daly 20-gauge I was shooting at that time. Bird season would be on and I planned to take full advantage of it, if only to feed us. Hippies were notoriously poor providers. I'd learned that, the hard way, in the Haight-Ashbury, where many spaced-out flower children would have starved to death were it not for Emmett Grogan and his Diggers, a hair-down-to-here benevolent society that every night collected leftovers from San Francisco's cafés and restaurants and distributed them free of charge—from garbage cans—to hungry street people.

We rented a van at the Albuquerque airport and rolled north. First stop was Bernalillo, where Roger had gotten wind of a commune established somewhere in the rolling hills near that old Spanish ranching town. Where precisely he did not know, hippies being as vague about directions as they were about language in general. Outside a bodega in town we spotted a pair of dusty, bell-bottomed, tie-dyed longhairs of indeterminate sex, mooching change and hand-outs from straight shoppers. They weren't having much luck. But at sight of Roger's hip-grunge attire they bright-ened. Sure, they knew the commune—they were heading that way themselves. We bought a supply of groceries—canned beans, chilis, tortillas, fresh veggies, sunflower seeds, a huge bloody packet of fresh-ground hamburger wrapped in brown butcher's paper, a few big jugs of cheap vino rojo, and plenty of munchables, enough to feed the whole starv-ing multitude—and after I picked up some ammo and a hunting license at the local hardware store, we headed into the dusty hills east of town.

The commune was located on public land at the site of a long-abandoned Butterfield stage station. You could just make out the twin ruts of the old stage route through the sage that rolled for miles and miles to the horizons. Not a tree in sight. Sandia Peak loomed far to the southeast, all 10,878 feet of it. Vultures turned hopeful circles in a hard blue sky. A half-collapsed adobe barn with an old rope-and-bucket well right beside it dominated the little valley where we stopped. The Butterfield folks, a century earlier, had ex-cavated sod-roofed stables into the hillsides around the barn. These the present occupants had reroofed with whatever they could scrounge—hunks of rusty sheet metal, flattened cardboard boxes, odd lengths of weathered, splintery, pewter-hued lumber, a roll of tarpaper found along the nearby highway. As we pulled up, a few of the longhairs—trailing the sweet incense reek of pot smoke—ambled out of the soddies to stare at us. They were a sorry sight: barefoot or shod in cheap sandals, half starved, sun-scorched, dirty, their jeans worn through at the knees, hair hanging limp and tan-

gled on the shoulders of threadbare workshirts that nonetheless bore colorful, indecipherable designs hand-stitched by
their wearers. When we brought out the groceries, faces lit
up (along with a few other things) and the fiesta began.

Everything save the snacks and the wine was dumped
into a huge communal pot and set to stewing over an
outdoor fire. Everyone on the premises had a musical instrument—guitar, mandolin, tambourine, Jew's harp, harmon-
ica, a battered accordion whose keyboard resembled a street
fighter's grin, even a tissue-paper-and-comb or two—and all
were soon jiving to a rhythmic raga beat. Kids danced freaky
barefoot patterns in the dust, breaking off now and then as
the mood struck them to fill tin plates with our fragrant
slumgullion. A few scruffy range horses, drawn by the
music, shambled in from the sage and stood just out of rop-
ing range on the fringes of the fiesta. The whole scene, it suddenly occurred to me, resembled a George Catlin painting
from the Great Plains more than a century ago, an Assini-
boine pipe dance, say, or better yet a rendering in ocher of
stick figures from the Lascaux caves of the Paleolithic.

After the feed, the communards wandered off to amuse
themselves. A tall, blond girl whose hair reached clear to her
hips walked toward the range horses, clucking sweetly to a
swaybacked, pregnant sorrel mare. The mare allowed her to
approach. The girl, whom I'd dubbed Maggie A Girl Of The
Streets, hiked up her loose, faded Mother Hubbard and
vaulted onto the mare's back. Then, sitting comfortably
astride the mare's broad barrel, she hied the horse forward
and off they plodded into prairie. "Cool!" said the two hippies we'd met at the bodega. I'd begun to think of them as
Frodo and Bilbo—they were hairy enough for hobbits. They
started clucking at the other horses—a small, walleyed pinto
gelding and a rangy, no-nonsense old buckskin that looked
like trouble on the hoof—but when the hobbits neared the

off-duty cow ponies, both turned and trotted away. Frodo and Bilbo ran after them.

Meanwhile Maggie was allowing the mare to wander where it wished, which was mainly in random circles through the bunchgrass. None of the horses wore halters, much less bridles, so there was no way to rein them. "You could try to steer her with your knees," I said.

Maggie looked at me dumbfounded. "Why should I tell her where to go?" she said. "She doesn't order *me* around, does she? I'm just bumming a ride, man. Let it happen."

Zen equestrianship . . .

Off in the middle distance, Frodo and Bilbo had caught up with the buckskin. While Frodo distracted the pony, Bilbo leaped for its back. Before he'd even touched down, the buckskin exploded in a furious, sunfishing, stiff-legged buck, bunting the hapless Bilbo high into the sky. Both ponies took off at a gallop for Sandia Peak. Bilbo stood up and began plucking prickly pear spines from his person. He was laughing. "There's a trip and a half," he said.

Meanwhile, in back of the collapsed barn, a hippie ball game was in progress. Frodo and Bilbo ankled over to join it. The longhairs had laid out not a diamond but a pentagon—a configuration much on their minds ever since Abbie Hoffman had tried to levitate the big one in Washington in protest against the Vietnam War. Four of the bases were slabs of sandstone from a nearby arroyo while home plate was literally that—a battered tin pie plate scrounged from the ruined barn.

A dozen or so hippies stood or squatted or lay on their backs toking joints in the outfield. There were no infielders. A shirtless, gangly kid in a San Francisco Giants cap and a pair of ragged shorts was on the mound. The woman behind the plate wore a catcher's mitt and little else. No one was at bat.

"What's the score, man?" Frodo asked.

"A million to nothing," the catcher replied.

"Who's winning?"

"We all are." She smiled up at him. "Wanna bat?"

Frodo picked up the scarred, splintery fungo bat.

"Let 'er rip," he yelled to the pitcher.

The Frisco Kid wound up and delivered a smoking fast-ball right down the pipe. Frodo swung and connected—a long, high shot to center field. The outfielders watched it drop in their midst. One of them said, "Wow." Nobody moved to field the ball.

Frodo trotted around the bases but got bored between fourth and home. He wandered back to the stew pot for another slurp of slumgullion.

"Does that count as an out or a run?" I asked the catcher.

"I guess I'd score it as a 'far out,' " she said. "But who's counting?"

As the afternoon cooled, I assembled my shotgun and headed out with Roger to try to fetch home some supper. One of the hippies saw me, ran into his cave, and emerged with a rusty lever-action .22 Marlin. "You hunt, man?" he grinned, trotting up to join me. "Cool. These dudes think it's square. They call me Pig. But how else you gonna get meat? Hey, I'll show you where the bunnies hang out—real big ones, man."

"You seen any quail on your wanderings?" I asked.

"Buzzy little fuckers, right? Blue? With like teeny-tiny cotton balls on their heads? Yeah, like a ton of 'em, in the yuccas, you know, man, like soapweed? But they're too fast for me."

"You ought to try bird shot," I said. "With a .22 you don't stand much of a chance."

"Lemme try your gun."

Visions of shredded feet, guts festooning the mesquite. My guts. "Maybe later," I said.

About a mile from the commune, in a thick stand of soap-weed, we jumped a covey of scaled quail. They scattered, heads low, running though the cover. "Trot on ahead and try to push them back to me," I told Roger and Pig. Pig was fast. He circled to the head of the soapweed patch and came hooting his way toward me, waving his arms. Six quail got up, straight back over my head. I doubled on them going away.

A chorus of whoops and right-ons suddenly filled the air. I looked back and saw about half the commune standing on a rise behind us. They'd followed to watch the excitement. We hunted on, walking up singles in the yucca patch. At one point a jackrabbit bolted out of the weeds, and I watched Pig swing on it, then drop the bunny with a nifty brain shot. He knew what he was doing. Reassured, I let Pig take the Daly and on his first flush he managed to fold a "cottontop" quail with a tricky, low, left-to-right deflection shot.

From the clear, cloudless sky came a sound like God on high working a rusty ratchet—the clattering call of sandhill cranes in migration. They were probably heading for the Bosque del Apache, south of Socorro on the upper Rio Grande.

Our quail, pan-braised in butter and sage over a slow fire, brought rave reviews from the diners that evening. Sunset lingered long into the evening, painting the shoulders of Sandia Peak a bloodred that faded only slowly to pink. Music and wood smoke, full bellies, sleep . . .

Next morning nothing would do but that I teach the commune the fine art of wingshooting. Against my better judgment I agreed. I had four or five boxes of No. 8s in the van. We had plenty of sandstone chips to use as clay pigeons, and the strong arm of yesterday's pitcher would serve in lieu of a trap. After running through strict safety instructions— principal of which was *No Pot!*—I demonstrated the close-range effect of a 20-gauge load on an antelope skull we found in an arroyo. The kids were properly impressed.

I ran them through the drill, a modified Churchill Method: both eyes open, mount the gun smoothly and firmly, hit the trigger the moment you're on the bird, and always, always swing through. Frodo was first up. He missed the first shot—the Frisco Kid's arm was in great shape that morning—but nicked a large flake off the second. The third bird he pulverized, a pale tan puff against the cloudless sky. Bilbo was even better. He smoked all three of his shots. These kids must be ringers, I thought. But when six of the first ten longhairs managed to macerate their targets, I was delighted. Either I was the best shooting instructor in America or, or . . . there was something in the air. Then I smelled it. Blow, weed, maryjane, grass—whatever you want to call it, it was bad news. They were smoking behind my back, like so many sneaky sixth-graders in the corner of the schoolyard.

In retrospect I believe that the first effects of the marijuana high had slowed things down for these kids so that through their eyes the chunks of sandstone seemed to be hanging fat, dumb, and happy out there on the end of their muzzles. It was like shooting tethered balloons. But then the pot took full charge, their reflexes slowed, they began to become mesmerized by the immediate: the reflections of sunlight on the slow-spinning "clays," the colors glinting off the Daly's smooth barrels, the pungent perfume of burned gunpowder hanging in the air. Sensory overload. Half the time they couldn't remember to hit the trigger. The other half they were firing wherever the muzzle happened to be pointing.

My moment of elation as a teacher had evaporated in a puff of smoke.

"That's it," I said. "A shotgun's a tool, not a toy." I picked up the shell boxes, grabbed the Daly, and locked them in the van. Roger and I left that afternoon for points north.

A year or so later I read in the *New York Times* that a number of hippies had died on a commune near Bernalillo, New Mexico. They'd died not of gunshot wounds, but of plague, the grim old Black Death, *Yersinia pestis,* which is endemic in prairie dog populations throughout the Mountain West. The prairie dogs had been sharing quarters in dugouts with the hippies, the article said. Fleas from the rodents had infected the longhairs, who were notorious for their lack of sanitation. I hoped that Frodo and Bilbo, Maggie and Pig, and the Frisco Kid had by then left the place. No way of telling . . .

A mad, sad story, but life is not a pot dream. Nor is death.

CHAMPION

His full name and title was Major Eduardo Francisco José Rodrigo Jesus Jaime Mora Alfaro, Director, Guardia Rural, Republic of Costa Rica, and it was just about a quarter of an inch longer than he was tall. We called him Major Moral for short. A plumpish coxcomb of thirty-nine, the major was, by his own admission, one of Costa Rica's champion hunters. "Me *campeón!*" he would announce during lulls in the conversation, throwing out his chest and thumping it. "Five years ago *campeón* of jaguar for all of Costa Rica! Last year, *campeón* of pig for the Atlantic Zone! Me *campeón!*"

Thump!

We were camped in a cow pasture at the western end of Cabo Santa Elena near the

139

Murcielago Islands—*murcielago* being Spanish for "bat"—up near the Nicaraguan border. It was a harsh and beautiful country, with barren hills thrusting up from the dense selva like the tonsured pates of buried monks. In addition to Major Moral, the party consisted of the major's brother, Elias, thirty-four, a spry and wiry electrical engineer from San José; the major's driver, Carlos Delfin, twenty-nine, a lithe *pistolero* who affected a black-and-yellow, jaguar-patterned hunting shirt; and the Brothers Bonilla—Cury, forty-two, the world's wittiest, most bloodthirsty certified public accountant, and Sergio, twenty-two, a second-year dental student.

Sergio was the most complex: fragile as an altar boy and possessed of a gloomy ecological concern for the future of his country's wildlife, he nonetheless was the most competitive and accomplished killer of the lot. No sooner had we arrived near the campsite than Sergio spotted a bronze-backed, spade-headed snake slithering into the brush.

"*Mocasín!*" he exulted, whipping out his .22 automatic pistol and popping four shots at the moccasin. It escaped unhit. A few minutes later, over beer and sardines, he was lamenting that, "We Costa Ricans are killers, not conservationists."

The self-accusation was as accurate as Sergio's usually smack-on aim. Hunting for sign during the lemon-colored twilight, we found the scats and pad marks of coyotes, the heart-shaped hoofprints of deer galore, plus the tracks of peculiarly Central and South American animals I had never before hunted, such as the splayed, three-toed prints of the tapir, which reaches six hundred pounds, and the almost human handprints of the coatimundi, a long-snouted relative of the raccoon. Wearing headlamps like those used by coal miners and armed with pistols, Cury and Sergio prowled the jungle after dark, flashing the amber eyes of an animal they were sure was an ocelot. But before they could raise their guns the eyes blinked out—the quick wary cat was gone, spots and all. Great lamentations, cascades of curses. *"Hijo de la Gran Puta!"*

Then they turned their beams on the surf of the Bahía Santa Elena, near whose shores we were camped, and Cury cast a handline for sharks. The hook was baited with a chunk of mortadella left over from supper. The sharks seemed to savor the sausage with more gusto than the diners had, but Cury was unable to hook them up. *"Putissima!"*

The rustling of countless hermit crabs, some housed in conch shells the size of softballs, echoed his discontent.

By first light the following morning we were hacking our way through the selva at the base of a tall, bald-topped hill to take our stands for a deer drive. Major Moral's four dogs—two beagles and a pair of liver-colored hounds—stood eagerly downwind of the guns, ready to course the hillside cover and push the deer into range. Sergio took the toughest, most direct approach to the hilltop, but his machete machismo proved fruitless. No sooner had he slashed his way through the morning-glory tangle guarding the hilltop than we saw two deer fade like smoke into the woods above. A bit more subtlety on the approach route might have bagged us a fair-sized buck.

But the morning was not a total washout. Elias Mora knocked off a coatimundi with a full-choked pattern of buckshot, reducing it to tatters. The beads of blood on its thick, dark coat attracted dragonflies longer than darning needles and black bumblebees the size of sparrows. "Even the bugs of Costa Rica like meat," Major Moral said.

The afternoon was a pursuit race as we chased Sergio on a long, hot, unproductive hike through the hills. The scenery, however, was magnificent—a cross between Kenya and Wyoming, with a scary hint of Vietnam in the tall, slashing grass. Banana-frond valleys rose to barren ridges. Clouds of gaudy *mariposas*—much lighter a word in Spanish than *but-*

terflies—gave way to breezy slopes where parrots flushed in stiff-winged indignation.

"Shoot, shoot!" the major screeched. *"Papagayos—muy deliciosos—*a good piece of meat!" But I couldn't see it and refused to raise my shotgun. The major ground his teeth and frowned quite horribly.

We wound our way up a streambed, pausing beside the few clear pools. The Ticos drank the water while this gringo wondered: *Agua pura, vita brevis?* Sensing my doubts, Sergio hacked off a few lengths of a bejuco vine and we drank the water that dripped from it.

"Good for the kidneys," our medical expert said.

After dinner that evening, Sergio suggested a night hunt. We drove slowly out of camp, searching the selva for feedback. Within half an hour Sergio's headlamp had frozen the eyes of a deer grazing no more than two hundred yards from the trail. He switched off the light and we clambered through dense thornbush and over downed hardwoods to get closer. Click! On went the light. The eyes were still there. No way of telling if they belonged to a buck or a doe but, as Sergio liked to say, "Here we have no conservation, only killing." Sergio blazed away, the two flashes of his shots freezing the deer in its final leap. The eyes thrashed out. It proved to be a spike buck weighing no more than eighty pounds, its antlers a scant three inches in length. Not a deer to be proud of, but then we were trying to do it Costa Rican fashion.

Lashing the buck to the roof rack to discourage hungry coyotes, we drove on toward the ocean and proceeded afoot. Sergio wanted to see if the green turtles were in yet. They usually lay their eggs this time of the year along the Playa Blanca, a five-mile, half-moon beach that flanked the Pacific just to the west of us. A waning moon washed the whole scene with silver. The streams feeding into the sea and the surf itself clattered with baitfish pursued by snappers, snook, and roosterfish, their high comblike dorsals slicing the moonlit water like so many scimitars.

After a mile or more of walking, we crossed the wide track of a green turtle that had come in from the water, and we followed it up to where she lay in her nest. The eggs were already dropping steadily. Sergio scooped a double handful of them into a plastic Ziploc bag. The turtle didn't seem to mind. Her breathing was harsh against the whisper of the surf. Her back and head were crusted with sand, but the gelatinous tears that have moved men for centuries with images of forlorn motherhood flowed through the crust as steadily as the eggs themselves fell. When the last egg had fallen, the turtle covered her nest carefully and waddled off a few yards to scrape out a false nest as a distraction to the coyotes that were waiting in the bush, anticipating their own feast of *huevos de tortuga*. Though we could not rightly blame the coyotes, since we too were looting the nest to fill our bellies, we walked around the nest to spook them off with human scent, then escorted the lady back to the sea.

She disappeared slowly, like a reef beneath a rising tide.

Back at camp with our plunder, we stiffened our resolve with a few raw turtle eggs. Here's the Tico recipe: Peel the Ping-Pong ball shell off the egg, drop the glutenous green yolk in a glass with a dollop of ketchup, a dash of Tabasco, a few grains of pepper, and a squeeze of lime, then gulp it down without wincing. Nothing readies a man for a walk among the snakes of Costa Rica better than *huevos de tortuga*. "Drink, drink!" the major exhorted me. "It will put lead in your *pistola,* for tomorrow . . ."

And certainly I would need it. All this slaughter was mere prelude to the grand finale: the weirdest, wildest duck hunt I've ever witnessed. On the final day of our outing, the major led us to the Tempisque River and a vast swamp underlaid with the foulest-smelling, gooiest mud in Christendom. Costa Ricans deign the use of skiffs or retrieving dogs in their duck hunting, the major explained—"Too soft, ees for sissies." He and the others would push around to the far side of the swamp while I waded into its middle from this side. The major's party would start shooting to flight the ducks. Then, as the birds swung around and around above and behind us, we would have the opportunity for some lively pass shooting.

As the others sloshed away, I contemplated the marsh before me: a fetid reach of saw grass, water lilies and dragonflies, snakes and caimans and mallards and blue-winged teal. I swallowed hard, then waded into the blood-warm water through clouds of mosquitoes, the 12-gauge Remington 1100 at high port arms. The bottom was uneven. I lurched. Ahead of me I spotted the V-shaped wake of a large animal. *Caimán . . . o cocodrilo?* No, just a nutria, thank God.

Suddenly I spotted the skinniest water snake I'd ever seen. It was nearly ten feet long, yet no thicker than a garden hose. I watched it slither up onto a grassy hummock not far from where I stood. Then it divided into two snakes, one chasing the other. The chaser zipped forward and grabbed the chasee by the head, then coiled itself around the other. The snakes were clearly of the same species: about four feet long, with green and tan racing stripes running the lengths of their bodies, black masks on their oval and hence nonpoisonous heads. I looked my way down the coiled twist of snake bodies and saw that the snake holding the other in submission had a little serpentine pecker sticking out of its belly. He proceeded to employ it in the time-honored manner. After copulating for a few moments, the guy snake shuddered, then released the girl snake. She zipped away, back to the water. The guy shot his black tongue a few more times as if in self-satisfaction, then slithered off in the opposite direction. Talk about Wham-Bam-Thank-You-Ma'am . . .

Then our own wham-bam got under way. Gunfire erupted at the far end of the swamp and in an instant the sky over my head was full of speeding, banking ducks. For an hour we had splendid shooting. Never were there fewer than a hundred ducks in the air at a given moment—the Yeatsian antithesis, the tightening gyre: a dozen teal caught between the guns, circling, circling, their delicate formation shattered and shifting to the impact of our shots, turning inward and ever inward until only three were left to wing out low toward safety in the snake-rife reeds.

We waded in to pick up the dead and wounded. A drake lay on his back, his paddles flailing good-bye to the sky. Major Moral picked him up and I saw that a single No. 6 shot had nipped off the top of the teal's head, exposing its minuscule brain. The lower mandible dangled like a tiny shoehorn. Major Moral held the duck high and grinned at me.

Ah yes, it was lonely and tough out there, armpit-deep in the warm, reeking water, taking the high doubles with one eye out for snakes, the other peeled for caimans. But Major Moral never lost his military bearing, never once broke step during the long marshy march. He is certainly the only man in Latin America who can strut convincingly while up to his sternum in snakes. How did he do it?

"Me *campeón*," Major Moral announced that night for the thousandth time, thumping his pouter-pigeon chest. "*Campeón* of ducks, and snakes, and caimans, and all other animals."

SEA GEESE AND DESERT WHALES

Toward sundown the geese began moving. We could see wedges of them sweeping down the desert shoreline, circling and settling in the shallow, reed-grown water of the shoals. Their soft voices came over the water on the sea breeze—a quiet, querulous "rouk, rouk, rouk." They were Pacific black brant—Branta bernicla nigricans—one of the smallest geese in the world but an incredibly fast, strong, and dodgy target on a gusting wind. Brant are about the size of a black duck and just as delicious, with dark heads and necks ringed by an inconspicuous white collar. This evening we were racing across the lagoon to one of the unoccupied shoals in a small, aluminum-hulled panga, the outboard at full throttle, hoping to get in position among the reeds before the first flight of brant arrived. My eyes were on the birds when it happened . . .

Suddenly the water to starboard erupted, as if someone had triggered a bottom mine, and a huge gray monstrosity—scabbed in patches of orange and yellow—surged into view not an arm's length away. It rose from the water to a height of perhaps ten feet and stared at me with one small, piggy eye. Then it opened its long, ugly maw and clapped its jaws. It had bad breath.

The monster was a California gray whale, also known as the devilfish, scrag whale, mussel-digger, or desert whale, and the cow's sudden appearance scared me silly. But she was only "spyhopping," poking her huge barnacle-laden head out of the water to see who was making all that racket topside in this, her preferred calving area. We were in La Bahía Magdalena, on the west coast of Baja California, one of three Mexican lagoons where gray whales spend their winters, bearing and rearing their young. The whale's unexpected appearance was only one of many surprises on that strange expedition.

Mag Bay, as it's more popularly known among gringo sportsmen, is about thirty miles long by five to ten wide—a huge, nutrient-rich lagoon protected from the strong, steady onslaught of Pacific rollers by two long barrier islands, Magdalena and Margarita, built almost entirely of white sand dunes. Its deeply notched shoreline offers plenty of beaches, inlets, marshes, and mangrove swamps, most of which serve as sanctuary to wintering waterfowl. But Mag Bay's shallow, food-rich waters offer world-class light-tackle angling as well. I traveled there often in the mid-1970s. There are swank resorts on Mag Bay nowadays, but back then we usually roughed it on a tugboat anchored off Puerto López Mateos, paying a few pesos a day for our lodging and running out at dawn in the skiff to shoot ducks and brant, then fishing the *esteros* all day for snook, corvina, halibut, leopard grouper, and spotted bay bass. It was hot work on the water and sometimes we cooled out at midday by diving for *langosta*—rock lobster. At dusk we would hit the brant again.

Both the fishing and lobstering were good, but the brant and the gray whales were out of this world. Both critters show up in Mag Bay sometime in January and for the next three months claim it as their playground. It's a sight to behold. Adult gray whales, which can grow to fifty feet long and weigh up to thirty-five tons, are the mottled color of a well-worn truck tire (though albinos are not uncommon). The body is usually covered with white, yellow, or orange patches of barnacles and whale lice, particularly on top of the head, around the blowhole and on the forward part of the back. The gray's head is narrow and arched along the upper surface, giving it a conical shape. The mouth is rimmed on each side with 130 to 180 relatively small baleen plates, which serve as strainers in which the whale gathers its food (mainly tube worms, mollusks, and shrimp). Primarily a bottom feeder, it can dive to 395 feet, but prefers much shallower water. While feeding it stirs up clouds of sediment from the seabed—gigantic discolorations that resemble bonefish "muds" and can cover many acres. A feeding whale filters this mud through its baleen plates, on which shrimp, tube worms, and amphipods collect for later eating. These big muds attract gamefish, eager to pick off anything edible that's escaped the whale's jaws, and we quickly learned to fish the edges of them—often with great success.

Three distinct populations of gray whales once existed. A North Atlantic subspecies was hunted to extinction around 1700; a Korean population in the northwest Pacific was fair game until 1968 and is now rare; the third group, the California grays of the northeast Pacific, is doing well for now.

Before whalers discovered their breeding grounds, there were somewhere between fifteen thousand and twenty-four thousand gray whales in the Pacific, and though whaling was legal, the killing of devilfish was not widespread. Then in 1857 Captain Charles Scammon discovered the Baja lagoons where California grays went to calve. The shallow water of these *lagunas* made the grays easy prey for the whalers. This was classic Moby Dick whaling, replete with lookouts shouting "Thar she blows!" and long chases in oar-powered whaleboats before the harpoons were hurled.

But the shallow waters of the hunting ground led to casualties among the whalers. A harpooned gray whale, unable to sound as it would in midocean, might turn on the boat that was plaguing it, smash it to bits, and then flail the floundering boat crew to death with its broad, heavy flukes. One whale in Magdalena Bay even chased a harpooner clear up on the beach, scooting along after the terrified tar on its long, powerful pectoral fins.

Still, it was an uneven match. By 1898 the gray whale population had shrunk to only two thousand. And when factory ships and cannon-propelled harpoons with explosive heads came into use in the 1920s, the game was nearly over. By the early 1940s gray whales were close to extinction. Then in 1946 the International Whaling Commission was formed and passed laws that prohibited the killing of gray whales. Nature recovers fast with half a break. By 1983 there were sixteen thousand whales in the Pacific and nine years later the population was more than twenty thousand. The whale population is still growing today.

The warm, shallow "nursery" lagoons of Baja California are perfect for gray whales to have their calves, which measure about fifteen feet long at birth and weigh some fifteen hundred pounds. Another female gray, called an "auntie," usually serves as a kind of cetacean midwife during this gargantuan labor process. The newborns immediately start suckling. A mother whale's milk is 53 percent fat—ten times richer than cow's milk—and the calf will need every bit of this fat to build up blubber for the long trip north. These whales are well traveled, covering twelve thousand miles in an annual round trip from their Arctic feeding grounds in the Beaufort, Bering, and Chukchi Seas to the Baja breeding grounds. By the time the whales leave the lagoons in March for their return voyage, the calves are nearly twenty feet long and have doubled their weight.

Grays are the most active of all large whales, spyhopping, lobtailing, and breaching all over the bay. They displace a lot of water. We were frequently drenched when they rose without warning beside the boat and splatted the water with their massive tail flukes.

Just as surprising were the brant, which initially pitched to our crudely painted Clorox-bottle decoys with kamikazelike abandon. After the first couple of days, though, it was almost impossible to toll them within gun range. Quick studies indeed.

Yet according to the waterfowling literature I'd read, brant, along with buffleheads, are the easiest waterfowl to hunt—reasonably predictable in their daily habits, and simple to decoy. "Both birds like to get shot," one authority writes, "and if you miss will often return to give you another chance, although both do seem to get tired of getting killed late in the season." Maybe that was it, I thought. These birds have run a gauntlet of gunners from their summer breeding grounds in the high Arctic clear down to the Baja, and of course they've wised up en route. But then I read that most Pacific brant fly nonstop from southeastern Alaska or British Columbia to the west coast of Mexico—a distance of at least three thousand miles, flying at an altitude of 750 feet over the open sea. Not many hunters could be banging away at them on such a flight path.

Black brant are probably the fastest geese in the world. Back in 1965 an ornithologist named Arthur Skogman

Einarsen clocked the birds at ground speeds of sixty-two miles per hour—more than half again as fast as Canada geese, which top out at thirty-six to forty m.p.h. Small and agile, brant have a much faster wingbeat—three or four per second—than their larger Canadian kin. They're true sea geese, spending nearly all of their lives on or over salt water, and breeding clear around the Arctic Circle. Their preferred food is eelgrass *(Zostera marina)*, but in 1931 a mysterious fungus destroyed most of the eelgrass on both sides of the Atlantic. Within a few years the Atlantic brant *(Branta bernicla hrota)* suffered a near-total population collapse. Where once they wintered in the Chesapeake region by the tens of thousands, and old-time market gunners used to sell them for fifty cents apiece, nowadays you're lucky to see a few hundred in a bunch. What's worse from the gourmet's standpoint, the Atlantic brant that survive have done so by feeding on sea lettuce *(Ulva lactuca)*, a leafy alga rich in iodine and iron that imparts a rank flavor to the birds' flesh. But as we saw and tasted at Mag Bay, the Pacific brant, which still have plenty of eelgrass to feed on, are not only abundant but as succulent as ever.

My gunning and angling companion on this trip was a childhood buddy named Harry Lenartz, who'd grown up to become one of California's most successful ophthalmologists. My most vivid memory of the Mag Bay adventure was the finale of that day when the spyhopping gray whale nearly capsized us. We made it to the shoal just minutes before the brant arrived. Our Mexican boatman debarked the two of us in waist-deep water, then raced back out to sea so as not to spook the brant. We waded ashore with shotguns and shell boxes held high over our heads, like Marines invading Tarawa. Harry sloshed fast and low across the shoal and hunkered down in the reeds. I found a flat rock, only slightly submerged, and sat down on it—only to feel the sting of a sea urchin's spines in my butt. I stifled a heartfelt scream. I had to. The birds were coming.

No decoys this time, and no goose calls. We trusted to faith. And it worked. The brant circled us only once, then committed—cupping in against the wind, tilting crazily from wing to wing, black against the hard blue desert sky, and chuckling happily to one another—*"Rouk, rouk, rouk!"*

I dropped two with my first shot, another with the second barrel. Harry's gun banged flat downwind of me and I caught the flash of falling birds out of the corner of my eye, and then looked over just in time to see him stand, swing, and take the prettiest triple I've ever seen. Three birds with one shot—all killed stone dead—directly overhead. They splashed all around him.

"Hey, Bob!" Harry yelled, grinning against the wind. "It's raining *Branta bernicla!"*

And with that, a gray whale rolled in the channel between us and the mainland, flagging its flukes in the sunset.

We ate well that night.

JAKE AMONG THE
TURTLEDOVES

We drift through the corn rows, both hot beneath the sinking Maryland sun, walking as softly as we can manage what with the crisp leaves and whispering stalks bent, in some cases, half underfoot by the sea breeze; working steady over the dry loamy soil that divides the rows.

Jake isn't wearing a bell.

After all, we're stalking—pussyfooting along, always alert, hoping to jump-shoot our targets within shotgun range.

My eyes are on the dog half the time, the other half searching for gray flickers of shadow ahead. Those little dove-pink head feints, those tiny bright brown beads that spell Zenaidura macroura . . .

The wind is from them to us, and from moment to moment I can see from the corner of my eye Jake's broad yellow-furred head come up, his

155

wet black nostrils flaring, and then his wide-set eyes, dark brown,
long-lashed, and very very serious, turning upward toward me—
  "They're out there," he seems to say . . .

We'd been frustrated that afternoon on a classic opening-day Eastern Shore dove shoot. Our host had stuck us at the station least productive, in terms of wind and flight patterns, for shots at the swift skeins of mourning doves sweeping in to feed in that field. I'd shot at only ten passing birds, fast and erratic targets as always, and killed six of them. Better than fifty percent, not bad . . . yet still it felt incomplete.

We still had six birds to go to fill an Eastern Shore limit.

By three that afternoon the shooting party had repaired to Joe Judge's sumptuous lodge for drinks and a dinner of fresh-caught Chesapeake Bay blue crabs boiled in salt water and seaweed, home-baked biscuits with plenty of farm-fresh butter, and new-plucked sweet corn. But Jake and I declined.

We still wanted to hunt birds.

So out we went into the corn- and bean fields . . . and walked them up.

Jake was my seven-year-old yellow Labrador. The breed alone attests to his excellence. But I'd been hunting with this big, fierce, gentle guy since he was eight weeks old, and I knew he could do anything I asked of him.

He learned his tradecraft under the tutelage of my old black Lab, Luke: how to be sudden death on woodcock, nearly as good on ruffed grouse, and a savvy, cool, eager, and do-anything retriever on waterfowl, in any kind of water or weather. He'd ferret his ninety pounds through muck and downed swamp timber to pick up wood ducks or widgeon or green-winged teal with no more indication of where they'd fallen than the direction of my muzzles when I fired.

But mourning doves on a dry, nearly windless afternoon, in early September, with the temperature pushing a hundred degrees?

Even the crows weren't flying.

Joe Judge could hardly keep himself from laughing aloud at the idea.

But still we went.

A recently harvested cornfield isn't the easiest venue in which to stalk doves. The birds would be hunkered down, feeding between the few rows of standing corn that the harvesting machinery had missed. But their eyes would be constantly alert to any approaching movement. The upright figures of an armed man and a big dog would signal our coming in time for the birds to flush well out of range.

As we crossed the first field, I saw perhaps two dozen doves swing in and alight among the corn rows two hundred yards ahead. Jake saw them too. He looked up at me for orders. "We'll just slope in at a shallow angle to them," I told him. "Don't look over at them, and keep a steady pace. They won't realize we're closing the range until it's too late." I hope . . .

I was talking to him, explaining our tactics, not so much in hopes that he'd understand what I meant, but to reassure him that we actually had a battle plan. I'm convinced that a good field dog, especially a Lab or a golden retriever, can learn more from its master's tone of voice than from any number of harsh, panicky commands or jolts from a shock collar. Jake stayed at heel, and slowly we closed ground on the birds. From the corner of my eye, I could see their heads bobbing now, one of them standing nearly upright to keep a beady eye fixed on us. Before leaving the lodge I had screwed in improved cylinder and modified choke tubes, anticipating long shots. One hundred yards to go, then eighty, sixty—only twenty yards more and we'd be within killing range of my 12-gauge Beretta over-and-under.

As we closed the last critical few yards, the ground underfoot grew damp and fell away into a gentle depression. A puddle of weed-rimmed rainwater lay in the bottom of this swale. The shallow depression would hide Jake from the birds, and if I bent low enough, they probably wouldn't be able to see me either. Jake knew we were near them, their scent filling his nostrils, and I suddenly thought of a trick we often use on woodcock and grouse when Jake has a good scent line on them. As we dipped into the swale I stopped and knelt, my free hand on Jake's shoulder. He looked up at me. I gestured out and around, describing a big three-quarter circle.

Any flushing dog's urge, of course, is to rush straight in at the birds, following the line of that delicious scent. But that would only flush them directly away from us. I wanted Jake to swing out wide to the right, then back in once he was past them, and approach them from the upwind side, forcing the birds in their panic to *flush toward me*. The old pincers movement, perfected by Field Marshal Erwin Rommel's Afrika Korps during World War II, but in this case applied to doves . . . My wise old black Lab Luke had learned to do this without any training on my part. And Luke had taught this tactic to Jake during the yellow Lab's first season.

Yes, Jake recognized the hand signal, his eyes lit up eagerly, and when I whispered "Go!"—he was off. Belly low, he swung out about fifty yards; then I lost sight of him as he circled the birds. I stuck two backup shells between the knuckles of my forearm hand, then stood up, gun at the ready, and walked slowly back into the doves' field of vision.

They were crouched low, not moving a feather, looking straight at me and ready to flush.

At that moment a ninety-pound blond thunderbolt flashed in from behind them—*outflanked!*

In a loud rattle of wings and whistling primaries, doves exploded in all directions.

I dropped one with the first barrel as it swept past to my right, then managed with the second barrel to catch two birds with a single pattern. I broke the gun and quickly re-loaded. No sooner had I snapped the gun shut than three more doves got up from the corn rows to my left. I folded two of them.

After Jake had retrieved the five doves to hand, we walked on in the direction that most of the birds had gone. One more to go for a limit. It came when an unwary single swept in from the treeline to my left. I quickly knelt and told Jake to "Sit!" The dove was clearly looking for the remainder of its flock, flying at half speed over the field. When I figured it was within range, I stood. The dove lit off its afterburners, but I scratched it down just as it was nearly out of range. Jake marked the retrieve and fetched the bird back. *Limited out, by God!*

We slogged back to the lodge in the twilight. When we got there, most of the blue crabs and corn were gone, half a keg of Harp beer had disappeared, and the party was at full roar. I quickly breasted that afternoon's doves, threw four of them under the broiler with half a flitch of bacon over each breast, found two unshucked ears of sweet corn, which I peeled, then wrapped in paper towel, and subjected to three minutes at full zap in the microwave. I carried a plate with our sup-per on it out on the porch, where amid the sprong of twang-ing foot-traps and the friendly roar of gunfire, Jake and I had two grilled dove breasts and a well-buttered ear of sweet corn apiece . . . and counted it a damned fine day.

OF DOVES AND WAR

My bloodthirsty young hunting partner Todd Seebohm lives in New Jersey when he's not visiting his grandmother—my neighbor—in Vermont. I'd taught him to shoot and fly fish starting when he was eight years old. He's now eighteen and a pre-vet student at Delhi College in downstate New York. Since Todd's home states consider the mourning dove (*Zenaidura macroura*) a songbird and thus forbid Todd's preferred method of ornithological study, I figured it was about time to introduce the lad to the joys and frustrations of a dove shoot. So on a Labor Day weekend, the two of us—Jake stayed home this time—ducked down to Joe Judge's place on the Eastern Shore for the season's opener.

For a while it looked like we'd have abort the trip due to the imminent arrival of

161

Hurricane Edouard, whose whirling winds—up to 135 miles an hour—were threatening to smash ashore directly on the Delmarva Peninsula, where we were headed. But Eddie proved a sporting gentleman and stayed offshore. Judge, whose farm we'd hunt, had told me that "clouds of doves" were gathering daily in his corn, bean, and sunflower fields, but when we arrived at Corsica Neck, near Centreville, Maryland, late in the afternoon of September 1, not a bird was to be seen. Usually the phone and power lines leading into Joe's place are sagging with the weight of four-ounce dove bodies at this time of day and year. It looked ominous.

"They're all across the river at Possum Point," Joe blithely explained when I put the question to him. "Don't worry, it'll be great shooting."

I walked over to the barometer. The mercury was down to twenty-seven inches. Edouard had just passed not 350 miles offshore, heading north, and the skies were sunny. But the falling glass, I suspected, had driven the doves wacky. But then, I thought, maybe the low pressure only put them off their feed temporarily, say yesterday and today. Tomorrow afternoon, when legal shooting begins, their appetite alarms will be clanging full blast.

Meanwhile there was the real business of a dove opener to attend to: the socializing. As usual Joe had a houseful of high-powered guests at Twin Ponds for this festive occasion. Bill Boesch, the president of American Airlines, was there: a quiet, soft-spoken gent and a consummate sportsman. So was Robert Dörnte, president and CEO of Shenker International, a large German shipping firm, and his director of surface transportion, Steve Wallack.

But the man I really wanted to talk with was big Ray Arnett from Stockton, California, currently vice chairman of the influential Congressional Sportsmen's Caucus. A lifelong outdoorsman and for eight years the commissioner of the

Golden State's Fish and Game Department (1968–75), Ray also served as President Ronald Reagan's assistant secretary of the interior for fish, wildlife, and parks from 1981 to 1985. All fascinating political stuff, I'm sure. But I'm a military history buff at heart and since Ray had served with the First Marine Division on Guadalcanal and in other island campaigns during the late unpleasantness in the Pacific, I knew I could pry some good war stories out of him if I asked the right questions and kept my ears open.

Ray's a big, impressive-looking guy in his seventies, lanky, well over six feet tall. He wore a recently grown Hemingwayesque beard, perhaps the better to help him spin a yarn like the master himself, and he didn't disappoint me.

Todd had headed immediately for his favorite diversion at Joe's place, the clangorous Dolly Parton pinball machine, but I made him shut it off and sit in on the evening's bull session. He might learn something. Joe calls these gatherings "Masters of the Universe Meetings," and tonight—after a delicious dinner of roast lamb, parsleyed potatoes, freshly picked green beans, and copious bumpers of red wine—the subject was World War II.

"We came ashore on 7 August 1942," Ray began, and it went on from there: the desperate night fighting on Bloody Ridge in September of that year, the waters of the Tenaru River running red with Japanese blood, the leeches, the jungle rot, the flash and boom of big Jap naval rifles all through the long cruel nights of the Tokyo Express runs, the bodies of U.S. sailors washing ashore after our disastrous naval defeat off Savo Island, the obscene crunch of land crabs dining in the darkness on friend and foe alike . . .

At one point Bill Boesch, a prudent man, snuck off to bed. Wicked Joe waited until he was asleep, then sent Todd in to rouse him and order his return to the conference table. Sometime during that long hypnotic evening I recall speaking fluent German with Robert Dörnte—the discussion had drifted to the European Theater—my eloquence no doubt inspired by the low barometric pressure, or something . . .

Todd had told me during the long drive down from Vermont that he'd visited the Gettysburg battlefield for a school project, taken many slides, and given a presentation to his class for which he'd received an A. I asked him if he'd added military history to his string of interests, which up to that point had included only guns, hunting, fishing, football, girls, and cars (he's now the proud owner of a used but newly painted grape-purple GMC extended-cab pickup). "Naw," he said, parroting the sentiments of his generation, "the only thing war does is kill people." Now, after the meeting of the Masters of the Universe, I asked him once again if he found any merit in battle. "Yeah," he said as dawn light flooded the lodge, "war's *way* cool!"

Not quite—but he's learning.

The dove shoot was nothing to write home about. By the time we took our stands in a sunflower field on Possum Point the following afternoon, the barometer had crept up half an inch and the sun was blazing with midsummer intensity. No breeze gentled the stinging white sky, and for a long while no doves flew. A man gets desperate at times like that and every tweety-bird, every hovering skeeterhawk glimpsed from the corner of an eager eye raised my hopes, then dashed them. Finally a lone pair of mourners hove into sight.

All up and down the line our guns greeted them—the Tokyo Express in static diminuendo. One bird fell while the other buzzed off in a hurry. It went on like that all afternoon, a few birds here, none there, then a wary loner checking the field out. Only at the top of the picket line was there any steady action. In the first two blinds hard by the Corsica River, Steve Wallack and Robert Dörnte got in a lot of shooting—Steve actually scratched down a twelve-bird limit. I was stationed at the midpoint of the line and got shots at a scant six doves in four long, humid hours, knocking down three of them. In the stand to my left I could hear Todd blasting away furiously and saw a couple of his birds puff and fall, but the sunflowers obscured a full view of the action. From time to time, the guides would appear with their dogs at heel to fetch the dead doves from where they'd fallen in the sunflower stand or the bean field beyond it. The Labs and a solitary German shorthair on retrieving detail were listless, hurting in that heat, their tongues lolling, noses dry. Scenting conditions must have been atrocious.

"How'd you do?" I asked Todd as we finally picked up and headed back to the lodge.

"I shot two boxes of shells," he said, grinning.

"And?"

"Well *[a bit doubtfully]*, I knocked down three birds."

"No," said Ray, who'd been stationed just to Todd's left. "I saw four of them fall."

"Yeah, but the dogs couldn't find the last one, so I don't count it."

Ray looked over at me and winked. "Good lad," he said. "But fifty shots, four birds? You realize, don't you, that dove shooting is the invention of the devil? He's a major stockholder in every one of the world's ammo companies. The more you shoot, the happier you make him. What he hates are guys like me and Steve who kill a bird with every shot and limit out in half an hour. But at least you're honest about it."

Well, as I've always said, he'll learn.

After a delectable feast of spicy hard-shell crabs, more corn on the cob, and far less wine than the previous evening, the Masters of the Universe retired early that night.

FAREWELL TO A SPORTSMAN

J oe Judge is dead, and I still can't believe it. No one who knew and loved him can believe it. Joe was one of those indestructible archetypes, the hero who lives forever. Our great good friend—angler and wingshot par excellence, yarn-spinner extraordinaire, the most generous man I've ever known, and master of the Twin Ponds Duck Club, one of the best waterfowling venues on Maryland's Eastern Shore—passed away in January of 1999 at the unfair age of fifty-seven. The previous summer Joe began suffering from intense pains in his lower back. He'd had these spasms before, but not this bad: Joe figured they were the work of fragments from a hand grenade that had blasted him in the jungles of Southeast Asia nearly thirty years earlier. But a biopsy showed evidence of a cancer that had already metastasized into his bones. Joe immediately underwent a series of massive, heroic chemotherapy and radiation treatments, but the best doctors in Washington and New York could not locate the initial source of the cancer. Thus it was only a matter of time.

That fall Joe called me at my home in Vermont and invited me down to Twin Ponds for what proved to be a final hunt. On the phone his voice still sounded strong as ever, and he was putting a brave front on the situation. He'd lost a lot of weight from the chemo, he said, and he had to use a walker to get around, but one of these days he'd be back on his own two feet. He couldn't shoot just yet, he said—the cancer treatment had weakened his shoulder. But he'd been out in the blinds with other hunters, watching them shoot. It was almost as good as the real thing. "Why not come down for Thanksgiving?" he said. Before the diagnosis Joe had bought a new farm at Church Creek on the other side of the Delmarva Peninsula, where the duck hunting was splendid. He was building a new lodge there, even better than Twin Ponds. "We've got tons of ducks on the new place, just like the old days," Joe said. "I want you to shoot it. Bring young Todd along. He's hunted geese and doves and deer and quail down here, but never ducks. You owe it to him for his outdoor education."

Todd picked me up in Vermont and we drove down to Joe's in his pickup. "Joe's going to look pretty bad," I told Todd along the way. "He's probably not going to make it. But he's a tough guy and he doesn't want anybody acting mopey or maudlin around him just now. He wants us to have a good time. Let's just have a lot of good gunning, like we always do at Joe's. The better we shoot the happier it'll make him."

We did. Joe was between chemo sessions during our visit and though his hair had fallen out earlier it was back by now. Same short grizzled dark hair and beard. The Joe of yore had been a tall, strong, graceful man, a lifter of heavy objects and the kind of guy who could dance around on the bow of a bouncing flats skiff like a boxer as he fought a world-class tarpon or bonefish on the fly rod. No more. He didn't look as thin as I'd feared, but it was painful to see him confined to a wheelchair. He forced himself to use the walker a few times during the four days of our stay, but each time it was an act of sheer courage.

"Flash him your buzzer," I told Todd shortly after we arrived. Todd smirked proudly, pulled out his wallet, flapped it open, and there it was: a bright shining gold badge proclaiming Todd Seebohm a member in good standing of the Chester, New Jersey, Volunteer Fire Company.

"By God, a fireman!" Joe said, beaming. "Bravest men in the world. You'd never catch me walking into a burning building to haul people out." Like hell, I thought. But that's Joe: always self-deprecating, always quiet about his own deeds. Always encouraging to the young, whatever their species. I flashed back to the day eight years earlier when Joe had introduced my year-old yellow Lab, Jake, to the realities of duck hunting . . .

Well before sunup on that autumn morning, Joe parked his truck at the edge of the Chester River and we hiked through the dark with Jake at heel. Wind from the north at thirty knots. Spartina thrashed and surf boomed on the rocks, sloshing and foaming at our feet—cold as the gunmetal dawn just breaking. Jake had never seen a johnboat before but he jumped right in at Joe's command. The blind too, when we got there, seemed as familiar to him as our living room back home. It was as if he'd been there many times before, and perhaps he had been, somewhere in the depths of the wondrous Labrador gene pool. Or maybe it was Joe's calming confidence, the feeling that emanated from him that this was what men and dogs were meant to do together.

Action came quickly that morning. Across the bay we watched a raft of ducks lift skyward into the first light for their breakfast feed. "Get ready," Joe said. "Here they come." He began to call . . .

Jake perked his ears at the strengthening gabble of duck talk, the whistle of wings getting louder as the flight approached. The young dog lay steady, only his shiver betraying the excitement he felt. Even his eyebrows were shivering. But he kept his head down, eyes averted almost purposely from the first ducks—greenheads and baldpates—that slashed overhead and circled back into the decoy spread. I looked up and saw them, cupped for the touchdown.

"Get 'em," Joe said. We rose and fired . . .

When Joe opened the door of the blind, Jake was out like a shot. He'd seen the angles we'd been shooting at and stared out over the water to mark the fallen ducks. At Joe's hand signal, he hit the water with a long, leaping splash and swam strongly through weeds and breaking waves—pausing only once to grab at a decoy, which he quickly rejected (and never bothered a decoy again). All told, Jake brought in twenty-five ducks that weekend, both for us and for others hunting Joe's ponds.

"You've got a good dog," Joe said. "You can be proud of him."

On Thanksgiving morning we rolled out well before dawn for Church Creek, our guide Rod Cawley leading the way. On the long drive through the darkness I sorrowed for Joe. Usually he would have been the man to give us our wake-up calls, to lead the way, tall and tough in his camouflaged waders, telling great mysterious stories of his adventures in Asia and Africa and South America as we rolled along the stygian transpeninsular highways, sipping strong coffee as he bulled the pickup down the wet two-track to the blind, wisecracking all the way. Now he was laid up in bed, fighting for his life. What were his dreams?

The water was black with ducks. We could hear them conversing in their busy chatter as the sky reddened over the Atlantic. When Cawley, who'd dropped us off at the blind, returned in a skiff to set the decoys, the ducks on the water flushed over our heads. Some flew so low we could have knocked them down with our gun muzzles.

But we were here to kill only singles and doubles. With the limit only four birds per man, we could afford to pick our shots. I can't recall every shot of the morning, but even with that restricted limit we had limited out in forty minutes. Todd shot well for a first-timer in a duck blind. My dog Jake, now nine years old, retrieved the birds with the aplomb of a veteran. The day could only have been better if Joe had been in the blind with us.

When we got back to Twin Ponds, Joe was up, sitting in his wheelchair on the lodge's wraparound deck, watching busy knots of bluebills and redheads trading up and down the Corsica River. He grinned when we told him how the morning had gone, relishing the description of every shot, hit or miss (and there weren't many of the latter). His wife, Donna, was cooking the Thanksgiving dinner—roast turkey, baked yams, two sweet steaming pies, superb as always. Over drinks and fresh oysters that evening, I took Joe aside and asked him what the long-term prospects were for him. "When I asked the doctor that question," Joe said, "he asked me . . . 'How tough are you?' " Joe's eyes suddenly filled. He shook his head. "But I'm fighting it, all the way."

We duck hunted again on Friday morning with equal success. The Eastern Shore's shotgun deer season opened at dawn on Saturday and Joe wanted Todd to shoot his favorite gun, a scoped Browning A5 autoloader, that day. He asked Donna to bring it to him so he could check Todd out on its operation. When she put it in Joe's hands, he tried to open the breech. He couldn't. He was too weak. Suddenly he laid the gun over his lap and spun the wheelchair so that his back was to us. His frail shoulders shook quietly as he wept.

Later he told Todd: "You'll see a lot of horns out there tomorrow morning, fours and sixes and even eights. But I don't want you to shoot anything less than ten points. This gun will kill any deer you aim it at. But don't settle for anything less than a trophy, know what I'm saying?"

Todd nodded his head yes.

The next morning, hunting with Rod again, Todd passed up an easy shot at a big six-pointer. Joe was proud of him. "That's a good young man there," he told me when we'd returned to the lodge and described the hunt.

Joe died on the afternoon of January 26. A mutual friend phoned me that evening with the sad news. I called Donna to express my heartfelt regrets. But what can you really say? "There were thirty-five people here when he went," she told me. "He lasted through the bird season. That's what he wanted. When it was finished, he felt it was time to go." Joe was cremated a few days later and his ashes cast upon the waters of the Corsica River, which flows past his lodge. From there they drifted down to the Chester River, thence into the Chesapeake Bay and from the bay to the oceans of the world.

I'd like to think that sooner or later an atom of the force that was once Joe Judge may permeate every body of water on this wild planet he so dearly loved. The world will be the better for it, as the world is surely better for his having lived.

SCRIBBLINGS IN THE SNOW

It snowed that night, just a light dusting of big, fat, lazy flakes that by sunup had laid perhaps half an inch of fluff over a base of twenty-odd inches. But the day broke clear and windless, the barn thermometer showed ten above, and the wooded mountain behind the house was now a tabula rasa—a clean slate on which to find inscribed some fresh, exciting stories. After breakfast my wife and I set out on snowshoes to read them.

Crossing the meadow we saw where a lone deer had picked its way down through the aspens toward the ice-edged brook, then after pausing to drink had forged uphill knee-deep through the snow to a gnarled old apple tree, there to mine for the sweet, wrinkled, frozen nuggets of fruit left over from last autumn's windstorms.

We saw where a red squirrel had descended a mature ash tree, then hopped its way at high speed—covering at least two feet between each tiny, bunched set of delicate footprints—to get to the safety of its next feeding station, a scraggly chokecherry that still bore some bitter fruits on its outermost twigs. The squirrel moved fast for fear of raptors. I'd seen a goshawk hunting the mountain slope that past week, zipping through the webwork of the upper canopy like a slate-blue lightning bolt, and every midnight of late we'd been hearing the murderous hoot of a great horned owl.

Next we pushed on into a stand of spruces, dense and dark, moving slowly, quietly on our snowshoes, hoping perhaps to flush a ruffed grouse from this favorite roosting place. But someone had beat us to it.

As we emerged from the edge of the spruces, the new-risen sun striking obliquely on the fresh snow before us, we saw the entire tragedy written in pale blue and white: The plump outline of a partridge in full flight—wings and fan widespread—lay graven in the snow. No tracks leading to or away from this icy intaglio. For a moment I was puzzled. What happened here? Then, overlaid atop the impression of the grouse's outstretched wings, we saw the fingerlike marks of broader wing tips. They looked to be three feet apart. Not broad enough for a goshawk, whose wings stretch nearly four feet from tip to tip, but too widespread for any lesser hawk or owl, they could only have been made by our mellifluous nighttime neighbor, the great horned owl.

He (or she) had hit the grouse as dawn was breaking, just as it launched from its roost in the sheltering spruce boughs, borne it down into the snow below while hooking it firmly with long, sure talons, then flown off for a hearty breakfast.

Sunrise and sudden death, scribblings in the snow . . .

You can learn a lot on snowshoes. Unlike cross-country skis, which because of their length restrict the winter woodsman to open, relatively straight trails, snowshoes allow you to penetrate the tangled depths of the woodland where the real wildlife action occurs. Birds and wild mammals are creatures of cover, always staying close to dense brush or the edges of thickets to avoid being eaten by those other woodland creatures that prey upon them for a living of their own. Try skiing through a patch of puckerbrush and you'll get my point. You'll be tripping over your own feet in no time, while I on my bearpaws or trail-model snowshoes will be dancing lightly over the pliant upper branches of steepletop or even multiflora rose, the webs serving to press them down as I walk—and in the process knocking off winter-stubborn berries and insect larvae for hungry songbirds to feed on once I've passed along my way: The Snowshoer as Wildlife Benefactor!

It wasn't always that way with me. I began walking the webs when I was about twelve years old, to prolong the hunting season while growing up in snowy Wisconsin. Winter came early, fast, and deep in those parts—well before the small-game season had closed. This was in the years just following World War II, and the only skis I owned were a pair of those long, heavy, wooden ones, U.S. Army surplus, with no steel edges and flimsy leather bindings. They were great for suicidal downhill runs, but in the deep woods . . . forget it. I was reading a lot of Jack London and James Oliver Curwood in those days, along with any related literature I could find about explorers, trappers, or sourdoughs snowshoeing through the High Latitudes. The greatest snowshoer of all time was probably John Rae (1813–93), a big, brawny Scottish physician and Arctic explorer for the Hudson's Bay Company, who could easily run a hundred miles in twenty-four hours on snowshoes. He once covered the forty-eight miles from Hamilton, Ontario, to Toronto in a mere seven hours, just to keep a dinner date.

Another great walker on the webs was the Mad Trapper of Rat River, who in the winter of 1931–32, wanted by the

Mounties (one of whom he'd already killed), led a combined force of Indians, white trappers, and the RCMP on a forty-eight-day, 150-mile chase through the Richardson Mountains on the Arctic Circle in temperatures averaging forty below. The Mad Trapper, whose name may have been either Albert Johnson or Arthur Nelson (or neither), was a small guy, only five foot nine and a half by 150 pounds, but he wore snowshoes that weighed ten pounds apiece and carried a pack as heavy as he was. When the Mounties finally killed him on February 17, 1932, in a firefight on an oxbow bend of the Eagle River, it took seven bullets to do it. With him he carried about twenty-five hundred dollars in various denominations and currencies (including alluvial gold), a Model 99 Savage 30–30 rifle, a sawed-off 16-gauge Iver Johnson shotgun, a Model 58 Winchester .22 rifle, appropriate ammunition, a pocket compass, an ax, a lard can and lid used as a tea pail, a dead squirrel, and a whiskey jack (for the last supper he never ate). A postmortem photo shows him snarling up at the camera, teeth bared through his grizzled beard, sweat frozen stiff in his ratty hair, dead eyes staring upward out of focus through slitted eyes still full of hate. A tough dude.

Inspired by such tales, I managed to procure a pair of ungainly bearpaw-model webs from the attic of a kindly neighbor. Those snowshoes were nearly circular, about three feet long by two and a half wide, so I had to walk kind of spraddle-legged at first—until I learned to take longer strides with them, while still keeping my balance. After many a chilly spill I even learned to trot at a goodly pace while holding my single-barreled shotgun in an Indian carry on one arm while swinging my other arm in counterbalance. I can't say I killed many grouse or rabbits on those snowy forays, but I did develop endurance, and a love for the stern, silent woods of winter.

Slogging across a frozen river one day, I came on a set of tracks that intrigued me and turned to follow them. They looked like the round, in-line footprints of a house cat taking a stroll on the crusted ice. A big cat judging by the size of the spoor. But what would any self-respecting tabby be doing outside so far from home on a subzero day like this? Maybe it was lost. Deciding to save the poor creature, I stepped up my pace, and five minutes later, rounding a bend, I saw the cat not fifty yards ahead of me—squarely built, with thick, spotted fur. She turned back to glare at me with fierce yellow eyes, then sprang into the brush along the bank. The poor thing had no tail!

The trail disappeared into a clump of brush that masked the mouth of a cave. From inside came a pitiful mewing, but louder than that of any kittens I'd heard before. Then on the air wafting from the cave came a sudden whiff of something rank—a faint cold hint of carrion. The mewing stopped. It was replaced by a low, menacing growl that seemed to come closer. The hairs on my neck tingled. I turned and walked quickly away, backtracking the cat's trail down the river to a deep patch of woods, where I found the gnawed carcass of a freshly killed yearling doe. Either I'd found the den of the toughest tabby in Wisconsin, or almost tangled with a mother bobcat . . .

Since then my snowshoes have led me to other memorable scenes. In the late 1980s, while covering the thousand-mile Iditarod dogsled race for *Sports Illustrated,* I had many opportunities to run the Alaska winter on webs. One sunny day, following the racers up the frozen Yukon in a DeHavilland Beaver, we spotted a pack of wolves devouring a moose in the riverside willows. The pilot put down on a sideslough and we strapped on our snowshoes, then trotted a mile back through twenty-below temperatures to observe the feast at close range. About that time the lead dog teams came mushing through. The wolves stopped eating, looked up gravely, and watched their domesticated counterparts go straining past, huffing and puffing with their tongues lolling loose. A big, grizzled wolf shook his head in what seemed to be disbelief, as if to say, *Ah, yes, the Northern Lights have seen strange sights* . . .

In the 1970s I accompanied Jim Whittaker and his climbing team up Mount Rainier, in January, to check out new equipment for their first (and failed) attempt on K2, the second highest peak in the world after Everest. For three days we climbed seracs and icy rock faces, dug snow houses, mushed miles through pristine snow at twelve thousand feet. I still have a pair of the prototype Sherpa snowshoes the expedition was testing—the lightweight aluminum frames have stood the test of time, of course, but the plastic webbing has deteriorated to the breaking point. Give me lacquered gut webs any day. I've been using my old Faber hunting snowshoes, four and a half feet long with upturned toes and birch frames, since the late 1950s and they still can break trail with the best of them.

On the Whittaker excursion we lived in flimsy tents through a man-killing blizzard. I'll always remember the trip from a remark made by Jim's wife one night when, replete from a meal of freeze-dried preservatives and too many cups of tepid orange pekoe tea, we all heard the call of nature. We went out into the raging storm and answered it as swiftly as possible. Back in the relative warmth of the tent, Jim and I were complaining on how chilling an experience it had been when Mrs. W. came in. She listened for a moment, then turned to us with a wry grin. "You guys are wimps," she said. "All you have to do is unzip and let fly. I've got to drop my pants, squat, and then knock off the icicles."

But the great joy of snowshoes, for me at least, is hunting ruffed grouse on them, and the difficulty of the flushes I'm likely to encounter. Nature has equipped *Bonasa umbellus* with its own built-in snowshoes, in the form of broad, flanged protrusions from the sides of its toes, allowing the bird to walk easily on even the lightest, deepest powder. But grouse don't like cold feet any more than we do. Many of your flushes are likely to be arboreal. I've always found tree-flushed birds hard to hit. They lose altitude the moment they take off, and almost inevitably I end up shooting too high. What's more, they'll fly in such a way as to keep the trunk of the tree between you and their cockeyed flight path, which is full of twists and turns since they're already at the altitude of the upper limbs of the surrounding trees when they launch themselves.

If the snow is two feet deep or more, you're likely to experience the most awesome grouse tactic known to the art of pteraplegia: what I call the Drift Flush. On really cold nights, grouse will take refuge under the snow, which serves as additional insulation against subzero, toe-freezing temperatures. A dog with a really good nose can often smell them under as much as three feet of snow. My old black Lab Luke had that knack. So too did Belle, the half-wild Irish setter who was my staunchest boyhood hunting partner.

Early one Saturday morning she and I were mushing uphill toward an aspen grove where I hoped to give some slugabed partridges a rude awakening. Belle bounded ahead of me through the snow-covered meadow, kicking up a rooster-tail of fine powder. Suddenly she stopped, dropped her snout down into a softball-sized hole in a gently bulging drift, and snuffled deeply. She locked up tight on point.

"Quit the clowning, you silly thing," I told her, not unfondly—she liked to play goofy tricks on me, mainly of the false-pointing variety. "There couldn't be a grouse in the middle of a meadow, and you darn well know it." But she stayed staunch on point. Just at that moment the early sun broke through a layer of clouds and illuminated the scene:

the setter a glowing, dark red statue etched against the frozen sea of pale blue drifts, with the gaunt, ragged thicket of popple as a backdrop. I mushed on in ahead of Belle—and the snow erupted like a mortar burst.

The ruff clattered out, straight on up through the aspens where its kinfolk took the hint and flushed wild, well out of gun range. I stood there throughout with my jaw hanging open and the 28-gauge silent in the crook of my arm. It was indeed a rude awakening.

In the half century since then, I've witnessed the Drift Flush only six or eight more times, and once—on a bird flushed back to me by the redoubtable Luke—even managed to scratch a grouse down, on an easy straightaway shot. Nowadays I pray each fall for a snowy winter. When we get one, all too rarely of late, the memory of those spectacular, unlikely flushes drives me out into the cold and the deep snow again and again, just for the possible thrill of seeing it happen again.

Often I don't even carry a gun. Nowadays, when the snow flies thick enough (anything more than eight inches is sufficient to justify the use of the webs), I'm content to course the miles and miles of woods and overgrown logging trails behind our house, accompanied usually by my wife and our dogs, Jake and Roz. The long and the short of it, indeed. Jake loves the snow, the deeper the better, but occasionally I have to rescue Roz from the deeper drifts, tucking her into my game pocket for a free ride through the softer stuff. We dress lightly, since snowshoeing is warm work: long johns, wool pants, two shirts, a parka shell, wool watch cap, gloves. For footwear, two pairs of socks, one of cotton or silk topped by another of wool, and high-topped boots to keep out the snow. I prefer a light shoepac with rubberized feet and leather uppers.

In addition to the Sherpas and the Fabers, we also own a pair of excellent trail-model Vermont Tubbs shoes, ten- by thirty-six-inchers. After a fresh snowfall, aided by Jake, I'll break trail in the longer shoes while Louise and Roz follow behind. Often we carry with us a copy of Olaus Murie's *Field Guide to Animal Tracks*, which contains drawings of the scat and footprints of everything from mice and voles to moose and polar bears.

On our lengthier hikes, we also bring along a fanny pack of sandwiches, apples, and a thermos of hot tea. It's pleasant to take a break high on Bear Mountain, which rises to thirty-three hundred feet behind our house. Tucked away out of the wind, we build a small fire and sip our steaming tea while watching the silent, snowy woods and valleys below. The other mountains of the Taconic range rise quiet in the hard blue light of winter, stippled with dark spruces and the faded russets of red oaks to which a few stubborn leaves still cling. Sometimes we'll see deer moving across the valley, or perhaps a raven creaking its way across the empyrean. Our house, far, far below, looks like a slate-roofed sugar cube at that distance, trailing a tendril of blue-gray wood smoke from the chimney.

I often think John Rae would have loved this scene. But the Mad Trapper? I doubt it. Then again, perhaps that's what he was seeking all along.

GRASSFIRES

On the prairie peninsulas of southern Wisconsin where I first started bird hunting half a century ago, grassfires were common. A railroad line, the Chicago, Milwaukee, St. Paul & Pacific, ran through the virgin tallgrass prairies just west of where I lived, the coal-burning engines of the locomotives throwing incendiary sparks from their smokestacks. Hardly an autumn went by without the familiar flare-up: first a yellow, bittersweet haze shimmying lazily in the distance; then a faraway grumble like the ghosts of buffalo stampeding out of the past, louder and louder; and finally from a roiling wall of smoke the beast itself would heave into view: a great crackling snake of flame sidewinding its way through the wind-crisped bluestem and bunchgrass faster than a man could run.

183

Prairie lore had it that on a strong northwest wind, a grassfire could outgallop a horse. Being a child of the Tin Lizzie Era, I never saw that happen, of course, though once I came upon the gutted, fire-scabbed carcass of a Model T Ford coupe in a gulch not far from the nearest road. The tires were melted, the upholstery reduced to a snarl of spring coils protruding through a bed of white ash, and even the wooden steering wheel was charred. I think it was a bootlegger's car from the Roaring Twenties, since I found dozens of exploded whiskey bottles in the sprung rumble seat of the coupe. No booze left, of course, not even the whiff of it on the air, but a couple of the jugs still bore faded labels proclaiming their contents Seagram's Crown Royal. No sign of the driver, either. Nary a bone. He'd probably driven down from Canada with his load in the middle of the night, hidden the car in the gulch at daybreak, then gone off to wait until dark to continue his delivery.

The way I liked to think of it, though, the bootlegger— let's call him Zack—is shortcutting his way across the prairie while the fire's already burning, taking advantage of the smoke to conceal his illicit mission. But then he's outflanked by the flames. He turns every which way trying to escape it. Now Zack's clattering along with the speedometer needle bumping forty, watching the flames in the rearview mirror get taller and taller, closer and closer, the Lizzie bouncing over ruts like a bronc on locoweed, Zack's eyes red and weeping from the smoke, the heat searing his lungs. Then the tires go all squirrelly, they feel mushy—my God, they're melting! He bails out only at the last moment, runs blindly to the road, and thumbs a ride into Milwaukee. Then he thinks: Big Izzy's really going to be pissed about this . . .

The grassfires were dangerous, to be sure, but they had a kind of wild beauty to them as well. At night from my bedroom window I would watch their progress on the prairie a mile away across the Menomonee River, a smoky firedance of ruby and topaz and opal, flaring up now and then when they hit a juniper patch or turned a wind-cured cottonwood into a blazing torch. "These scenes at night become indescribably beautiful," George Catlin had written way back in the 1830s, "when their flames are seen at many miles distance, creeping over the sides and tops of the bluffs, appearing to be sparkling and brilliant chains of liquid fire (the hills being lost to view), hanging suspended in graceful festoons from the skies."

The fires burned slowly after sunset when the air cooled and the wind died down, and watching them one evening it occurred to me that by morning the flames might reach a particularly troublesome patch of cover that I knew sheltered a big flock of prairie chickens. The swale was flanked on one side by a dense stand of multiflora rose shrubs, tall as a man and fanged like a nest of vipers. Whenever my neighborhood pickup team of half-wild Irish setters, Rusty and Belle, quartered into the grass the birds simply legged it through the rose thicket and flushed from the far side. I couldn't see them when they flew, only hear the frustrating clatter of their wings. But if I stationed myself on the far side of the thorny barrier and let the fire serve as my flushing dogs, I'd likely get some fast and furious pass-shooting.

I already knew from my reading that the Indians had used fire as a hunting tool long before the white man came. Woodland tribes like the Shawnees and Iroquois used it to drive deer, the Seminoles burned swatches of the Everglades to flush alligators, while the Plains tribes—Sioux and Cheyenne, Crow and Arapaho—pushed whole herds of buffalo over cliffs and into rivers by means of wind-driven prairie fires. The Digger Indians of California and Oregon even fired the tules to collect the bite-sized pupae of big pandora moths, which they gathered from the ashes already cooked (they were said to be quite tasty, like the witchety grubs that Australian Aborigines also collected by burning). Indeed, over many millennia the Indian practice of widespread, intensive fire-hunting had shaped the prairies themselves, keeping the forests at bay and extending the grasslands across the Missouri and Mississippi into the forested East. The vast, grassy barrens of western Kentucky, where D. Boone and other eighteenth-century Long Hunters killed deer, elk, and bison for the eastern markets, were formed by ages of Indian fire. In a letter to John Adams dated May 27, 1813, no less an authority than Thomas Jefferson, a savvy amateur naturalist, suggested that fire-hunting was "the most probable cause of the origin and extension of the vast prairies in the western country." In fact, the prairie peninsulas I hunted in Wisconsin had been created by Indian fires.

That at any rate was my quasi-historical justification for the unsportsmanlike experiment I was about to undertake. That it was also damned foolhardy I was soon to learn.

I was up and out of the house well before first light. Knowing that dawn would bring up a breeze, I wanted to be in position before the fire came racing into the rose cover. Rusty and Belle must have heard or smelled me as I passed, and they came galloping from their doghouses eager for the fray. Across the river we followed the railroad tracks northward for a mile to the low patch where the rose thicket grew. The river made a big oxbow bend here, passing under the right-of-way on two black iron trestles a few hundred yards apart. The thicket was about a hundred yards west of the river and the tracks. Usually I approached it from the northwest, but today I hiked straight through the knee-high bluestem to the back side of the thicket. The grass was dry: No dew soaked my Levis. As we neared the roses, Rusty and Belle looked puzzled. They kept wanting to skirt the thicket and push into the cover where the birds were. But the leading edge of the fire was still a quarter of a mile off to the northwest, and the bitter smell of the night-damped smoke made them more obedient than usual to my commands. "Sit and stay!" I told them in a drill sergeant's voice—but wisely reinforcing the order with a couple of toast crusts from my game pocket.

All was proceeding as planned. Sure enough, soon after the sun popped over the horizon a northwest breeze sprang up, gentle at first, but strengthening as the morning warmed. It was a scary sunrise, the sky stoking quickly from ash gray through amber to a brilliant flame red. The sun itself was huge, warped and magnified by the smoke in the air to the shape of a giant blood orange. The fire pepped up, rolling fat waves of blue-gray smoke toward us. My eyes started to water. Belle sneezed. Yellow flames danced merrily through the smoke, and the crackle grew louder, from the sound you might hear from a casually crinkled piece of cellophane to the popping of a string of cheap Chinese firecrackers. Through the din we could hear the prairie hens talking, not frantic yet but a bit apprehensive. I'm sure they already knew that the tall, awkward figure with the loud stick and his two rapacious, four-legged, red-coated sidekicks were in place downwind from from them. Pinned between the threat of fire and the lesser threat of a kid with a gun, they were puzzling out their best escape route. It was an easy choice.

The grass in the swale where the roses grew was taller than that on the rest of the prairie, maybe waist-high. When the first flames hit it they doubled in height and the crackling grew to a throatier rumble. The wind suddenly gusted, blowing straight and acrid into my face. My lungs convulsed and I started to cough. My eyes streamed tears. I heard the birds get up—a clatter like a million city room typewriters gone berserk—and then they were pouring past me, a stream of long, fast, dark blurs banking and cackling as they flew. I couldn't see to shoot. Panic grabbed me by the bowels. When the fire hit the roses, dried by a long hot summer and the smoky winds of the past few days, the thicket exploded in a wall of flame, exploded with the roar of a lion.

I turned and ran. Rusty and Belle were well ahead of me, pelting with tucked tails toward the trestles over the river. I could hear the fire roaring at my back, feel its radiant heat through my hunting coat. The hair on the back of my neck felt singed, and any moment I expected my eyebrows to flare. All I could picture in my mind was the image of that burned-out bootlegger's car, the ribs of its upholstery poking through the ashes. Like my own ribs would look if I fell. How I hung on to my gun I'll never know. When the dogs reached the river they plunged in and swam to the far side. I leaped from the bank, hit the water, and promptly sank knee-deep in mud. No way I could swim, not without losing the gun. I crouched under the bank, up to my nostrils in the chilly, mucky Menomonee. Flames flickered in the dry grass atop the bank, dropping fiery ashes on my head. I slogged in a crouch, quick as I could, through the shallows to the shelter beneath the iron trestle. There I hunkered down, cold, wet, scared, and miserable. And cursing myself for a damned fool.

The fire burned out when it hit the combined barrier of railroad and river. I had to wait a couple of hours before going home to let my clothes dry, but they were still damp when I got there. I'd hidden the shotgun, as usual, in the dugout "fort" we'd built in the field across the street. When I came in the kitchen, my anti-hunting mother said, "Bobby, you're all wet!"

"In more ways than one," I told her . . .

It was a whole week before Rusty and Belle would hunt with me again.

HIGH ON THE WILD

I've been thinking a lot about Ernest Hemingway this past year, which marked the centennial of his birth on July 21, 1899. Few literary figures make much of an impact on the world of the outdoor sports, yet for me and many others, Hemingway's words not only captured the essence of what we feel when we're out in the wild with rod or gun, but imbued the very acts with high existential meaning. "Big Two-Hearted River," arguably Hemingway's best short story, freighted as it is with dark, unspoken fears and dreams and the promise of salvation waist-deep in an icy river, baptized anyone who read it in the cold-water religion of trout. It converted whole generations to a love of fly fishing.

Yet by all accounts Hemingway loved wingshooting even more than trout fishing. Why then did he never create a pteraplegic parallel to "Big Two-Hearted River?" Apart from passing references in three short stories and a rather rambling essay in *Esquire* ("Remembering Shooting-Flying: A Key West Letter," published in February 1935), he never wrote much about bird hunting.

In "The Three-Day Blow," Nick Adams and his pal Bill sit around in Bill's Michigan cottage on a blustery, rainy autumn day, talking baseball and books, the delights of fishing and the drawbacks of marriage. Nick's just broken up with a girl named Marge (see "The End of Something") and is feeling deep regret. He's even considering going back to her. After a couple of drinks, they decide to join Bill's father, who's down in the swamp bird hunting.

They stepped out the door. The wind was blowing a gale.

"The birds will lie right down in the grass with this," Nick said.

They struck down toward the orchard.

"I saw a woodcock this morning," Bill said.

"Maybe we'll jump him," Nick said.

"You can't shoot in this wind," Bill said.

Outside now the Marge business was no longer so tragic. It was not even very important. The wind blew everything like that away . . .

Against the wind they heard the thud of a shotgun . . .

Moral: Bird hunting, even on a rainy, windy day, is a sure cure for heartbreak.

In "A Day's Wait," an older Nick is in rural Arkansas, taking care of his young son, who's in bed with a fever of 102. While the boy dozes, Nick takes his own mind off his concern for his son with a spot of bird hunting.

It was a bright, cold day, the ground covered with a sleet that had frozen so that it seemed as if all the bare trees, the bushes, the cut brush and all the grass and the bare ground had been varnished with ice. I took the young Irish setter for a little walk up the road and along a frozen creek, but it was difficult to stand or walk on the glassy surface and the red dog slipped and slithered and I fell twice, hard, once dropping my gun and having it slide away over the ice.

We flushed a covey of quail under a high clay bank with over-hanging brush and I killed two as they went out of sight over the top of the bank. Some of the covey lit in trees, but most of them scattered into brush piles and it was necessary to jump on the ice-coated mounds of brush several times before they would flush. Coming out while you were poised unsteadily on the icy, springy brush they made difficult shooting and I killed two, missed five, and started back pleased to have found a covey close to the house and happy there were so many left to find on another day.

When he gets home and takes his son's temperature again, it's a little higher: 102.4 F. The boy asks when he's going to die, and Nick realizes that his son—raised in France—is confusing Fahrenheit with Centigrade, where forty-four degrees is fatal. *"You poor Schatz," I said. ". . . It's like miles and kilometers. You aren't going to die. That's a different thermometer. On that thermometer thirty-seven is normal. On this kind it's ninety-eight."*

The boy, reprieved from a death sentence, lets go of himself *"and he cried very easily at little things that were of no importance."*

Moral: The world is dangerous, confusing, unsteady under our feet. Keep your eye on the target and don't allow yourself to be misled.

The posthumously published short story "I Guess Everything Reminds You of Something Else" is set in Cuba, where Hemingway lived on and off from 1939 to 1959. There he competed weekly in live pigeon shoots where the birds were launched at speed from an array of mechanical traps. You never knew beforehand which trap would spring, and had to kill the pigeon before it cleared a low fence not many yards off. A lot of money changed hands in the betting. In this story, the narrator's youngest boy, called Stevie here but probably Hemingway's third son Gregory, is a natural wing-shot, competing on even terms with grown men and professional shots at the age of twelve.

At live pigeons, in competition, when he walked out on the cement, spun the wheel and walked to the metal plaque that marked the black stripe of his yardage, the pros were silent and watching . . .

"Ready," he said in that low, hoarse voice that did not belong to a small boy.

"Ready," answered the trapper.

"Pull," said the hoarse voice and from whichever of the five traps the grey racing pigeon came out, and at whatever angle his wings drove him in full, low flight above the green grass toward the white, low fence, the load of the first barrel swung into him and the load from the second barrel drove through the first. As the bird collapsed in flight, his head falling forward, only the great shots saw the impact of the second load driving through onto the bird already dead in the air.

But in addition to being a great wingshot, Stevie is also a very promising writer. He shows his father a prizewinning short story he wrote at school and though there's something vaguely familiar about the piece, the narrator admits that he couldn't write that well at Stevie's age. The boy promises his father a second story, but never delivers it. *It was seven years later that his father read the prizewinning story again. It was in a book that he found in checking through . . . the boy's old room. As soon as he saw it he knew where the story had come from. He remembered the long-ago feeling of familiarity. He turned through the pages and there it was, unchanged and with the same title, in a book of very good short stories by an Irish writer . . . Now he knew*

that boy had never been any good . . . And it was sad to know that
shooting did not mean a thing.

Moral: Plagiarism is a worse sin than missing.

Hemingway, who's been critically lambasted in recent years for being too "macho," was in fact a very sensitive man. But I don't believe that the Stevie incident, disillusioning as it was (if indeed it actually happened), could have embittered him so deeply against bird shooting as to prevent him from writing a transcendental story about it on a par with "Big Two-Hearted River." After all, he kept on bird hunting right to the very end. But a little-known incident in 1939 may well have done so. It certainly put the quietus to a major story he planned on the joys of western bird hunting.

In the summer of 1939, Hemingway and his soon-to-be third wife, Martha Gellhorn, accepted an invitation from the Union Pacific Railroad to spend some time at the company's new Sun Valley Lodge in Idaho. It was Hemingway's kind of country for sure. Great fishing on Silver Creek and the Big Wood River. Pheasants and Huns and ducks galore in the surrounding hills and valleys. Elk, deer, and bear in the nearby Pahsimeroi Mountains. Taken in hand by Sun Valley's publicist, a handsome young westerner named Gene Van Guilder, Hemingway quickly fell in love with what Sun Valley had to offer. Drifting Silver Creek, he had the best of three worlds: jump-shooting mallards in the sidesloughs, going ashore to walk up pheasants, or, when that got a bit old, picking up a fly rod and sight-casting to the creek's wary five- and six-pound rainbows.

As Lloyd "Pappy" Arnold, who was Van Guilder's chief photographer, reports in his 1968 memoir *Hemingway High on the Wild*, "Then, coming up from pheasant shooting one night, with a few ducks in the loot, he handed Gene a press agent's gem: He'd write an article on Idaho's great shotgunning; he knew he could plant it for winter publication with his good friend Arnold Gingrich at *Esquire;* make it long enough to run as a series of two or three."

It was early autumn, and hot. The big flights of migrant waterfowl that blanketed the fields, sloughs, swamps, and interlaced creeks of the valley each fall had yet to arrive. To scout out locations and ensure that everything was just right for Hemingway's "potlatch," as they called it, Van Guilder, Arnold, and a Sun Valley employee named Dee set out on the nearby Snake River in a canoe one late October weekend, while Hemingway remained behind in Suite 206, working on *For Whom the Bell Tolls.* He promised to pray for some good old-fashioned duck weather the following weekend.

The shooting was spotty, but on Sunday it picked up. "By about one o'clock we called it quits," Arnold writes, "a few birds short of our limits. While we paddled the half-mile up the west shore, ducks started to stir . . . I paddled stern, Gene forward—it was his turn to shoot if something passed close enough to a little tule-fringed bay we ducked into. Our companion, whom I'll call Dee, was the midship passenger, having finished a fair morning in a makeshift blind on one of the islands. Something did come along shortly, drifting down on the water. Gene thought the little ducks were teal, the best of eatin' ducks, bar none; the backlight glaring the water fooled him. When in easy range they skirted the low tules concealing us—buffleheads, little diving ducks—I said, 'Let 'em go, Gene.' My voice didn't raise them, and I thought he would let them go. Then, tightly bunched, they took off, straightaway, and Gene fired both barrels. Six birds down, but two were only winged, and under they went.

" 'Now we have some chasing to do, mark 'em. . . .'

"I was cut off by a violent roll of the boat, a sharp thud on its bottom, a single shot . . . Poor Gene had triggered it himself. To flush the ducks and shoot, he stood fully upright in the narrow prow, without feeling the slightest movement of the boat. In easing himself down, he turned to grasp the gunwale with his right hand, his gun held high in his left. He was frozen in this half-turned, half-crouched position when my horrified eyes saw the hole just under his right shoulder blade. The smoking muzzles of Dee's double-barrelled 12-gauge were directly in line. . . ."

Hemingway wrote a eulogy to his friend Gene Van Guilder and delivered it at the graveside in the shabby little Ketchum cemetery on November 1. It concluded: "Best of all he loved the fall . . . the fall with the tawny and grey, the leaves yellow on the cottonwoods, leaves floating on the trout streams and above the hills the high blue windless skies. . . . And now he has come home to the hills. He has come back now to rest well in the country that he loved through all the seasons. He will be here in the winter and in the spring and in the summer, and in the fall. In all the seasons there will ever be. He has come back to the hills that he loved and now he will be a part of them forever."

Hemingway never wrote the story on western bird hunting, and that's our great loss. He lies buried in Ketchum cemetery not far from Gene Van Guilder. "Come home to the hills."

"HUNGER IS THE KEY"

Rusty, a staunch, solid Brittany spaniel, was locked up tight in heavy cover, his beeper urging us on: "Hurry! Hurry! Hurry!" We pelted down through the overgrown field to where the dog stood, rigid as marble, his nostrils aimed like gun muzzles into a dense tangle of aspen whips and brier. My friend Jeff kicked at the brush and, sure enough, it exploded as a gorgeous, long-tailed cock pheasant took flight, his metallic cackle breaking the morning stillness.

An easy straightaway shot—but none of us carried guns.

Instead we employed a more ancient weapon.

As the pheasant reached maximum airspeed, high over the field and well beyond gun range, three other avian forms flashed out of the surrounding trees and converged on the doomed cockbird like so many dark, darting lightning bolts. Our Harris hawks were on the job. One of them hit the pheasant with a solid *whump!*, clearly audible to us a hundred yards back up the slope. A puff of tan feathers bloomed in midair, and the pheasant squawked once in sheer, shocked terror as it sloped down into the trees at the far end of the meadow. The hawks—a big, flame-eyed female named Moet, who had "footed" the pheasant with the knuckles of her huge, powerful yellow talons but failed to bind on, and her two smaller wingmen, Clint and Austin—followed their quarry down . . .

It was a moment of awful, awesome beauty.

For years I'd been reading about the joys of falconry, in the works of such fine, evocative writers as J. A. Baker *(The Peregrine)*, Steve Bodio *(A Rage for Falcons)*, Dan O'Brien *(The Rites of Autumn* and *Equinox)*, and T. H. White *(The Goshawk, England Have My Bones,* and of course *The Sword in the Stone)*, but I'd never had the opportunity to accompany a falconer and his hawks in the field. Then I met Dr. Jeffrey Piper. Jeff's an ophthalmologist in Rutland, Vermont, a tall, red-bearded midwesterner with a fondness for all things British, including best guns, bird hunting in all its forms, well-trained pointing dogs, single-malt Scotch, rich port wine, haute cuisine (he's a marvelous cook), and, most recently, hawking. After moving to Vermont from Pennsylvania in 1996, he began studying the avian art at renowned falconer Emma Ford's British School of Falconry, which a few years ago opened a satellite American campus in Manchester Village, Vermont. Jeff's wife Kim works with my wife, Louise, at the Northshire Bookstore in Manchester, so it was inevitable that Jeff and I, with our mutual love of bird hunting, would get together. Last October Jeff invited me along for three days of sporting clays, wild bird hunting, and a fast and furious driven pheasant shoot at Tinmouth, which was to conclude on the fourth day with a morning afield following the hawks. The shoot was conducted by Ed Kozak's excellent Shorthair Tours, a Pennsylvania-based operation. But a magazine deadline denied me the chance to go hawking. Instead Jeff and I met a few weeks later at Tinmouth for my first taste of falconry.

With us that Saturday were my writer friend Philip Marion, who, though he doesn't shoot, will at a moment's notice drive all the way from Maine or New Hampshire to western Vermont for the chance to spend a morning afield behind dogs, so long as the gamebirds are flying; and Jeff Piper's falconry sponsor, Diane Mahaney, a licensed falconer employed by the Ford school. Diane, who hails from Sharpsburg, Virginia, is a slim, fit, eager young woman with short dark hair, pale green eyes, and an almost mystical ability to read the moods of her hawks. She proved capable of explaining the arcana of falconry not only clearly and understandably (to this layman), but inspirationally as well. You can feel the respect she holds for these raptors, an unreciprocated feeling, as she quickly points out. "To a manned hawk, we—either pointing dogs or people—are nothing more than moving bushes that produce gamebirds. They follow us through the woods knowing that, sooner rather than later, the beeper will go off, and a pheasant or rabbit will pop out of the cover. Don't expect doglike loyalty from a hawk. Hunger is the key. The need to fly, the need to kill."

Never used in falconry before the 1960s, Harris hawks have since become the raptors of choice among British and American falconers, especially beginners. They cost less than half the price of peregrine falcons ($450 for an untrained Harris female), they're readily trainable, versatile, and strong enough to handle bigger gamebirds, like chukar partridge, pheasants, and even—on occasion—that elusive king of wild upland birds, the ruffed grouse. Harris hawks are broad-winged yet long-tailed, clad in a rich, bay-colored plumage, with bright yellow eyes, beaks, and claws. They're originally birds of the American Southwest, native to mesquite and chapparal country from West Texas to eastern California, ranging on into the high, bleak reaches of southern Colorado, Nevada, and Utah. Big country like that, where game is spread thin, demands teamwork for predators to make a living. In the wild, Harris hawks learned through the vicissitudes of evolution to hunt in family groups, teaming up to capture lizards, snakes, desert quail, songbirds, and ground squirrels, and sometimes even cottontails, jackrabbits, or massive European hares.

As with all hawks, female Harrises are larger than the males. On the morning of our hunt, Moet (named for the classy French champagne but known as Mo to her friends) tipped the scales at 1 pound, 12¾ ounces, 9 ounces more than Clint, 8 more than Austin. Harris hawks are classed as a monotype: *Parabuteo unicinctus,* a kind of cross between broad-winged hawks like the ubiquitous redtail *(Buteo jamaicensis),* which soars and circles at low altitudes, then dives down on its quarry, and long-tailed, short-winged accipiters such as the goshawk *(Accipiter gentilis),* which seeks its prey by swift, fierce, direct flight through the lower levels of cover, dodging and twisting all the way. The Harris combines the best of both techniques.

Harris hawks hunt well in small groups, unlike true falcons (kestrels, merlins, peregrines, prairie falcons, and gyrfalcons), which tend to be aloof, high-soaring loners. And Harrises, once they're cast off from the falconer's gloved wrist, will follow a pointing dog along at treetop level, perching now and then as dog and men work the ground. Then, when the game is flushed, they zoom down as if aerobatically choreographed, double- and triple-teaming their quarry, almost certain death from short range. If they miss on the first pass, they will follow the quarry until it pitches in again, usually only a short distance. And if a hawk flies out of sight, it can often be relocated with a portable telemetry unit tuned to the miniature radio transmitter secured to its ankle.

"The life span of hawks in captivity can reach twenty-five years," Diane Mahaney told me. "They're fed reliably and not exposed to as many hazards as a free-flying hawk, though a wild, banded redtail I heard of proved to be twenty-three years old. Most mortality among wild hawks, as with all birds, occurs in the first year of life. Accidents in flight, starvation, bad weather, predation by other, larger raptors or coyotes—it's a tough world out there."

But does the pampered captive hawk appreciate the care its falconer offers—the weatherproof mews where it can roost in safety at night, the spacious, wire-fenced and -roofed "weathering" where it may enjoy the sun during its nonflying days, and even take an occasional bath, the carefully measured and regulated diet of day-old cockerel chicks, quail, beef, liver, rabbit, ungutted rats or mice, or a nice chunk of a pheasant she herself has killed? Don't count on it.

"Falconers claim that the only way to lose a Harris hawk is to drive home faster than it can fly," Jeff Piper says. "But that's an exaggeration." At the slightest miscalculation on the falconer's part, even the steadiest, most reliable hawk can disappear like smoke on a routine hunt. You might have trained your bird perfectly, accustomed it to return to your wrist by swinging a pheasant-wing "lure" sweetened with a piece of meat, or perhaps the shrill blast of an Acme Thunderer, but if you overfeed your hawk and then fly it on game, it might well amble off beyond the horizon, heedless of all the lures and police whistles in the world.

They are, after all, still wild at heart.

In Vermont, as in all states, the rigmarole involved in getting a general falconer's license makes gun hunting, with its rather simpleminded "hunter safety" test, look easy. After

more than a year of lessons under Diane Mahaney's prac-
ticed eye, Jeff Piper is finally ready to take a stringent written
exam on his knowledge of falconry. If he passes it, he will
pay the state $250 for an apprentice license. Then come two
more years under Diane's supervision. He must build a
mews and an outdoor "weathering" according to exacting
standards, and next, trap a wild hawk, probably a redtail (the
most widespread hawk in North America), and "man" it—
i.e., train the bird to sit on his fist, eat from his fist, and jump
from the ground to his fist, increasing the range until it is flying on a "creance," which is a long tether. Finally he must
"enter" the bird to game—get it to hunt for him. Like Harris
hawks, redtails are relatively easy to train.

The legal hawk-trapping season in Vermont runs from
September 1 to late January, during the fall migration. Jeff
says he'll use a harnessed pigeon to toll his wild redtail
down from the sky. The harness is fitted with loops of mono-
filament fishing line, which should snag the hawk's talons.
An alternative method would be to confine the pigeon in a
"Bal Chatri"—a protective cage fitted with similar loops. If
all goes well, a wandering hawk, seeing the helpless, fluttering quarry, should stoop on the cage and be snared. Then the
fun begins . . .

O n our day afield with the hawks at Tinmouth, we took
five pheasants in the course of a four-hour hunt. Every bird
Rusty pointed ended up in the game bag. All that morning, it
seemed, we were tearing through the woods at breakneck
speed, homing in over hill and dale to the sound of Rusty's
beeper where he'd locked up on another bird. In the words
of Johnny Horton: *We ran through the briers and we ran through
the brambles, we ran through the bushes where a rabbit wouldn't
go. . . .*

The hawks followed at treetop level, waiting until one or another of us worked in to the point and flushed the pheasant. Then the hawks swept in to knock it down. The truly tricky part came next: getting the pheasant away from whichever hawk stood over it, wings spread to "mantle" its prey, plucking breast feathers in preparation for the feast to come. It was imperative to get the pheasant in the bag before the hawk could eat enough to lose its desire to hunt on. Jeff and Diana handled that exercise, distracting the hawk with a small piece of meat (brought along for that purpose) held between the knuckles of one gloved hand, then with the other hand whisking the pheasant away and slipping it into a game bag. Dangerous legerdemain: A hawk on its kill will instinctively spike with its talons any creature unwise enough to interfere with its meal. Size is no protection. The hawk, once aroused, fears nothing on this earth.

The teamwork of Mo, Clint, and Austin that day was superb, the aerobatics a delight to behold. But do I plan to take up hawking? It's a whole new world to be sure, with an arcane language all its own, a fascinating blend of history, technique, and technology. And the wild, fierce hawks are an existential inspiration in themselves. We can never really know them.

Twenty years ago, I'd have entered that world in a minute. But I'm afraid I'm not hungry enough for it now. A little too old and set in my ways, I guess. I'll have to stick with my shotguns and flushing dogs, but I wish I'd experienced the excitement of hawks much, much earlier.

THROUGH A GLASS, DARKLY

So here it is: the twenty-first century with all its hopes and horrors. Will this new millennium prove to be the turn of the ebb tide for bird hunters, or the dawn of a brave new era? No crystal ball is clear enough to make any accurate prediction, but if the final decades of the second millennium—say, from the end of World War II to the present—are any indication of what lies ahead, I'd have to say that things are going to get a lot worse for us in the years to come, and maybe they'll never get any better.

Looking at the big picture, the millennium just past was a grim one in terms of outdoor stewardship. It was marked and marred by the Industrial Revolution, which triggered an ever-accelerating despoliation of the planet: deforestation from Europe and

Southeast Asia through sub-Saharan Africa to the Americas, the resultant spread of deserts, the pollution of lakes, rivers, oceans, and the atmosphere, not to mention the extinction of entire species of creatures once hunted by man, ranging from the aurochs and the dodo and Steller's sea cow, to the passenger pigeon, the heath hen, the Carolina parakeet, the ivory-billed woodpecker, and the near eradication a century ago of North America's bison and pronghorn antelope, more recently of the Asian rhinoceros, Bengal tiger, snow leopard—ad sickeningly infinitum.

And that's just the big stuff. Edward O. Wilson, the Pulitzer Prize–winning Harvard scientist who is one of the world's leading authorities on everything from the lives of the ants to the death of nature, believes we're undergoing yet another of the planet's great periodic global extinctions—this one attributable entirely to man. In a book called *The Diversity of Life* (Harvard University Press, 1992), Wilson describes how human population pressures, particularly in the developing nations of the Third World, are destroying other species of life at a disastrous rate. Human beings are literally overwhelming nature. By the year 2020—less than a human generation from now—no fewer than a fifth of the earth's existing species of plants and animals will be extinct, by Wilson's *conservative* estimate. Wilson estimates that because of the runaway destruction of the earth's tropical forests alone, the planet is losing twenty-seven thousand species a year: seventy-four each day, or a little more than three species an hour (even while we sleep).

The main cause of these depredations is clearly human overpopulation. The world I was born into sixty-eight years ago had two billion people in it. Now there are three times that many, all demanding full bellies, roofs over their heads, steady jobs, swift transportation (the classier the better), and, in the more affluent corners of the world at least, plenty of leisure time to trash what's left of the wild. America's parks and national forests are jam-packed as never before with campers and RVs, dirt bikes and four-wheelers; the amplified drone of hiphop reverberates from canyons and mountain peaks where once only the eagle screamed.

In our own small, specialized world of wingshooting, we've seen the development of certain omininous trends that speak forbodingly of the future. Wild gamebird populations have for the most part declined steadily and steeply throughout the twentieth century. The spread of suburban and exurban development, coupled with the filling of wetlands for yet another few million shopping malls, have destroyed great swatches of upland bird cover and paved over countless acres of waterfowl breeding grounds. Ruffed grouse populations rise and fall on a seven- to ten-year cycle, but the highs over the past half century have sunk to the point where they equal the lows of earlier cycles. Woodcock numbers continue to decline by 5 percent a year. Wild bobwhite quail are in ever-shorter supply throughout the South. America's two subspecies of prairie chicken (*Tympanuchus cupido*), which were so abundant only a century ago that they were hunted for the market, are now extinct through much of their former range east of the Mississippi, and in short supply even where huntable populations still hang on. Mourning doves, ducks, and migratory Canada geese on the Atlantic Flyway are all declining. Though the Canada goose is in trouble, its cousin the snow goose is undergoing a ruinous population explosion—ruinous for the wetlands and fields these "flying rats" feed in, since they rip out plants by the roots, and their overabundant, nitrate-rich droppings often burn the soil, leaving long-term devastation in their migratory wake. About the only bright spot in the picture is the comeback of the wild turkey. But the turkey is not a bird one normally shoots on the wing, so for the ardent shotgunner its resurgence is no boon to speak of.

Half a century ago, when I was cutting my bird-hunting teeth on the prairies of the Middle West, you rarely saw a

POSTED sign. Big hunks of grassland and woodlot were still open to anyone who felt the urge to wander them, with or without a gun. Even more surprising, in retrospect, is the fact that no one looked askance at a gun-toting man or boy dressed in rough clothes, even when he was riding a streetcar to the end of the line where the good gunning began. Today the very sight of a gun, even an elegant, twenty-thousand-dollar English double, is enough to make most of our fellow citizens freak out and grab for their cell phones to call the cops. "Maniac on the loose! Heading for the local school-yard!"

The enclosure of common lands (i.e., the posting of America) compelled us through the last decades of the second millennium to rely more and more on "shooting preserves" to find our sport. Most of these private-club-like game parks are pleasant enough places, where we can talk the talk with our fellow sportsmen, work our dogs on abundant gamebirds, shoot clays or pheasants or quail till our shoulders ache and our hearts are content (or at least until our checkbooks squeal for mercy, and we howl for another single-malt Scotch, please—no ice). But believe me, pardner, it ain't the same as shooting wild.

Pen-raised birds, no matter how thoroughly they've been exercised, don't fly with the same strength and canniness as wild birds. They've lived their brief lives, cozzened and un-culled, in the security of wire cages, been fed by timetable, not had to wander through real-life weather and a world teeming with bird-hungry predators just to get a drink of water. Most of them have never even lived through a winter. Even the best-conditioned ringneck in Christendom is going to feel groggy after having been rocked to sleep by the keeper, and waking up under the bulging eyes and wet, twitching nostrils of good old Spot the Setter isn't going to help matters. When he finally takes to the air he's going to fly high, straight, and fatally, flailingly slow—easy pickings. Too easy.

Pen-raised gamebirds are to wingshooting what hatchery trout are to fly fishing—a pale, tasteless imitation of the real thing. In short, bad news.

Well, that's a pretty bleak picture of the future. What can we do to make it brighter? We can fight for the retention and wise use of public lands, we can manage our own land for better propagation of wild bird populations and urge our neighbors to do likewise, we can support the Federal Conservation Reserve Program, which pays farmers for land left fallow and thus capable of supporting wildlife, we can join gamebird-specific organizations like the Ruffed Grouse Society, Pheasants Forever, and Ducks Unlimited both to get information on all these fronts and help their researchers to gain more information pertinent to the battle. Most importantly of all, we can combat the ugly image of the slob hunter by behaving responsibly afield. After all, we're gentlemen, aren't we?

Or else we can move to Montana.

THE BIONIC GUNNER

What's the single most important element in the upland bird-hunting equation? Some might argue in favor of gun fit, others a keen-nosed, well-trained dog, while yet a third good case could be made for sheer stamina. (As Frank Woolner said in his excellent 1970 book *Grouse and Grouse Hunting:* "Guns don't kill grouse. Legs kill 'em.")

After more than half a century in pursuit of upland birds, I've come to a different conclusion. To my mind, what kills more grouse, woodcock, pheasants, quail, or doves than any of the above is good eyesight. Think about it. Let's say you've pounded the hilly coverts all afternoon, your dog has locked up on a solid, certain grouse point, and you're sure from a thousand previously successful shots that your gun fits you like a sweaty T-shirt. The bird explodes from the aspen whips, hell-bent for heavy, leafy cover. You have only an instant to focus on it, mount the gun, and snap off your shot. Unless you have the bird solidly fixed along the swinging plane of your gun's sighting rib, you're going to miss.

For most of my life I've been blessed with good eyesight. When I was a kid, my eyes tested not at a mere 20/20, but 20/10—good enough to qualify me for a career as a navy jet jockey, if I'd wanted it. I opted instead for three years of sea duty as a line officer in amphibs and minesweepers, and once on a morning watch in the mid-Pacific managed to astound our ship's combat information center by spotting the topmast of an approaching freighter when it first peeked over the horizon, eighteen miles away—long before radar could pick it up. "Old Eagle Eye," my wife and kids and shipmates used to call me.

Then in 1974 when I turned forty, I began to notice that book publishers had suddenly begun printing their offerings in blurry type. It could be read only if I held the tome at a greater-than-normal distance from my eyes—first a foot and half away from me, than later at full arm's length. One night my wife, noticing my bizarre reading posture, remarked: "Pretty soon you'd better learn how to turn the pages with your toes. Either that or go the eye doctor."

I went, and learned that I was suffering from presbyopia, which my dictionary defines as "the inability of the eye to focus sharply on nearby objects, resulting from hardening of the crystalline lens with advancing age." To add insult to injury, the word stems from the Greek *presbus*, which means "old man." In short, I was farsighted. But the problem was easily solved, at first with the use of then highly stylish "granny glasses" for reading, later by wearing soft contact lenses. But as the years wore along, my natural lenses got harder and harder, even as other parts of my anatomy got softer and softer, and soon I was wearing bifocals. (Simultaneously, as the hair on my

head grew thinner, great luxuriant thickets of it sprouted from
my ears and nostrils—nature's misguided notion of compensa-
tion, I guess.) I started seeing the eye doctor every year or two
for a routine adjustment of my prescription.

Thus, when I went for a long-overdue visit last June, ex-
pecting no more trouble than coughing up another huge wad
of cash for new pair of glasses, imagine my horror when the
good doctor looked up from behind his gleaming, space-age
Thingamajig and said: "You've got a cataract forming in
your right eye." Though I'd been having difficulty driving
at night, when the glare of approaching headlights created
a confusing halo effect even on low beam, I really hadn't
noticed any other problems with my vision that glasses
couldn't correct. That was probably because my dominant
eye is the left one. I shoot off the left shoulder, and checking
back through my gunning journals I found that my "batting
average" had actually improved over the past few years—
from about 55 percent for every bird shot at in 1993 to 62 percent in 1998. But once the diagnosis had been made, I became
acutely aware of other subtle changes. My depth perception
was minimal, and even with my glasses on, while holding a
book at arm's length I could not read even large print with
my left eye closed.

The ophthalmologist recommended surgery to remove
the cataract. Ah, laser surgery, I thought, a high-tech piece of
cake! I was wrong. No cataract surgery is performed with
lasers, which are only used for other, less drastic corrective
procedures.

To remove a cataract, the surgeon cuts a tiny incision in the
side of the anesthetized eyeball, penetrates to the base of
the pupil, breaks up the crystallized natural lens, "vacuums"
the pieces out, and inserts in its place a rolled-up IOD (a
plastic "intraocular device," or artificial lens) equipped with
tiny feet that, once the IOD unrolls, lock into the eye and se-
cure it in the proper position. No stitches are needed to patch

up the surgical channel. For a week or ten days after the surgery, the patient must take eyedrops to prevent infection, refrain from lifting heavy objects, and scrupulously avoid shocks to the head or upper body that might displace the IOD. That would mean no shooting for at least a week or two after the operation.

I decided to schedule it for November, after the woodcock season in Vermont had closed, and just before the state's sixteen-day deer season opened. That way I could get in five or six weeks of shooting before having to hang up my gun. I rarely hunt birds during deer season anyway, not wanting to risk my dogs to that invading army of wild-eyed Rambos who increasingly, I've found, shoot first at any sound or movement in the woods and look for horns only afterward. By the time deer season ended and my eye was healed, I would have the whole month of December to hunt grouse and see if my shooting was any better.

On a sunny, crisp November afternoon, not without great trepidation I must confess, I presented myself at the Cataract and Laser Center in North Adams, Massachusetts, and submitted to the procedure. It was like an assembly line. The waiting room was jam-packed. It's not unusual for an ophthalmologist to perform a dozen or fifteen cataract surgeries in the course of a single day. I and a small group of other patients were shrouded in surgical gowns and little shower caps, trotted into a prep room, and dosed for an hour with about two hundred various eyedrops to both numb our eyeballs and dilate our pupils—at the end, my right pupil was almost the size of the entire iris, only a tiny rim of which could yet be seen.

When my turn came, I was whisked into the OR, laid out on a table, hooked up to an anesthetic drip, told to "watch the bright light" (by this time, all lights were brighter than any I'd ever seen before), and a great gleaming machine descended upon me like the proverbial Juggernaut. My doctor, masked to unidentifiability, leaned over and went to work. I felt a slight pressure on the right side of my eyeball, then noticed a shift in the light as he broke up the lens. An instant later, it felt, the light shifted back again to the way it had been. "Okay," the doctor said. "It's done. You're outta here."

What? The whole damned thing had taken, I later figured, a little under twenty minutes. It took all the rest of that day and part of the next for my dilated right pupil to return to its normal dimensions, but apart from the inconvenience of wearing sunglasses even at midnight, there was no strain, no pain.

The following afternoon I went to the eye doctor again for him to check the results. "Your right eye is now 20/20," he told me after completing his tests.

And indeed it was. Suddenly I could see again like Old Eagle Eye. Nowadays I wear a soft contact lens in my left (presbyopic) eye and nothing in the bionic one. Oh sure, I still need granny glasses to read, but that's no problem. What's most important is that my shooting has indeed improved. In October, before surgery, I was hitting 60 percent of the birds I shot at. During December, with my bionic eye in full play, I hit three out of every four grouse that flushed within range.

I'm eagerly awaiting the development of a cataract in my left eye. Who knows; maybe after another dose of surgery I'll be shooting 100 percent!

THE BIG ONE ONE

I've said it before and I'll say it again: It's just not fair!

Today is my great, good gundog Jake's eleventh birthday. It seems only yesterday that I brought him home from his birthplace in Zeeland, Michigan, a fat, clumsy little yellow Lab puppy who looked more like a butterball than a prospective hunter. He had everything to learn and a whole sprawling world of gamebirds ahead of him.

I'd gotten him then—in the fall of 1989— because my dog of the moment, a superb black Lab named Luke, had himself just turned eleven and I knew I couldn't count on more than another season or two of hunting him. My plan was to have Luke help me train the new pup, and he did: by example. On Jake's very first outing, the afternoon of our return to my home in Vermont after thirteen hundred miles of nonstop driving from Michigan, he stumbled along with us on his big-pawed legs, dragging his fat belly over downed tree trunks and through mucky swales as the older dog located, flushed, then retrieved a woodcock from a favorite covert of ours behind the house. At that magical moment, a light went on in Jake's eyes that has yet to dim, even though he's now the human equivalent of a very senior citizen.

Three weeks after that initial exposure to what it's all about, Jake found, flushed, and tried to retrieve his own bird, another woodcock. The old black Lab was having none of it, however. Outraged at the puppy's effontery, Luke insisted on fetching the bird himself. But all the while the puppy was learning valuable lessons from Luke: how to quarter ahead of the gun, read the wind with his nose, check every possible tuft of cover for a tight-lying grouse or woodcock, hold at the flush, watch the flight of the bird and its fall when I was lucky enough to hit it. He learned to mark the bird down and, later that season when Luke deigned to permit it, how to pick one up with a tender mouth so as not to ruffle so much as a single feather. One trait of Luke's that he never adopted, though, was the sneer of utter contempt the black Lab threw at me when I missed an easy shot. For that I'm grateful.

Two years later, Luke passed on to the Great Grouse Covert in the Sky and Jake became my Number One Dog. He's fulfilled the role to perfection. Though he's never matched the black Lab's uncanny ability to flush birds back over my gun, he's been much better than Luke on ducks and geese. A powerful swimmer who brooks no nonsense even from wounded Canada ganders that fight back, Jake once fetched twenty-five ducks in a row from an icy patch of water on the Chesapeake Bay where the waves wore white-caps and the crosscurrents spun like a whirlpool. Ice doesn't faze him: He eats his way through it. Mud? He loves it, sometimes returning from a morning on the duck marsh looking more like a Dove bar than a dog. On the evidence of my gunning diary, Jake has been a more steadfast retriever on upland birds as well. I don't believe he's ever lost a grouse, woodcock, quail, or pheasant that I've hit. A number of times, when I'm sure I've missed a shot, he's insisted on a thorough search despite my orders to "Hunt on!" and returned a few minutes later, sometimes from as far as a hundred yards away, with a wing-tipped grouse or woodcock in his mouth, and a twinkle in his eyes that says, "I told you so!" I quickly learned to trust his judgment.

When Jake was three years old I wrote a couple of books about his upbringing and training. *Upland Passage: A Field Dog's Education* was the adult version, with lots of hunting and Labrador retriever history in it. *Jake: A Labrador Puppy at Work and at Play* was for children aged eight and up. Many people fell in love with Jake, and I was soon deluged with calls from local mom-and-pop breeders who wanted him to stand stud. I'd never gone that route before with one of my dogs, but I felt an obligation in this case. All those kids out there who wanted Jake look-alikes . . .

What the hell, I figured, Jake might enjoy an off-season hobby.

I vetted the prospective mothers carefully, insisting on certification of good eyes and sound hips, the works. I checked out the breeders as well and made liaisons only with people I was sure of. As a result he sired more than a hundred first-rate pups. His biggest litter was twelve. All of them ended up in good homes. Many of Jake's offspring live in my neck of the woods, and they're immediately identifiable as his progeny. The same big, anvil-shaped heads, wide, warm, intelligent eyes, long legs, heavy shoulders, and deep chests. The same sweet dispositions. My young friend and occasional hunting buddy Todd Seebohm, the grandson of our neighbor down the road, has one of Jake's sons, whom he chose to name Luke, in honor of Jake's mentor. Luke the Younger is a testament to his daddy's blood lines. He not only retrieves like a champion for Todd, but he insists on helping Todd's grandmother, Ruth Moore, bring in the mail and even fetches logs from the woodpile behind the house when the family stove gets hungry.

So now Jake's reached The Big One One, and again I'm faced with the hard, ugly fact of mortality. "If life were fair," I wrote at the outset of *Upland Passage*, "hunters and their gundogs would have identical lifespans—learning, peaking, and declining together, step for step, one man, one dog hunting along on a trail toward that Great Grouse Covert in the Sky." It doesn't work out that way. When I got Jake, I was fifty-five years old. I'd always lived a rough life, taking lots of chances in many rough places, and figured—maybe even hoped— that I'd shuffle off this mortal coil before he would. But now I'm sixty-six and still kicking. In dog years he's seventy-seven. His muzzle has gone bone white, he's getting deaf (should I have insisted that he wear ear protection during the hunting season?—No way!), and he's slightly arthritic in his left foreleg. After a strenuous workout in hot, humid weather, his breath comes in short pants. But then again, so does mine these days. And at least he still has all his hair, which is more than I can say. We're both slowing down and there's nothing we can do about it. Time calls the shots from here on out—"That old bald cheater, Time," as Ben Jonson so aptly described it.

Jake's good for another couple of seasons, maybe more, but I'm reluctantly beginning to think of acquiring a replacement, just as I did with Luke. It's painful.

I think back on all the good dogs I've hunted with through the years. Rusty and Belle, the wacky Irish setters of my boyhood; Peter, my first black Lab and the first gundog I ever trained from scratch; Max the German shorthair and Simba, the big, tough, deadly yellow Lab; Buck, a sweet black Lab who died too young when a friend (herself now dead) let him out one Sunday morning without my knowledge and he wandered onto a highway . . . I still can't think about Buck without cursing.

Then Luke, and now the best of them all, Jake.

Do I want to go through this heartache again? I've known men who gave up bird hunting when their favorite dogs died. Never before could I understand it. But now I'm beginning to. A dog, after all, is more than just another hunting tool. I'd much rather my guns wore out in a dozen years than my dogs. There's something wrong with a world where even a good pair of boots lasts longer than a great gundog.

On the other hand, maybe I'm just being a soppy sentimentalist. It would be nice to have a puppy around the place, despite all the fuss and training a new dog entails.

It *would* be worth it, wouldn't it?

We'll see how the season goes.

THE EVERLASTING LAB

. . . Pow! . . .

The grouse died in midair and plum-
meted earthward just over the ridge ahead
of us. But I didn't hear the usual satisfying
thump as its body hit the ground. Both the
dog and I were puzzled. When my black
Labrador, Luke, and I came up to where
we'd marked the bird's fall, I found out why.
The grouse had fallen into a thick patch of
multiflora rose—two hundred square feet of
thorny green hell. We could see it dangling
about two feet off the ground, stone dead
but hung up on the long, wicked spikes that
stud the wild rose from root to branch tip.
No way either of us could fetch it out of
there without losing at least a pint of blood.
Or so I thought.

Luke studied the problem. He circled the
copse—once, twice, and halfway around

223

again—then looked up at me as if to say, "Don't worry, Boss." I watched him pick his way through the thorns, stifling a yip when they raked his nose, ears, or underbelly. With infinite pains (in more ways than one) he finally, gently, extracted the bird and picked his way back to where I stood. Blood streaked his sides and muzzle, dripped from his torn ears, but when he laid the bird in my waiting hand he broke into a wide, proud, Labradorian grin. I never loved him, or his breed, more than at that moment.

Judging by registration figures, the Labrador retriever is far and away the most popular dog in America. Last year (A.D. 2000) the American Kennel Club showed 172,841 registered Labs leading its list of the top 148 breeds—more than twice as many as the runner-up golden retriever (66,300). By contrast, the German shorthaired pointer ranked twenty-fourth overall and third among gundog breeds, with 13,224, followed by springer and Brittany spaniels (10,918 and 9,230 respectively). The classic pointing breeds were far down the AKC list—English setters placed ninety-first in overall popularity with 684 registrations, and pointers one-hundredth with 521.

This raises an interesting question. Why would a dedicated upland bird hunter like myself prefer a Lab to the more surefooted pointing breeds? Wouldn't a more traditional dog such as an English setter or pointer, a German shorthair or a Brittany—actually the dog of choice in my part of New England—produce more birds for your gun?

Of course it would, but not the way I like to hunt them. I certainly admire the walking-on-eggs caution a good pointing dog exercises in its craft, its beeper allowing plenty of time for the shooter to get in position, but I'm not really out for a high body count. I much prefer the spontaneity of hunting behind a flushing dog. There's a kind of existential rhythm to pounding along fast behind your dog, seeing him get birdy, tail going spastic, then having him check back to make sure you're ready before he plunges in to flush the bird. It all happens so fast. The birds seem to materialize out of nothingness, already moving like feathered lightning, and are as quickly gone—or dead. Hunting behind a Lab you must learn to shoot like a quick-draw pistolero, from any position. You may not get as many shots or hit as many birds, but you never lose any wounded ones—not if you hunt with a Labrador.

The Labs I've hunted with over the years (five of them so far) have had a greater sense of dedication to the chase than any other breed I know. I can see many moods in a Labrador's eyes—seriousness, joy, anticipation, anxiety, gravity, sometimes even scorn or contempt, but most often love and its jolly twin, playfulness. Am I being anthropomorphic—attributing human emotions to a creature incapable of them? Perhaps—but then again, I'm an anthropoid.

Where did this paragon of dogdom come from? No one knows for certain, but as early as the sixteenth century a strong, black, sleek-coated, web-footed dog, perhaps the ancestral Labrador retriever, was already common to the West Country lowlands of Devonshire, where the principal means of livelihood was waterfowl hunting and fishing. Seamen from Devon must have brought these superb water dogs with them to the New World when they began fishing the Newfoundland banks in the early sixteenth century, if only to aid them in their fishing and in hunting the abundant game they found ashore.

British sportsmen in the early 1800s saw black dogs of the Lab's general description being used by commercial fishermen on the Avalon Peninsula around St. John's, Newfoundland, and recognized their potential as a hunting breed. The Avalon fishermen, who knew the breed as the St. John's dog or the Newfoundland water dog, took the dogs with them in their dories when they were working longlines. Fish sometimes came off the barbless hooks of the dropper lines as the main lines were pulled into the boat. These "water dogs" would leap overboard on command to fetch the escaping fish. They'd also swim out from a dory to pick up net floats and bring them back for hauling. Clearly this skill at working in frigid, storm-wild waters could be suited to a sport hunter's benefit.

By 1814, the appellation *Labrador* began to be used for the breed—Labrador being a part of the province of Newfoundland, and certainly its wildest, most game-rich region. Colonel Peter Hawker, England's premier gunning authority, called the Labrador dog "by far the best for every kind of shooting. . . . Their sense of smell is scarcely to be credited. Their discrimination of scent, in following a wounded pheasant through a whole covert full of game, or a pinioned wild fowl through a furze brake, or warren of rabbits, appears almost impossible. . . . For finding wounded game, of every description, there is not his equal in the canine race; and he is a *sine qua non* in the general pursuit of wildfowl."

Today's generic Lab may not be the top flushing dog in the business—the smaller springer spaniel probably holds that honor, if only because it can winkle out birds from closer, tighter cover. But as my game journals show, you'll never lose a bird when you're shooting over a Lab. When it comes to retrieving, not even a Chesapeake can match a Lab for smarts or biddability. I've never had to repeat a hunting lesson with any of my Labs—show it to him once and he'll remember it all his life.

But there was one hunting technique I never had to teach Luke, and to this day I can't figure out how he perfected it. In

our third season together, I began to notice that most of the
birds he flushed—grouse, pheasants, quail, or woodcock—
were flying straight at me. I was flustered at first, trying to
snap-shoot them as they exploded from the cover and
zoomed directly overhead. Needless to say, I missed most of
them. But then I learned to pivot at the flush and take the
birds going away—a lead-pipe cinch in most cases. The percentage of these flushes, though, seemed far higher than the
law of averages would dictate. I checked back through my
game journals and discovered that over the past two seasons
Luke had been putting close to 65 percent of the birds he
flushed straight over to me. I began watching him closely
when we were afield and saw that when he scented a bird in
cover, instead of working in directly toward it, he would circle out to one side or another, get the bird between himself
and me, then move in to put it up.

I knew I could never train a dog to do that. Where would
you start? Then came Jake, Luke's quick study. By the end of
that first season, wonder of wonders, Jake was beginning to
circle out from close-lying birds and flush them back in my
direction.

In his own right, through the years that followed, Jake
himself has taught other Labs to hunt in this gratifying
style—hell, he even taught my uncontrollable Jack Russell
bitch, Roz, to flush tight-holding woodcock straight back to
my waiting gun.

If I can keep this cycle going, dog after dog after dog, I
may well have created a perpetual hunting machine, but one
with a loving heart, a lightning-quick mind, and above all an
unconquerable soul: The Everlasting Lab.

Luke lives! And so will Jake, forevermore.

THE HUNTER IN MY HEART

In some strange way the birds we kill fly on forever. Perhaps it's the broken arc, the interrupted parabola, the high zig through the alders that never quite made it to zag—all those incompletions crying out to be consummated. But something there is that keeps them airborne if only in our hearts, their wings forever roaring at the base of our trigger fingers. The partridge that puffs to the shot string this morning at the edge of some frost-crisp apple orchard in the hills of Vermont is the selfsame bird—but totally different, of course—as the very first dove we ever knocked down, a lifetime ago, over a midwestern cornfield. And watched in disbelief the pale feathers spill from a saffron sky.

"Sometimes, drunk or dreaming, I see the world crisscrossed in a webwork of avian force fields, the flight paths of ghost birds winging on *out as if they'd never been hit. In the end, of course, they will weave our own rough winding sheets. . . ."*

When I wrote those words some years ago, for a sporting anthology called *Seasons of the Hunter,* I had no idea they'd come back to haunt me. I was trying to explain, perhaps excuse, the wingshooter's inner need for completion—the culminating kill—and his simultaneous regret at having snuffed out yet another bird's life. Joy and sorrow both in the same instant. It's a delicate psychological balance, but as with all things in life, easily upset.

For a number of years I've been caught up in an agonizing internal debate: Should I or should I not swear off killing woodcock? No bird has given me more pleasure, through a long, satisfying lifetime of bird hunting, than *Scolopax minor,* the plump, pint-sized, russet-clad, long-billed, bug-eyed solitary of the uplands. As Jorrocks, the rough-and-ready fox hunter who graced the works of the nineteenth-century English sporting writer Surtees, often said of wily Reynard and his kin, "I loves 'em, I loves 'em, I loves 'em . . . and I loves to kill 'em." For years I've shared that emotion, but lately it's been eroding, at least as it applies to woodcock. Now when I pick one up after a successful shot, cup its warm musky body in my palm, and watch those big dark eyes begin to glaze, I feel mostly sorrow. These wings will no longer whistle . . .

Though woodcock aren't yet in danger of extinction—U.S. Fish and Wildlife surveys indicate that licensed hunters each season bag nearly two million birds over the bird's migratory range, east from the Mississippi to the Atlantic, and from southern Canada to the Louisiana bamboo thickets hard by the Gulf of Mexico—they've been declining over the past dozen years or more at an annual rate of from 3 to 5 percent. Hawks, owls, coyotes, foxes, skunks, and house cats kill a whole lot more woodcock than even the best of wingshots, so human predation isn't a major reason for this steady, ongoing decline. What's doing it is loss of habitat. To thrive, woodcock need young successional forests dotted with brushy, overgrowing meadows, but we are allowing our woodlands to get too damned old—not just in New England, where I live, but throughout their entire range.

Whatever the statistics show, it should be clear to any bird hunter that woodcock are in serious trouble. My gunning journals show that over the years I've been killing three of every four woodcock I've fired at, a far higher percentage than I shoot on ruffed grouse. It's almost too easy, and that's certainly too many woodcock killed over the course of a season.

On the other hand, I love to walk the autumn woods behind my dogs in search of these birds. I love it when the dog makes game and noses into a thick patch of cover, his whole demeanor changed, intense now, more than intense—vibrant. Nostrils wide, eyes gleaming, tail erect, he probes the thorn whips and red and brown leaf-blanketed undergrowth. It's almost impossible to see an unmoving woodcock against the forest floor. It holds tighter than any other gamebird, sometimes not flushing until a dog's jaws, or a hunter's boot, are only inches from where it crouches.

I love the unexpectedness of the flush—even when I know it's coming, the flurried, thunderclap whistle of blurring wings still delights and surprises me. You never know which way a woodcock will fly. I've had them take off directly at my face, then reverse direction in a wingbeat to line out through a maze of head-high interlaced branches that you'd think wouldn't permit the passage of a sparrow. To hunter and bird alike, the adrenaline rush is instant, intense, and the neophyte gunner's instinct is to mount his shotgun and fire immediately, like a quick-draw artist in a western gunfight. But that's sheer folly. The shot pattern is still too tight at close range to allow much chance of a hit, and even if you did center the bird at so short a distance, five or ten yards, the still-clotted shot would tear it to bits, leaving only a mangled gobbet of bloody meat and feathers with a wing and perhaps the long-billed head still attached.

You kill woodcock to eat them, and to waste even one in the course of a season feels to me like a mortal sin.

You must wait until the bird is fifteen or twenty yards out before firing. By that time, it's dodging through the branches as twistily as a mourning dove, and gets harder to hit with each thrust of its wings. To connect on a long shot is a blessing.

Or is it? The more I've learned about woodcock and their ways over the years, the more I've grown to love them. Every thinking hunter feels a spasm of regret when he's killed what he came for, and perhaps the bird hunter feels it longer and more deeply than most.

Yes, it's rewarding to walk the woods for these birds, to enjoy the dog work, to take pride in one's knowledge of cover and skill with a shotgun, and God knows it's a delight to eat woodcock. But can all of this make up for having snuffed out the life of a bird one truly cherishes?

I can argue to myself that my love of hunting grows from an instinct, a million years of human evolution as a hunting animal. But I know that that's begging the issue. I no longer care to hunt big game—deer, elk, moose, and the like— though I did when I was younger. I've never had any desire to hunt bears or mountain lions. So why do I still hunt birds, particularly woodcock?

There's a truism among hunters that the older we get, the more remorse we feel about killing. That spasm of regret the young hunter feels at taking a game animal's life becomes, with age, first a nagging repugnance, and then finally an outright revulsion. It certainly seems to be true.

A dear friend of mine, a former game warden in Kenya who killed hundreds of elephants and buffalo in the course of his duties as a game control officer, and who later became one of the most successful safari outfitters in East Africa, now tells me that he regrets every animal he ever killed. He gets tears in his eyes when he speaks of them.

The popular explanation for this, of course, is that the closer we get to our own demise, the more abhorrent the idea of killing any fellow creature becomes to us.

I think it's more complicated than that, though. No clear-thinking man or woman today still believes that some Old Testament God created "lesser animals" for the exclusive pleasure and use of humankind. We've ceased to recognize a clear-cut dichotomy between humans and other creatures. We know now that we too are animals, and not necessarily the only ones with self-awareness. I'm not arguing that a creature as different from us as a six-ounce, pea-brained timberdoodle has a "soul." But woodcock do have a distinctive, unique essence, a collection of traits and modes of behavior, that I find downright charming. And though I also love to pursue them, flush them, shoot at them, cook them, and eat them, I love that essence more.

So here is my pledge to *Scolopax minor* and all his kind: I vow that beginning this season—the first of a new millennium—I will no longer raise my gun at you in anger, no matter how tough or tempting the shot. Grouse, quail, and pheasants, yes; doves, ducks, and geese, of course. Maybe even the odd English sparrow or starling or barn pigeon.

But woodcock, nevermore.

Of course, whether I can keep that promise on every flush remains to be seen. In the heat of action, men are likely to forget their best resolves and follow their instincts. And then again, even if I *can* control my trigger finger, maybe my dogs won't let me.

POSTSCRIPT

Now on to an confession I'd rather not make. On my third day afield during last fall's grouse and woodcock season, I hunted my friend Ed Carmel's covert. So far I had kept my vow. Not a single woodcock had fallen to my gun. But it was not a true test of steadfastness, because on the two previous days my dogs hadn't flushed any. Still, I knew they would on Ed's land. That sixty-five-acre parcel of sidehill alders, spring seeps, blackberry brambles, overgrown meadows, and abandoned but still productive apple trees always produces a bumper crop of both woodcock and grouse. It was an ideal day, sunny but crisp, not too hot for Jake and Roz to work at full vigor. Jake knows that covert like the bottom of his food bowl, and sure enough, on his first pass through a favorite patch of briers and saplings, two woodcock got up. My instincts, honed over more than half a century of upland shooting, took charge and I found myself swinging fast on an easy left-to-right passing shot, well within killing range. The instant before I hit the trigger, my willpower clicked in. I checked the swing and let the bird fly off unscathed.

It felt odd. Even as my sanctimonious superego was preening itself on adherence to my promise, something in my guts, or maybe my nerve ends, said this was all wrong. The hunter in my heart felt cheated. "Be a man," I told him silently, "a promise is a promise. Don't be greedy."

My host Ed Carmel, who doesn't hunt but loves to follow me and the dogs while we do, said he'd seen a grouse cross one of the trails he brush-hogs through the covert each fall.

The bird had crossed less than an hour earlier. We ambled on down the trail in that direction. Soon Jake's nose located the grouse in question and I saw it hop up into a small, leafless apple tree. Young birds will do that. Of course I wouldn't shoot it standing there motionless, but even when I yelled at it to fly, waved a free arm at it, and stamped the ground like a petulant teenager, it stayed put. I walked up, hoping to make it fly for a fair shot. The closer I came, the more clearly I could see that it was a young bird, a hen, not yet fully grown. We'd had a rainy spring and summer, and I suspect the grouse had a second hatch as they often do when their first eggs and chicks are killed off by wet, cold weather.

She was a beautiful little bird on a beautiful Sunday afternoon, the sunlight illuminating her eye like sparkling amber as she stared down at me. Jake and Roz were zooming around the apple tree where she perched, their noses to the ground—but still she wouldn't fly. I came up to within five feet of her, could have batted her with the muzzle of the gun if I'd reached far and fast enough. "Fly, bird, fly!" I yelled again. But it was no go.

"God, she's beautiful," Ed said beside me now. "I've never seen one this close before, not unless you'd killed it."

"I can't kill her," I said, "not having looked in her eye, even if she flies like a comet." I broke the gun and dangled it over my forearm. Then Jake, following our eyes, looked up and spotted her. Seeing the dog almost eyeball to eyeball, the grouse finally flushed. Rather than ducking immediately around and behind the tree trunk and winging on out like a corkscrew, as most treed grouse will, she flew straight down the trail, never varying her flight path an inch to either side. The easiest straightaway shot one could ever hope for, a lead-pipe cinch, a dead cert. But we watched her disappear, unshot at, and she took our blessings with her.

Again the hunter within protested, but not quite as loud as before. He had other plans . . .

"There'll be another bird," I said, both to Ed and to my inner self. We started back up the trail, then headed into thick brush along a stone wall, with fragrant apples rotting underfoot. Now Roz got into the act. She darted ahead into a patch of brush and I heard a bird flush. It was the distinctive piping whir of woodcock wings. The bird came out in a gray-brown long-winged long-billed blur.

Before I could even think, my gun was up, swinging, swinging through, and then going bang, and the woodcock tumbled, thumping dead on the ground among the rotting apples.

I picked up her up, warm and soft in my hand, blood bubbling from her long slender bill.

My vow had been broken, as I feared it might.

"In the heat of action, men are likely to forget their best resolves and follow their instincts . . ."

I killed no more woodcock that day. I had tried to live with a vow I suspected I could never keep. I'll try again to live up to it as the seasons progress, but I'll lapse from time to time, I'm sure. The hunter in my heart will have his way.

THE LAST HUNT

When Jake turned twelve last July, I decided the time had finally come to train a replacement, but this time a black Labrador, not just to alternate the color scheme but in hopes that the new dog would prove as exemplary in the field as my last black Lab, Luke. The breeder in Zeeland, Michigan, who had produced Jake for me fortunately had a newborn litter. I chose another male, whom I named Bart, as in Black Bart the California stagecoach robber. The puppy arrived at our door in late September. He was a piece of work all right, handsome, intelligent, and so black that he went invisible at night when my wife and I took him out for the last walk of the day. Jake and nine-year-old Roz were a bit put out at first at the arrival of this stranger on their hearthstone, but soon Jake adjusted to his presence. Roz still seemed aloof, though, and indeed she was off her feed. She was losing weight, and at first I attributed it to jealousy over the puppy's arrival. But the weight loss and lack of appetite continued, even after she learned to tolerate Bart, so we took her to the vet. There an ultrasound exmination revealed cancer in her pancreas. Pancreatic cancer moves fast . . .

OCTOBER 29, 2001

E-mail to my friend Tom Davis in Green Bay, Wisconsin:

Dear Tom,

It looks like my lovely little Jack Russell, Roz, only nine years old, has pancreatic cancer. Jack Russells normally live to fifteen at least, sometimes eighteen or even twenty years old. She's been a delight and a strange but wildly keen little bird dog, especially on woodcock. She won't eat, and I'm afraid I'll have to have her put down sometime soon. It will break my heart.

I'm just back from a two-hour hunt with Roz in her favorite woodcock cover. I kept thinking of it as her last hunt. That's why I wanted to take her alone today. But when we got in the truck, along with the gun, her bell collar, my shooting vest, boots, all the proper gear, she acted disturbed, kept looking around for something. What she wanted was Jake. It was our time-honored custom. I went in and got him, leaving the puppy at home, and we headed out. The first hour produced nothing, though the dogs worked their hearts out.

A beautiful fall afternoon, most of the leaves gone, temps in the low fifties, blue skies with racing white clouds but just a light westerly breeze on the ground. We were at the bottom of the cover, and turned for the truck. Just then Jake got birdy, moved into a hunk of puckerbrush, and up popped Mr. Woodcock. I could have sus-

pended my vow to spare these birds and killed him on the first rise. But this was Roz's hunt and I wanted it to be her flush. We marked the bird down, about seventy-five yards ahead of us.

We hunted back uphill, angling to the northeast, through dense briers and beggar's-lice, doghair aspen and maple whips, low old crooked black apple trees that had laid a floor of miniature bowling balls for us to walk over. I called Jake in to heel and hied Roz on ahead. She knows hand signals and followed my gesture into a thin stand of weeds. I could see her tail start to buzz and the bird got up, low, and I killed it with the first barrel. Jake broke away from me at the shot, but Roz got to the bird first. I called the Labrador back, and for the first time in her life Roz had the honor of the retrieve. A male woodcock as I'd surmised at the first flush. Then we went back to the truck and had a drink of water and a dog biscuit or two. They're quite tasty if you love your dogs as much as I do.

I hope it's not her last hunt, but if it was, it couldn't have gone better.

Best--Bob

Tom replied:

Hi Bob--

I'm honored that you chose to share the story of what may have been Roz's last hunt. I can see it all, and I can feel what was in your heart. What a lovely way to remember her.

I'm not sure how relevant it is, but you'll recall that shortly before Timothy McVeigh's execution there was a lot of media attention focused on who was to be allowed to witness it. My wife and I were talking about it, and she said, "I just don't think I could watch. Do you?" My short answer was "yes," and I explained that after holding my beloved dogs in my arms as they died, feeling the last rippling tremors ebb from their muscles, hearing the sigh as the final breath left their lungs . . . well, compared to that, I didn't think I'd have much of a problem watching that coldhearted son-of-a-bitch check out. "Collateral damage," indeed.

You're clearly making the most of the time you and Roz have left--which, of course, is all you can do.

Best regards,

Tom

Next day I replied:

Tom,

Thanks for your thoughtful message. Here's some good news for a change. We took Roz to the vet this morning, where she received a shot of some magical elixir that has given her back her appetite, and she is once again eating-- everything she can get her mouth around. The vet says she's feeling no pain from the cancer. I asked if it was time yet to put her down. The vet, a wonderful woman named Jean Ceglowski, looked shocked and said: "I'm not ready to do it yet. We'll keep her alive as long as we can keep her eating." Then she shook her head sadly. "Why do bad things always happen to the nicest dogs? I love this little girl . . ."

Best--Bob

But it was a short-lived hope.

NOVEMBER 5, 2001

A chill, grim, gray autumnal morning. Most of the fall color has blown, only a few yellow popple leaves flickering in the north wind. Up on the mountain, the red oaks glower.

An e-mail to close friends:

This is a very sad day for us. We had to put Roz down this morning. The pancreatic cancer moved into her liver. Last night she started shuddering and panting, her abdomen hot and distended. She couldn't even drink water. We gave her a Bufferin, then when that wore off about 1 a.m., a quarter of a codeine pill. We were up with her most of the night, took her to the vet at 8 a.m. It was time. She went peacefully in about two minutes. We're having her cremated and will spread her ashes in her favorite woodcock cover and hang her collar and hunting bell in a tall, tall tree.

Both Jake and the puppy have been very quiet and know there's a change. They, especially Jake, will miss her for a while. We'll miss her forever.

Louise and Bob

From John Holt, Livingston, Montana:

Bob,

I'm terribly sorry to hear about Roz. In my heart, your home in Vermont and Roz are one and the same. She had enough personality to fill even a 10,000-square-foot house, and was as good a dog as I've ever known. I can't think of what to say other than my heart goes out to both Louise and you . . .

I'll think of Roz as I walk along the Yellowstone this morning.

John

From Matt Mullins, Hebron, Indiana:

Dear Bob,

So sorry to hear about Roz. Something about a terrier just chews its way into your heart. I have been there, feeling the weight suddenly drop into your hands as the needle does its horrible work. Of all the broken bones, and sutures put in my hide, nothing hurts worse than that. When the time is right, a new puppy heals the hole in your heart without taking away the joy of what was.

Best--Matt

From Dan Gerber, Santa Ynez, California:

Dear Bob,

I'm so sorry about Roz. It's the kind of thing you and I have both been through so many times, and it never gets easier, though it's a vital part of our relentless training in life, and we have all those memories. As Rilke said, "but having been once, only once, it can never be cancelled." I came up with something a while back, thinking in that particular instance of my late wife Virginia and the thoughts and memories and love I still harbor for all the years we had together. "Love for the new is love for the old." I don't know if I came up with that or pulled it somewhere from memory. But it applies certainly with our dogs. My love for Jake's littermate, Willa, has been a continuation of the love I had for my first yellow Lab, Lily. In fact, I used to, and occasionally still do, call her Lilla--that abiding spirit through so many dog bodies. And I guess we too are abiding spirits through sucessions of bodies (beings). The energy carries on, finding new forms.

Love--Dan

And that's the end of it. Rest in peace, my darling . . .

POSTSCRIPT (FEBRUARY 5, 2002)

But of course there is no end to it. Memories of Roz flash through my head and my heart every day. Each time I drive down to the general store in town I recall the way she always rode standing up in the passenger seat, her front feet braced on the dashboard, muttering to herself with her ears cocked, on the lookout for something to yap at. If a squirrel or a chipmunk dashed across the road ahead of the truck, Roz went ballistic—"Lemme at 'em, lemme at 'em . . ." On wintry days like "this one, with snow on the ground and the temperature down below freezing, I remember our snowshoe hunts, Jake chuffing ahead of me to break trail, sniffing out grouse under the snow, and Roz following behind, struggling through drifts that sometimes buried her, burrowing through them like a giant mole until she was exhausted and I had to pick her up and carry her in my game pocket. Roz made a wonderful hot-water bottle in bed on cold winter nights like these, curled up warm between me and Louise, though sometimes she chose to do isometric exercises in the wee small hours, stretching out crosswise in the middle of the bed with her front paws in the small of my wife's back and her rear ones braced against my rump. Then she would push, and one—or sometimes both—of us would be pushed out of bed by a mighty mite that weighed no more than a full shopping bag.

It's now exactly three months since Rozzie's passing, yet still I dream of her every night: dark, sad dreams in which she is lost, long overdue at the back door; I blow the police whistle again and again, yet she doesn't come. I am suffused with sorrow, tears in my eyes, frustrated and forlorn. Then at last, far and faint, I hear her hunting bell tinkling in the distance. It comes closer, closer, and then I see her galloping fast through the field toward the house, legs going like tiny pistons, her ears flapping, she's grinning her wide Rozzie grin, and my heart bursts with joy. . . . Wish fulfillment, they call it.

And then I wake up, and she's still dead, and I miss her so that I can barely breath. Oh, Roz, my dear sweet Warrior Princess . . .

The Lord giveth, and the Lord taketh away.

STARTING ALL OVER AGAIN

I'd forgotten how much sweat and anxiety the training of a new gundog entails, but perhaps that's all for the better. Otherwise I might never have made the acquaintance of Kent Hollow Black Bart—a wonder-dog if ever there was one. As in, "I wonder if he'll ever catch on . . ."

My new Labrador retriever is a handsome young fellow, black as Satan and smart as the proverbial whip. But he definitely has a mind of his own. In fact, he's had it right from the instant he appeared on our doorstep. Due to the temporary disruption of air cargo flights following the cataclysmic events of 9/11, Bart's arrival was delayed by eleven days. Bart's breeders—Grace and Myron Morris—generously decided to drive him to my home in Vermont. Grace stayed home to tend the kennels and Myron undertook the odyssey. It took thirteen hours, door to door.

When Myron's diesel-fueled VW Beetle chugged into our driveway one afternoon at the end of September, Bart was nearly ten weeks old. The ideal time for a puppy to be weaned from the attentions of its mother and introduced to a new home is seven-and-a-half weeks, no more than eight at the outside. Some nitpickers say the ideal time is precisely forty-nine days. At this magic moment, the pup is balanced on a very delicate cusp between obedience and independence. If caught at the right time, the puppy is primed to transfer the bonds of love and respect that it has with its mother to whomever next takes it in hand. Let that transfer be delayed too long, though, and the pup will develop a stubbornness of mind and behavior that's very difficult, if not impossible, to overcome. Whatever the case, the pup won't be near as "biddable" as it would have been at forty-nine days on the dot. Or so say the experts.

No sooner had Bart been released from his traveling crate on that memorable afternoon than I called him over to me. He came at a joyful gallop—stumbling over his outsized paws, tail flailing, coal-black eyes alight with glee, his capacious mouth, bristling with needle-sharp milk teeth, grinning from ear to ear. It was just as if he knew me, knew that I would be the firm but kindly master of his fate from that instant onward . . .

Then he bit my hand.

"It's just a love bite," my wife explained, but still it drew blood. That was fine with Bart. He licked off the blood, grinned up at me, and waited for more to well from the wounds.

Oh well, I thought as I wrapped a handkerchief around my mangled mitt, at least he's a peppy puppy.

While Myron and my wife chatted about the journey, I took Bart out into the big field behind the house to let him

run the cobwebs of travel from his infantile system. He followed dutifully at my heels for about a hundred paces, as a
bonding puppy should, but then sprinted ahead—nostrils
flared and ears cocked, as if he were making game. Often
there are woodcock to be found in the brushy edges of the
field and for an instant my heart leaped with joy. He's
whiffed one—a God-given natural! And when Bart skidded
to a halt, locking up into a perfect if puppyish point, I nearly
swooned.

But it was not to be. What he'd pointed was a mound of
doggy-do deposited that morning by Jake. I'll spare you the
ensuing details, and the four-letter imprecations that accompanied them, but puppies are by nature coprophagous (look
it up if you don't know Greek). Ah well, I thought, when I'd
cuffed him away from this bounty and calmed myself down
a tad, the poor boy was just a mite peckish, as the Brits say.

It was too late for a proper hunt that afternoon, but the following morning—after accustoming the pup to the sound
of gunfire with a session at the foot-trap—I took Jake and
Bart up to a productive covert of mine. It was already prov-
ing a bumper season for ruffed grouse. The previous winter
had been mild, the spring dry, and there was food galore in
the woods—loads of apples, barberry, thornapples, beech
mast, acorns. There were grouse everywhere, many of them
naive birds-of-the-year. The coverts fairly reeked with hot,
fresh partridge scent, and the heavy dew of morning glistening from every sprig of puckerbrush only enhanced it.
For any right-minded dog, I reckoned, this would be like
walking into a pie factory just as the oven doors spring
open. My theory has always been that a puppy can learn
more from the example of an older dog than any man can
teach him, and this would be the perfect morning to prove
it. I'm sure Jake agreed. After all, he'd learned the skills of

his upland craft from the master, my old and unbeatable black Lab, Luke.

Within moments of leaving the truck, Jake got birdy, backhair lifting, tail slashing, nose high at first to catch body scent, scanning the air, then low to the ground as he neared his quarry. As always in this critical situation, he walked as if on eggshells. As always he checked back to see if I was in position. As always I nodded to him, "Yes," and he stepped in for the flush. A grouse roared out from under his nose, I shot, and the bird tumbled in a spray of iridescent feathers. "Fetch dead." Jake tore off for the retrieve. It felt good, as it always did—good day, good dog, good bird, and the great good relief when the teamwork plays out.

Bart had been standing beside me, watching all this with the air of a serious scholar. As Jake ran toward the fallen bird Bart's eyes lit up and he followed. He gets it! I thought. O joy! I'd witnessed this epiphany often before—a new pup learning the meaning of the game from the deed itself. The excitement of the scent, the careful steps of the approach, the sound of the flush, the climactic burst of flurried wings punctuated by the blast of the shotgun, all fear or doubt forgotten in the stumbling fall of the gamebird. On the instant, the pup learns the meaning of life: The Climactic Retrieve, which this thrilling prelude has made possible.

But Bart had other game in mind. As Jake carefully sniffed out and mouthed the fallen grouse, the pup kept running his own course, paying no heed to nuance or ritual. He lurched and gallumphed toward the nearest apple tree, where he smartly retrieved and devoured—a rotten Winesap, worms and all.

It was disappointing to say the least. Jake flushed half a dozen more birds that morning, grouse and woodcock, but Bart remained fixated on apples. And on the drive home, as if to emphasize the point, he regurgitated them all over the floor of his Vari Kennel. The future did not look promising.

Obedience training and hard work with the retrieving dummy over the next few weeks taught Bart the meaning of "Come" and "Sit/Stay," "Heel," "Fetch," and "Give." After the first few sessions I was sure that he knew what those commands meant. Sometimes he actually obeyed them! On other occasions, though, he'd get that wild, devilish glint in his eye and the only thing that could lure him back to his senses was the offer of a dog biscuit. But bribery does not a gundog make. Was this just puppy playfulness, or did some deep-seated, ineradicable obstinacy lie behind it? Or worse yet, a simple lack of interest where gamebirds were involved?

In the field, over the next three weeks, Bart showed some improvement. Instead of sticking to my heels he learned to follow his canine mentor, dogging Jake's every footstep, quartering with the older dog as he "frisked" the coverts for birds. But as yet Bart hadn't flushed even a woodcock on his own. In fact he ran just inches past a few birds that Jake later turned back to flush. At Bart's age, according to my shooting diary of 1989, Jake had already put up half a dozen wood-cock and four grouse by himself. And old, jealous Luke had actually allowed Jake to retrieve a few of them. At this rate, I was rapidly despairing of ever making a hunter out of Bart.

Then, out of the blue, came Bart's salvation. One Sunday morning my friend and occasional gunning partner Jeff Piper called to invite me on a walk-up hunt with him and his good buddy Bill Iovene at the Tinmouth Hunting Preserve. "Bring Bart along," Jeff said. "He might learn a thing or two. Planted pheasants are easy."

It was a bright, crisp morning at the height of the fall color season. Jeff and Bill had left their excellent German shorthairs in the kennels as we forged out into the first patch of pheasant cover: a long, wind-dried stand of field corn at the top of a ridge just south of the clubhouse. I walked the middle of the cornpiece, with Bill just ahead to my right and Jeff to the left. The plan was to call Bart back and forth between us as we proceeded through the corn, thus getting the pup to cover the entire swath. Somewhere along the way he was bound to flush a longtail.

It went as planned, but at first not as well as I'd hoped. We weren't ten yards into the cornpiece when a hen pheasant got up right under Bart's feet. He looked nonplussed, watching her go. She flew straight ahead for a few loud wingbeats, then curved to the right, rising against the hard blue sky well ahead of Bill Iovene. He deferred to my shot. I dropped her.

But Bart was still standing in place, grinning at the sky, Mr. Goofball. He gave no evidence of having seen or heard the pheasant fall. Then he sat down and busily scratched behind his ears.

We led Bart out to where the pheasant lay in the frost-glazed grass of the adjacent field. She was lying on her back, still kicking. Bart trotted up merrily—What new wonders do you guys have in store for me?—then shied away in horror at the sight of the pheasant's beak and claws. He leaped back from her, a clear three feet.

Oh no, I thought. *I've gotten myself a dog who's not afraid of guns—in fact he's gun blasé—but instead he's BIRD shy!*

I felt like weeping.

"Not to worry," Jeff said, picking up on my disappointment. "The bird's bigger than he is, after all. It fell from the sky like a dragon, at least as he sees it. Let's just show him it's not a threat."

He took the dead pheasant by the neck and twitched it away from Bart through the thawing grass, as if the bird were fleeing. *"Look, Bart!"* he said in a high, puppy-wooing voice. "She's *a-skeered* of you! She's trying to get away! *Get her, boy!* Grab her, *quick*, before she takes off!"

Bart was doubtful at first, but in a while he approached the pheasant. He sniffed her long and hard. He backed away a step or two, watching warily for any signs of life, then suddenly he shed his infantile fears. The rich, hot, primordial scent overwhelmed them. His eyes lit up, but with intelligence this time. He tore into her as he would a pound of raw steak . . .

Later that morning I killed another pheasant, a big, bright cockbird that fell stone dead to bounce on the frozen ground in a flurry of feathers. Without a moment's hesitation Bart ran out to retrieve it as if the bird were the Holy Grail. As he trotted back to me, dragging the pheasant by its neck, he was growling a low, satisfied growl, deep in his chest. From that morning on he's been death on any gamebird that runs, flies, or falls. He loves the hunt in all its rewarding fullness, be it for grouse or woodcock, pheasants or quail or ducks or chukars. All it took was patience. Mainly on my part, as I learned from Jeff Piper.

You've got to take your time with pups, especially those with a spark of the devil in their eyes.

Death in the Tangled Syntax: A Tale of Revenge

A SHORT STORY

A SWOLLEN, LOPSIDED Hunter's Moon slid down the glassine slope of the evening sky like a gobbet of pus from a suppurating wound. Below in the valley, a mournful Holstein tolled the knell of parting day. A coonhound yowled in reply. The short hairs rose involuntarily along the back of my neck and I could feel goose bumps hammering at the nap of my clammy, sweat-soaked Damart long johns: "Lemme out, lemme outta here!"

But I had a score to settle—with the Leader of the Pack.

I force-fed a fat brace of Federals into the gaping maw of my thorn-scarred Stevens Model 311 double and carefully aligned them so that the arched lettering on their bases matched perfectly side by side. "Double-O Buck." The 12-gauge shells glared back at me like the brassy eyes of an owl gone gaga. I knew I was stalling, putting off the moment of truth by pretending that this minor, meaningless detail meant something, but it was important to me that the shells lined up in the chambers with absolute perfection. Call it a quirk—hell, call me superstitious—but I knew I'd need all the luck I could muster this death-fraught October evening.

The gun snapped shut with the solid finality of a finely machined garbage can lid. I thumbed the safety forward, clenched two backup shells white-knuckle tight between numbed fingers cupped on the forend, and stepped into the thicket . . .

My childhood pal Buddy Wilkins was generally acknowledged the best woodsman in Hubley's Gore, if not the whole of New England. Until yesterday, that is. Over the years he'd killed bears and bobcats by the dozen, whitetails by the score. I'd hunted ducks and upland birds with him since we were in grade school and never seen him miss—not once! Not even on supersonic grouse in heavy cover. He'd long since stopped counting the elusive wild turkeys he'd blasted into Never-Never Land—huge, long-spurred, barrel-chested gobblers, each and every one, and none with a beard less than nine inches long. "Ayuh," Buddy used to say to the gang of envious hunters around the barrel stove in the Gore's general store, "I set myself a rule long ago. If a turkey-bird ain't got a beard as long as my pee-pee, he ain't worth the powder." Then Buddy would flash that nut-brown, fur-toothed grin of his and swagger out to his rust-gnawed pickup into the noonday sun, a giant, fire-feathered gobbler dangling from each Vibram-palmed paw.

The birds' bloody, shot-torn heads trailed eyeless in the dust.

The silence that inevitably followed was thicker than a yearlong mud season. You could hear the sound of grown men eating their livers in envy, their whining grumbles loud as rats on a good day at the dump. Finally someone would sigh and squirt a gobbet of snoose juice on the stove. "Ayuh," he'd moan when the sizzle died, "that Buddy, he's the cat's pajamas."

But then the Pack got to Buddy and stripped those PJs off of him. In more ways than one.

The Pack . . . Yeah. We had coydogs the size of dire wolves in the Gore back then—bold, canny canines that had filtered down from Canada over the years, picking up useful increments from the gene pool of the wolves and domestic dogs they met and mated with along the way. Huskies and Landseers gave them their size, Airedales their feistiness, Labradors their smarts, and pit bulls their wicked tenacity. Lambs were just crumbs on the breadboard to those supercanine predators, whole sheep mere hors d'oeuvres. Clint Meecham, a struggling drover of woollies, once saw a coydog run down a full-grown Corriedale ram in a sidehill pasture on Abednego Mountain—at high noon on a sunny day at that—then grab it by the back and carry it kicking and bleating, like a woolly retrieving dummy with sound effects, crosswise in its jaws up to the slavering Pack waiting in the woods. Clint took a poke at the marauder with the Ought-Six he always keeps racked on the rear window of his pickup, but the long-fanged sheep killer must have had his eye on the gun. He sidestepped just as Clint fired, yawned, cocked his leg at the dust kicked up by the bullet, and pissed on it. Then trotted off disdainfully . . . gone before Clint could even rework his bolt.

The Pack quickly developed a taste for dairy cattle, the more highly bred the better. Gentleman farmers began finding their best Swiss Browns lying gutless in the pastures of a morning, udders ripped by relentless jaws, ragged bloody potholes where the rump roasts would have been, tenderloins stripped as neatly as if by a master chef's Thiers-Issard high-carbon filet knife to feed the always-hungry bellies of the Pack. It didn't help to stable the herds at night, either. The Pack took to killing in broad daylight, driving the cows into a fence corner, hamstringing half a dozen of the juiciest heifers, then gobbling as much still-living meat as they could before the angry farmhands, aroused by the plaintive bellowing of the herd, could arrive with their rifles.

Bill Morton, the town's most successful dairy farmer, hired out-of-work townsmen to keep watch over his herd, but the Pack faked them out of their barn boots. The Pack's leader, a massive one-eyed brute with a distinctive white blaze in his lionlike ruff, sent part of his gang to growling and slinking just barely into sight at the far end of the pasture. When the hapless gunner's attention was diverted, he and the rest of the Pack would kill a cow or three, eat their innards out, and drag the lightened carcasses back into the woods for the main course.

None of the townies cared to go in there after them.

"You jist oughta hear them at their dinner," said Curly Brickhouse, one of the guards. "It makes the sawmill sound like naptime in kindygarden. I ain't goin' up against that 'Blaze' dog. Not at close range, I ain't." Curly, a redhead who stood six-six without his shoepacs and had shoulders as wide as a John Deere's rear wheels, did not know the meaning of fear. Or if he did, would spell it "f e r e." "Maybe one a you fellers wants to try it?"

The men around the stove avoided his eyes. A few spat between their boots.

"Mebbe we oughta contact Fishengame," Herbie Clutterbuck said timidly.

The others merely glowered at him. Fish and Game is a dirty name in backcountry New England. Asking a game warden's help would be tantamount to dealing with the enemy, or worse—like inviting the late Cleveland Amory to a deer jacking party. Word would get out and every flatland flower-sniffer from Boston to Manhattan would be on the Gore's case, whining and sniveling about "animal rights" and the gentle, misunderstood nature of "God's Dog."

No, the town would have to eradicate the coydog threat on its own.

The selectmen hired Buddy Wilkins to do it. His acceptance of the assignment (at five dollars an hour—a buck and a quarter over minimum wage at the time, and thus the highest salary in town) was the worst mistake of Buddy's life. Indeed, it was the end of it.

At first Buddy had spurned the job. "I ain't no farmer," he told the Town Fathers. "Them coydogs ain't eatin' my cows 'cause I ain't got none. I make my livin' with my gun, my traps, and my fish pole. Old Blaze ain't no skin off my butt. In fact I kinda like hearin' that Pack yippin' and a whoopin' up there in the hills of a midnight—they sing me to sleep nicer'n my momma ever did."

But then the Pack hit Buddy where he lived. Buddy had killed a beautiful ten-point buck early in bow season, a deer that dressed out at a hundred and ninety-three pounds on the town clerk's scales. After parading the buck through town in his pickup and accepting the grudging compliments of his neighbors (and the hot-eyed approbation of the Gore's few unmarried beauties along with a flutter or two from the eyelashes of some married ones), Bud hung the buck head-down from the rope-worn meat pole outside his shack at the edge of town. From a distance the shack looked like a ghostly, outsized brier patch, with all the weather-bleached deer racks nailed to its walls. Then he kicked back in a lawn chair with a platter of thin-sliced fast-fried deer liver (heavy on the melted lard), a raw yellow onion, and a square-faced jug of Old Duke red to admire his first legal deer of the season.

That night, as Buddy snored blissfully in a haze of wine vapors, dreaming of deer the size of Irish elk, Blaze and his mates unhitched the buck from the meat pole and ate it on the front stoop. When Buddy awoke at first light, eyes blurred and head throbbing with Old Duke's revenge, he stepped out of the cabin to "water the weed patch"—and sprawled head-first in the dew. The thing that tripped him was the buck's well-chewed head. The rack and its tines, thick ivory-tipped towers just yesterday, had been splintered to toothpicks by the coydogs' jaws, and one of the buck's clouded eyes dangled dolefully from its socket. Buddy stumbled to his feet, his own optics redder even than they had been on awakening.

"Blaze!" he yelled up at the forested hills. "You're doomed!"

An echo bounced back to him ... *Doomed, Doomed, Doomed* ...

Somewhere up on the mountain, a coydog chuckled.

Doomed indeed. From the evidence I was able to gather after the Gore's selectmen called me onto the case, Buddy Wilkins spent the last days of his career in a whirlwind of vengeful activity, using every iota of his hunting skills to track down and destroy the hated Pack. He pounded the hills like a bipedal pile driver, scouting for sign. Once he found it, he shifted gear into a pantherine prowl, tracking the crafty devildogs with the alertness of a Bronco Apache who'd smelled paleface scalps. He slept on the trail, rolled in a threadbare Hudson's Bay four-point blanket to fend off the frost of star-bright autumn nights; he snared what he needed to eat—snowshoe rabbits, partridges, now and then a wild turkey, more often a red squirrel or a blue jay—fearful that a shot from his deadly .22/250 Ruger would scare off the Pack. He built his few cookfires small, of wind-dried hickory slivers pared from deadfalls. He drank his water ice cold, unboiled, from the high-country brooks, heedless of the risk of giardiasis despite abundant sign of the bank beaver whose droppings vector the disease. He slept very little. Whenever he heard the Pack singing, he moved on them.

Yet in three full weeks of peerless, nonstop woodcraft that would have done an African Wanderobo tracker proud, only once did he come in sight of the Pack. And only once did he shoot.

It was the last shot of his life.

The crack of the .22/250 came clearly to me, carried sharp and crisp through the cold, dense night air and the frost-rimmed glass of my new double-pane Andersen rear window where I'd been sitting up late, reading the latest Peter Hathaway Capstick classic, appropriately titled *Death in the Silent Places.* At first I thought it was a tree branch cracked by the cold. In the dead of winter here, when the mercury hits twenty below, whole trees have been known to explode, and the hollow where I live sounds like an artillery duel in the Hürtgen Forest. But it wasn't that cold yet, a scant twenty-three above on my barn thermometer.

Then I heard a far, faint scream.

Buddy!

I ran out of the house and stared helplessly up into the mountains. There it came again—a high-pitched, almost womanish scream (but deeper, more agonized than a bob-cat's shriek), a scream that led off into throat-clogged, liquid sobs and gagging. It lasted only a minute, but to me, down below, listening and trying to zero in on the location, it felt more like an hour.

Finally there was silence. But not for long.

A howl of coydog triumph rang out through the ice-bound woods, joyous over the dark, brooding hills and shadowy hollows, joined slowly, tentatively at first by other, higher-pitched yips and whoops until the entire Pack was singing a canine chorus of "We Are the World"!

It took me nearly an hour to get up there, pounding hard through the doghair aspen and willow brakes of the lower slopes, splashing knee-deep through ice-edged brooks, then up through the big, gray, smooth-barked beeches that loomed against the stars like grasping monsters. Briers ripped my flesh and I could feel blood trickling down my face, slow and thick as Grade B maple syrup hot from the sugaring pan. And the sting of cold sweat in the cuts.

I smelled him before I saw him—a stench blended of fresh blood, raw meat, fang-torn intestines, and the cold, despairing stink of doom. It was enough to gag a dump rat. They'd eaten all of him but his gallbladder, a big toe, his nylon bootlaces, and the long johns he'd worn for the past two weeks. I found his fleshless skull ten yards away in the weeds. Only Buddy's eyes stared up at me, puzzled, baby blue, asking Why? Why? Why *Me*?

Nearby was his rifle, its stock and forearm scarred by powerful jaws full of teeth the diameter of .375 H & H Magnums. Buddy Wilkins was dead all right. I scraped what was left of him into a Two-Ply Hefty Steel-Sak and headed back down the mountain. Dawn was just breaking when I reached the general store.

I slopped Buddy's mortal remains onto a ground cloth tidily spread on the town constable's driveway. After he and the village dads had retched their guts out, they asked me to take over the hunt. "We know you've purty well given up huntin', Pete," the senior selectman said, scuffing his highcuts in the gravel, "but you was as good or better than Buddy in his day. And you was closer to the late lamented than any of the rest of us."

I still hunted grouse and woodcock, though thanks to the Pack there were very few of them in the woods anymore, but it was true that I'd given up deer hunting. I was disgusted by the degradation of the sport: road hunters chugging the town's backroads like a rush-hour traffic jam on the Long Island Expressway, potbellied geezers roaring through the woods on fat-tired four-wheelers. "Brush shots" and "sound shots" had made the woods about as safe as H-Hour on Omaha Beach. The sight of four-inch spikes, sixty-pound button bucks, and, God help us, prime young does draped proudly over the roof racks of out-of-state Tahoes and Range

Rovers had gotten me grinding my teeth like a gutshot warthog.

But Buddy had been . . . well, my buddy.

I accepted the assignment. I would hunt down the Pack not only to avenge Buddy's death, but to spare the lives of those countless deer, household pets, dairy cattle, and especially the gamebirds the coydogs would certainly kill without quarter in the years to come.

Or maybe the Pack would kill me . . .

The first order of business was to assemble my gear. When you're hunting game that runs both ways, you can't be too careful. Taking a cue from the "leopard katundu" Mr. Capstick describes in his masterful memoir *Death in the Long Grass*, I loaded a backpack with the scuffed old racing leathers I'd worn in my motocross days, dug up a wide, thick, spike-studded dog collar that belonged to my late lamented Doberman, Mad Max, threw in a half gallon of hydroperoxide for disinfecting any razor nicks I might incur on my delicate epidermis and a quart of Old Overshoes in the event of sudden toothache. I assembled an emergency medical kit containing a few heavy, curved, stainless-steel surgical needles and a hundred-yard spool of Johnson & Johnson Dentotape Waxed Ribbon Floss for mending any rips Old Blaze & Co. could inflict on my person. I wished I'd had a Kevlar jockstrap to throw in there: Judging from what they'd done to Buddy, these coydogs had touch of the honey badger in their makeup.

Now for the weapons. From the mess that had been my onetime playmate, and the location where I'd found it, I'd quickly deduced that the Pack caught Buddy unawares, while his head was down following their trail. They'd surrounded him, lying low in the briers that flanked the trail, then jumped him all at once from no more than six feet away. He'd gotten off only the one rushed shot—probably a nonfatal hit, since I'd found a clump of coydog hair bloody at the roots not far from the death scene—and he hadn't been able to reload. In fact, a live round was jammed at an angle, partway into the breech, the bolt handle up and moving forward when the coydogs stopped him forever. He'd clearly have been better off with a shotgun at that range, something short-barreled with an open choke, like my old Stevens double, the gun I'd creamed woodcock with since the age of twelve. I had a Remington 1100 and a classic Winchester Model 12 in my armory, but autoloaders and pumpguns can jam on you and I wasn't about to cut down the thirty-inch barrel of the priceless cornshucker, not even to raise the odds on my survival in a close fight. So the Stevens it was.

But maybe I ought to bring a rifle as well. Though Buddy hadn't made long-range contact with the Pack in two whole weeks of stalking them, that didn't mean I couldn't. He probably hadn't used varmint calls. Bud was a meat hunter, plain and simple, and if he couldn't chow down on what he killed, he wouldn't waste good bullets on it. I'm pretty proficient at calling in those predatory paramedics, though. House cats and stray dogs, skunks, foxes, and even hawks respond to my crippled bunny squeaks like yuppies to a Ralph Lauren outlet. I decided finally on my Mannlicher-Schoenauer 6.5 mm 1961-MCA carbine, a seven-and-three-quarter-pound nosepicker that kicked out its ninety-three-grain soft-point Spitzers at nearly four thousand feet per second and laid a lethal load of better than a ton on anything you aimed at up to a football field away. Hell, if W. D. M. "Karamojo" Bell could dump "jumbos" with it—African elephants, that is, in White Hunter jargon—I ought to be able to stop a few plume-tailed pooches, man-eaters though they might be. I'd carry the shotgun in hand and the Mannlicher slung, since the only chance I'd have to use the rifle would be if I spotted the Pack before it saw me. The last item I hung on my already creaking frame was a well-honed K-bar combat knife that my dad had used to disembowel a Nip major who'd had the temerity to charge at him with a samurai sword on Iwo nearly half a century ago. The Jap, he always said, was sushi before you could say "Banzai!"

I left the house shortly before noon and picked up the trail at the spot where the crows were cleaning up what I'd missed of Buddy. It was a sunny afternoon, crisp at about forty degrees, and the wind, thank God, was out of the northwest— the very direction the Pack had loped off in after their midnight snack. One of them indeed had been nicked by their victim's single shot. After a bit of judicious squinting, I found dime-sized drops of coydog blood, gone a lacquery reddish brown as it dried, glittering on the fallen leaves. The paw prints associated with the blood trail showed sharp and deep wherever the animal crossed bare mud. They measured nearly four inches long, almost double the size of a western coyote's.

This was either Blaze or the Hound of the Baskervilles.

For an hour, two hours, I followed the spoor, slowly, cautiously, tenderly as a bomb disposal expert defusing a Doomsday Machine. I walked on the outside edges of my Clark's Desert Boots—I'd chosen them for this stalk over my Gore-Tex-lined Russells because their soft soles would be quieter—adopting the silent stride of a Masarwa Bushman on the trail of a paunch-reamed pachyderm. Sweat dripped down my neck.

I stopped well short of the spot where the Pack's trail broke out of the woods into an overgrown meadow. An old stone wall, its upper boulders spilled loosely in the sun by a century of frost heaves, marked the edge of the field. I'd killed many a deer here over the years, lying in ambush along the wall until a suitable buck came out to munch frost-sweetened apples under the ancient Winesaps that studded the far edge of a long-forgotten orchard. I knew that the field rose sharply to my right, ending in a steep, broken tumulus of shale ledges. Bobcats sometimes sunned themselves up there on nippy fall days like this one. Why not coydogs?

The Leitz Trinovid 8x35's, their knobby leather covering worn smooth as the Whore of Babylon's pectorals by years of handling, came eagerly to my eyes. With the touch of a forefinger I tweaked their blur into gin-clear focus on the ledges. At first I saw nothing—just gray rock and wind-dried weeds swaying in the breeze. Then something twitched. And another something, gray-tan, fuzzy-edged, triangular, like the top of a furry Marconi-rig sail just peeking over the horizon, twitched a few inches away from the first. I peered closely. Sure enough, the tips of two coydog ears. Once I'd spotted the first pair, the rest were easy. The Pack was lying up on the ledges, digesting Buddy Wilkins. They were down in a crease behind the deepest ledge, out of the light northwesterly breeze, enjoying the heat of the weak October sun reflected down onto them by the rock wall behind them. I eased the Mannlicher off my back and wrapped the sling. Then I slid the camo-patterned backpack up onto the warm boulders of the fallen wall and snugged down behind it, to use it as a rest for the rifle. The range was pushing two hundred yards so I'd have to hold just under an inch high through the Redfield 2–10X post-and-crosshair variable.

No sweat.

The question was, how do I get them to stand up so I can zap them?

The answer: my trusty P. S. Olt Model Number T-20 Fox-Coyote Call, a seductive four and an eighth inches of brown and black hard rubber that had over the years lured more slavering, slit-eyed predators toward a free lunch of death than I could rightly remember—wily coyotes, funky foxes, even once (up in British Columbia) a coal-black hundred-and-sixty-pound timber wolf that I swear yipped "No fair!" when I punched his lights out with a .300 Weatherby Mag at nearly a quarter of a mile. I could play the siren song of a moribund bunny on that instrument like the late Dexter Gordon blowing "Body and Soul" on the tenor sax.

So I did. The ears perked up—five pairs of them, cocked and swiveling to locate the pitiful squeak that, to the Pack, must have sounded like the wheels of a dessert cart in a hundred-dollar-a-customer restaurant called Le Lapin Deliceuse. One of them stood up, a young coydog about the size of a full-grown Chesapeake. I squeaked again and three more rose to their feet, ears angling toward me, drool beginning to dribble in glistening strings from their ripsaw lips. Then the fifth one, a bitch that must have been the Pack's matriarch. But no sign of Blaze. Where was he—already out and away, sneaking belly-down under cover to circle around behind me? My muscles tensed with the voltaic jolt of sudden terror that sparked through me and I almost leaped to my feet, rifle in hand. But I controlled it. Nothing I could do about him right now. The first order of business was to wipe out the killers I could see.

I already had a round up the spout. Ladies first, I thought. I laid the post on her left eye—a pinpoint of black death frozen in amber—picked up the slack in the two-stage trigger, and touched off. At the break of the sear, I didn't even feel the kick of the 6.5x68 cartridge or hear the bullwhip crack of the bullet. Big Momma's head snapped up, leading her in a back flip that would have won a unanimous ten in the Coydog Olympics. Already I'd worked the bolt, barely sensing the wink of the brass as it spun sideways trailing a tendril of spicy blue smoke. I nailed two of the younger coydogs before they could jump, both through the shoulder, taking their lungs out in gouts of tissue that resembled Pink Panther fiberglass insulation. The other two were running now, bellies low to the ground, using every bush, every swale of the meadow to conceal themselves. But I swung with them, the rifle steady as the Midnight Special on a newly ballasted roadbed, and picked off the first one as he showed himself at thirty-five miles an hour just beyond an apple trunk. I gave him about half a coydog's lead and rolled him in a slurry of fur, earwax, bone, and bright brain tissue—

a perfect head shot. His brother slowed as he neared the still-kicking body, a fatal mistake that sent him crashing in flames like a Messerschmitt 109 in the Battle of Britain. Five for five in as many seconds. Only one round left—but this was no time for self-congratulation.

Where the heck was Blaze?

Just about on me was where.

I still don't know what it was that made me spin around—a scuffed leaf as he launched his Great Leap Forward? The crack of a twig? The scream of a nearby blue jay scared witless by the huge coydog's sudden materialization? But there he was, hurtling through the air straight at me not a yard away, huge and shaggy as a werewolf out of the Inferno, his jaws like a wide-open iron maiden spiked with ivory-hued stilettos that hadn't been purchased from Hoffritz. I swung the carbine as hard and fast as Barry Bonds coming around on a huge, fuzzy fastball. The muzzle took Blaze in the belly just as his fangs ripped into my forehead. I fired and smelled scorched hair, burned meat. My head smacked the boulders behind me and starshells exploded in my skull with the fiery finality of a George Plimpton fireworks extravaganza. The reek of something that wasn't quite Alpo filled my nostrils. I could feel the inexorable pressure of Blaze's jaws compressing my noggin like a giant nutcracker popping a rotten pecan. Everything went black as an NFL backfield . . .

By the time I dog-paddled my way to the shores of consciousness, the sun was nearly down. My head felt the size of a prizewinning Hubbard squash at the Iowa State Fair and my once-nifty L.L. Bean safari jacket bore a close resemblance to a croker sack stuffed with freshly ground steak tartare. Crows had gathered on the bare branches above me and were eyeing my leaky carcass like a bunch of outdoor writers at a buffet lunch. I grabbed a quick belt from the bottle of Old Overshoes, and when none of it leaked out of the holes in my throat I knew I would live. After slapping a few stitches into the worst of my many slashes, I grabbed the scattergun, loaded my pockets with Double-O shells, groaned my way into the racing leathers, buckled the spiked dog collar around my frazzled throat (better late than never), and set out in what remained of the light on my quest for vengeance. Despite my wounds, or perhaps because of them, I was madder than a taxpayer on the ides of April.

Blaze's blood trail had more curves to it than the *Sports Illustrated* swimsuit issue but I made good time, spurred along by rage and injured pride. I wasn't about to let this Pooch from the Pit of Hell get away with attempted murder. Not just my pride but that of every hunter who'd ever drawn a bead on dangerous game—from the earliest Australopithecus in Olduvai Gorge through Jim Corbett of Kumaon fame to J. H. Patterson who killed the infamous Man-Eaters of Tsavo to, well, Pete Capstick himself.

Perhaps an old Africa hand named Bob Foran had put it best in the title of his grim memoirs: It's all a matter of *Kill: Or Be Killed.*

I followed the tracks at what might be termed a coydog's trot, racing the dying of the light toward my quarry. Down through the long grass of the overgrown meadow, eyes peeled sharp for the first hint of movement. Into the dark, clawing reach of the ancient apple orchard. Across a brook where Blaze had paused for a long drink—sure sign that I'd gutshot him when he jumped me. The light fading all the time, leaking out of the day like the bloody water through Blaze's perforated belly. Then I saw ahead of me, as dense and dim as a remedial reading class for college football stars, the place where he'd gone to ground: a thicket of wild rose briers and thorn apple scrub more impenetrable than *Finnegan's Wake.* Blaze rose from the cover and stared at me, not ten feet away.

It looked like the end of the line, for one of us at least.

And then it happened.

Just as I raised the death-dealing tubes of my scattergun, I felt the first symptoms of the most dreaded disease an outdoor writer can contract.

Catachresis!

But don't let the dictionaries kid you. They define it as "1. a. Strained use of a word or phrase, as for rhetorical effect. b. A deliberately paradoxical effect. 2. The use of a wrong word in a context."

It's a hell of a lot worse than that.

My brain began to swell like the Goodyear blimp at a World Series game. My pulse raced faster than the opening lap of the Daytona 500. Ghetto blasters redlined in my ears like lunch hour on Sixth Avenue and the tap dance of my trigger finger would have put the legendary Mister Bojangles to shame. My eyesight faded like a Taiwan T-shirt in hot water. I could hear about as keenly as a cracked-out teenybopper at a Def Leppard concert. The taste of fear clogged my throat like the dregs of a copper refinery.

Blaze attacked with a snarl as vicious as Ken Starr facing Monica Lewinsky . . .

But not to worry—I had him covered like a prude at a nudist convention. The double load of chilled buckshot caught him square on the chest and he erupted to its impact like a teenager's pus-filled zit.

It took me a while to dig myself out of the slimy pile of mixed metaphors and overstressed similes, tangled synecdoches and jangled jargon that spilled from the ruptured guts of the late great predator in the course of his well-earned demise. But dig it I did. Then, with the trusty smoothbore cocked jauntily over one shoulder and the jug of Old Overshoes gurgling merrily in my other hand, I sauntered down the mountain toward home through an autumn evening as purple as . . . well, as purple as a swatch of gorgeous Capstickian prose.